PRAISE FOR

THE GIRL WITH THE LOWER BACK TATTOO

"Amy Schumer's book will make you love her even more. For a comedian of unbridled (and generally hilarious) causticity, Schumer has written a probing, confessional, unguarded, and, yes, majorly humanizing nonmemoir, a book that trades less on sarcasm, and more on emotional resonance."

—*Vogue*

"*The Girl with the Lower Back Tattoo* is laugh-out-loud funny when Schumer wants it to be . . . but more often, it's surprisingly honest and raw . . . If you're here for humor, of course, you won't be disappointed . . . But on the whole, this book is far less a portable joke factory than it is a real, deep dive into Schumer's life, and what it's like to be an imperfect woman and content and proud of yourself despite that."

—*Entertainment Weekly*

"[An] excellent new essay collection . . . Schumer, the celebrity, shedding Schumer, the schtick . . . an unapologetic paean to self-love. In that, *The Girl with the Lower Back Tattoo* finds a new way for Schumer to be radical: It treats feminine self-confidence not in the way it is too often regarded, as a BrainyQuotable truism or an inborn gift or a fuzzy aspiration or, indeed, a source of shame, but rather as a skill like any other—something that is developed and worked at and thus, most importantly, earned."

—*The Atlantic*

"This is your happy hour with Amy Schumer. You'll get everything from tips on how to be a stand-up comedian, to the story of her one one-night stand. It's *Bossypants* meets *Trainwreck* meets your long weekend."

—*The Skimm*

"*The Girl with the Lower Back Tattoo* is an alternatingly meditative, sexually explicit, side-splittingly hilarious, heart-wrenching, disturbing, passionately political and always staggeringly authentic ride through the highs and lows of the comedic powerhouse's life to date."

—*Harper's Bazaar*

"Beyond the many powerful and empowering take-aways of *The Girl with the Lower Back Tattoo*—from loving the hustle to self-love—perhaps the most overlooked is that of a woman's right to not only make mistakes, but to make art out of them."

—Salon.com

"If you find yourself feeling guilty for laughing at her pain, just keep in mind she's probably laughing with you, unapologetically, in true Amy Schumer fashion."

—*Vulture*

"It's hard to top the title of this essay collection, but what's inside is best of all. Yes, Schumer is as honest and hilarious on the page as she is onstage."

—*Glamour*

"A poignant yet shockingly amusing book."

—Lena Dunham, *Lenny*

"[Schumer is] a concert pianist of comedy: keeping a steady rhythm of jokes with her left hand, adding deeply political, immensely feminist flourishes with her right . . . [She] knows what people want her for: she knows they like her jokes, and her delivery, and her vulnerability. But she also knows what she wants them for: to read, to listen, and to understand the world as she sees it. And she might end up changing it a little before she's done."

—*The Pool (UK)*

"Schumer chronicles her life with digestible stories that impart powerful messages through a kind of logic of the opposite: she makes mistakes so that we can learn from them."

—RollingStone.com

"Amy Schumer exposes herself—hilariously—in *The Girl with the Lower Back Tattoo*."

—*Vanity Fair*

"Surprisingly moving and unsurprisingly hilarious."

—*Esquire*

"Schumer keeps it real in *The Girl with the Lower Back Tattoo*. [She] is a talented storyteller . . . Readers will laugh and cry, and may put the book down from moments of honesty that result in uncomfortable realistic details from her life. More important, the essays challenge readers to harness their own stories and rest in the fact that they're good enough. Experience the world. Be bold. Love your body. It's OK to fail and make mistakes. And lower-back tattoos can only make you stronger."

—*Associated Press*

"[A] raunchy, revealing new memoir."

—*O Magazine*

". . . [T]he book does contain laugh-out-loud—occasionally graphic—dating anecdotes. It's made funnier when infused with Schumer's vivid, occasionally stream-of-consciousness writing style . . . Still, make no mistake: This is not solely a breezy beach read. With little notice, the essays whiplash from hilarious to grim as Schumer lays bare some of the most traumatizing moments of her life."

—*The Washington Post*

"In line with its genius name, *The Girl with the Lower Back Tattoo* tackles the arduous task of explaining how Amy Schumer of Long Island became Amy Schumer of *Vogue*'s cover and internet think pieces, packed with the characteristic self-effacing humor and unfiltered raunch you crave."

—*The Daily Beast*

"Schumer weaves a brave, vulnerable tale without falling into the usual celebrity traps of neediness and defense . . . It's an exercise in either vanity or courage when a celebrity offers a self-reveal. In this case, it's mostly the latter. And even the parts that veer into the former are witty enough to make you glad you stuck around."

—*The Chicago Tribune*

"Schumer shuts it down. Be like Schumer."

—Buzzfeed

". . . we knew [*The Girl with the Lower Back Tattoo*] was going to be good. And boy, did she deliver. Sprinkled with her famous humor, Schumer's book provides comical anecdotes that makes it feel like you're chatting with your bestie while downing a pint of ice cream and bottle of wine (yes, both at the same time), while also touching on some very intimate and dark moments that may raise your eyebrows in a different way than you're used to when it comes to Schumer."

—E! Online

"Revealing."

—People

"[Amy Schumer's] prose, like her popular comedy act, is plucky, forthright, hilariously raunchy—and honest. Amid ill-fated dates, alcohol-induced blackouts, and late-night eating binges, Schumer, in these candid, well-crafted essays, wears her mistakes 'like badges of honor.'"

—Publishers Weekly (starred review)

"A funny, highly revealing recollection of memories, relationship rehashes and career experiences."

—USA Today

"Schumer takes her readers through reminiscences by relating events that have most likely happened to all of us, and she engages readers, shedding new light on her motives and practices . . . A hilarious and effective memoir from a woman with zero inhibitions."

—Kirkus Reviews

"Amy Schumer bares her soul in *The Girl with the Lower Back Tattoo*."

—*NPR*

"Schumer is revealing and vulnerable, but it's her willingness to be unapologetically herself that makes the book such a wonderful and engaging read."

—*The AV Club*

"A hilarious and deeply emotional book."

—Cosmopolitan.com

"The comedian's essay collection isn't just bitingly funny—it's also raw, honest, and often heartbreaking. We dare you to walk away without even greater understanding and respect for Schumer."

—*Entertainment Weekly*'s "Must List"

"Some of the prose . . . could rival Oliver Sacks or Paul Kalanithi. *The Girl with the Lower Back Tattoo* would still be a success if it wasn't funny, because it is so unashamed and human."

—*The Guardian (UK)*

"This book is what a selection of personal essays and letters should be, witty, sometimes casual, sometimes achingly sad but always entertaining. This rich, unashamed and slightly strange book should be on your shelf if you have ever wanted to be inside Amy Schumer's head."

—*Funny Women*

THE GIRL WITH THE LOWER BACK TATTOO

AMY SCHUMER

POCKET BOOKS

New York   London   Toronto   Sydney   New Delhi

Pocket Books
An Imprint of Simon & Schuster, Inc.
1230 Avenue of the Americas
New York, NY 10020

First Pocket Books paperback edition October 2018

POCKET and colophon are registered trademarks
of Simon & Schuster, Inc.

For information about special discounts for bulk purchases, please contact Simon & Schuster Special Sales at 1-866-506-1949 or business@simonandschuster.com.

The Simon & Schuster Speakers Bureau can bring authors to your live event. For more information or to book an event contact the Simon & Schuster Speakers Bureau at 1-866-248-3049 or visit our website at www.simonspeakers.com.

Interior design by Jaime Putorti

Manufactured in the United States of America

10   9   8   7   6   5   4   3   2

ISBN 978-1-9821-1098-7
ISBN 978-1-5011-3990-1 (ebook)

Photo credits appear on page 379 and should constitute an extension of this copyright page.

For Kimby and Jasy

CONTENTS

THE
GIRL
WITH
THE
LOWER
BACK
TATTOO

A NOTE TO MY READERS

Hey, it's me, Amy. I wrote a book! This is something I have wanted to do for a long time because I love making people laugh and feel better. Some of the stories you'll read in here will be funny, like the time I shit myself in Austin, and some will make you feel a little blue, like the time my sister and I were almost sold into sex slavery in Italy. JK. Neither of these stories are in this book, even though both actually happened, unfortunately.

Speaking of, everything in this book really happened. It's all true and nothing but the truth, so help me God. But it isn't the *whole truth*. Believe it or not, I don't tell you guys everything.

This book isn't my autobiography. I will write one of those when I'm ninety. I just turned thirty-five, so I have a long way to go until I am memoir-worthy. But for now I wanted to share these stories from my life as a daughter, sister, friend, comedian, actor, girlfriend, one-night stand, employee, employer, lover, fighter, hater, pasta eater, and wine drinker.

I also want to clarify that this book has NO SELF-

HELP INFO OR ADVICE FOR YOU. Over the last several years, I've been asked to write articles on topics like how to find a man. Or how to keep a man. Or how to rub a man's taint at the right time. I don't know how to do any of that stuff. I'm a flawed fuckup and I haven't figured anything out, so I have no wisdom to offer you. But what I can help with is showing you my mistakes and my pain and my laughter. I know what's important to me, and that is my family (not all of them, for Christ's sake, just some of them). And getting to laugh and enjoy life with friends. And to, of course, have an orgasm once in a while. I find at least once a day is best.

So anyway, I hope you enjoy my book, and if you don't, please don't tell anyone.

Wish me luck!

AN OPEN LETTER
TO MY VAGINA

First of all, I'm sorry. Second of all, you're welcome.

I know I've put you through a lot. I've had hot wax poured on you and the hair ripped from you by strangers. Some of the strangers have burned you even though I told them you have very sensitive skin. But it's on me for going to a shady-looking place in Astoria, Queens, that you thought may have been a drug front. I've been responsible for getting you yeast infections and UTIs and have worn stockings and Spanx for too long, knowing it could cause you problems. And I want to apologize for Lance on the lacrosse team, who treated you like you owed him money with his finger. That sucked, and I'm totally with you in being pissed. But you've also had a lot of nice visitors, right? Huh? You have to admit we've had a lot of fun together. I even fought to be able to call you "pussy," which I know you prefer, on television.

I've honestly done my best as I've gotten older

to only let people visit who will be kind to you, and I feel like I've done my part to keep you healthy. I know that sometimes I let people in you without a condom, but, in my defense, it feels better that way and it was only the people I was dating and trusted. Well, mostly. But we really have lucked out, haven't we?

I'm also sorry for the time I had sex with my new boyfriend and we couldn't find the condom afterward and then three days later I realized it was stuck in me and I had to "bear down," as they say, and fish it out. That must have been a real bummer for you. Or maybe it was fun to have a visitor for so long? Either way, my bad!

So what do you say? Let's grab a beer together. Okay, fine, nothing with yeast. And you're buying.

MY ONLY
ONE-NIGHT STAND

I've only had one one-night stand in my life. Yes, one. I know, I'm so sorry to disappoint anyone who thinks I walk around at all times with a margarita in one hand and a dildo in the other. Maybe the misunderstanding comes from the fact that onstage, I group together all my wildest, worst sexual memories—which is a grand total of about five experiences over the course of thirty-five years. When you hear about them all back-to-back it probably sounds like my vagina is a revolving door at Macy's at Christmastime. But I talk about these few misadventures because it's not funny or interesting to hear about someone's healthy, everyday sex life. Imagine me onstage saying, "So last night I got in bed with my boyfriend and we held each other in a supportive, caring embrace, and then he made sweet love to me." The crowd would walk out and I'd walk out with them.

And besides, even *I* sometimes confuse my

onstage sexual persona with my reasonable, sensible, real-life self. Sometimes I try to convince myself that I can have emotionless sex, the kind I'm always hearing about from men and Samantha on *Sex and the City*. And I have my moments, but 99.9 percent of the time, I'm not that way. I've never even hooked up with a guy after one of my shows. Isn't that sad? I've been touring for twelve years and not once have I met a guy after I've performed, brought him home, and even made out with him. Nothing. I know some male comics who say they've never gotten laid without the girl seeing them perform first. It's the exact opposite for me. I'm not in this for the dick. I enjoy sex the normal amount, and most of the time it's with someone I'm dating, and I just lie there in Happy Baby pose making it sound like I'm having a good time. When I'm single and one-night stands present themselves, I'm usually still a fairly self-protective chick, and the thought of some mystery cock entering me doesn't get my pulse going. Well, except for this one time . . .

I was on the road doing a tour and traveling between two horrendous cities: Fayetteville, North Carolina, and Tampa, Florida. I'm not scared about writing that and making those people mad, because I know for a fact that no one who lives there has ever read a book. JKJKJKJKJK, but kind of not K. When you go between cities like those two, you get the pleasure of flying on the tiniest short bus in the sky, which for some reason is still called a plane. You have to duck to get on, and you can hear the propellers the whole flight, and also the faintest sound of someone singing *"La la la la la bamba,"* but you hope that the latter is just in your head.

It was early morning and I was hungover. As I said, I'd been doing a show in Fayetteville and there is nothing to do there afterward except drink until your eyes close. I got to the airport as I usually do—with zero makeup or bra, wearing sweatpants, a T-shirt, and flats. I'm not someone who looks adorable in the morning. I would argue I look exactly like Beetlejuice—the Michael Keaton character, not the Howard Stern regular. I was enjoying this lovely time in my life when no one took pictures of me unless I photobombed them. I was just a wonderful thirty-one-year-old girl who was opening and closing her mouth, realizing she'd forgotten to brush her teeth—well, less forgot and more I'd left my toothbrush in Charleston and it didn't occur to me to buy one in North Carolina. One way for me to verify that I drank too much the night before is if I wake up with red-wine teeth and enough eyeliner smeared underneath my eyes that I resemble a tight end for the New England Patriots. The point is, on this particular morning, I looked heinous and smelled like curry, and if someone had put a dollar in my coffee cup, thinking I was homeless, I would have thought, *Yep*.

I got to airport security and there he was: a six-foot-two-inch strapping strawberry blond of about thirty-five years. My first kiss was with a redhead so I've always had a weakness for them. He was the most beautiful man I'd ever seen, and I was immediately turned on just looking at him. Quick side note: THAT NEVER FUCKING HAPPENS. Every day, men look at women walk by in skirts and tight jeans and get tiny erections, or at the very least some sort of arousal. But for women it's a rare occurrence to see a dude and think, *Dayummmmm!* I was looking him up and down, trying to find one inch of him that wasn't Gaston from *Beauty and the Beast*, and there was nothing. All he was missing was the ponytail and the bow on said ponytail.

I audibly sighed, and before he walked through the metal detector, he looked at me. All the blood rushed to my vagina, and I smiled at him before immediately remembering I looked like Bruce Vilanch. (For those of you who don't know who he is and are too lazy to Google it, just picture a barn owl wearing a blond wig.) I got through security and walked to my gate—and *boom!* There he was again—looking even hotter than before. He was wearing a crew-neck long-sleeve shirt that was just tight enough around the chest so you knew what was up. It was abundantly clear that underneath his shirt was a place where you would want to rest your cheek and breathe in all his pheromones until he took you like Marlon Brando in *Streetcar* or Ryan Gosling in annnnnyyyyythiiiiinnnnnngggg.

I ran to the bathroom to try to find makeup in my purse, which is an actual bottomless pit when I need something (and at all other times). I'm not lying when I say my purse has all the contents of an actual ostrich's nest. I'll never do a celebrity magazine "What's in your purse?" story because people would see the array of fun, gross surprises in there and probably think I needed to be hospitalized. I found some blush and ChapStick, and thought, *Perfect. That's all I need to take me from a two to a four.* I looked in the mirror and saw the rosacea I'd created, and laughed at myself. Fuck it. I rolled my sweatpants up to half-calf height, thinking, *Let's highlight my strongest zone.* I brushed my teeth with my finger and splashed water all over myself. I walked out like I was on a runway and floated right past him. He at no time, for even one second, looked at me in the terminal.

I bought some gum and a magazine with Jennifer Aniston on the cover and boarded the plane, defeated. I got to my tiny window seat and started reading about how Jennifer was going to die alone and it wasn't fair, and there he was again, boarding the plane. He walked down the aisle and I watched him, his arms bulging and his huge hands gripping his bag as he navigated his way between the seats. I was thinking, *Maybe when he walks by, I can pretend to sneeze . . . and fall on the floor in front of him . . . and he will trip and fall inside of me.* Then I saw him look right at the seat next to me.

No, I thought. *There is no way he is in the seat next to me.* No, no, no. But YES! *Game, set, fucking match*, I thought, *IT IS ON.*

I never ever talk to people on airplanes. It's a

huge gamble that has resulted in such things as James Toback (Google him) telling me, "You don't really know a woman until you've eaten her ass," before we even took off, and a woman showing me pictures of her dead bird for three hours. But on this flight, I turned right to him.

"Hi, I'm Amy."

He smiled, revealing a tiny gap between his front teeth. I love a gap more than anything on a man. "Hi, I'm Sam," he said, in an English accent.

I soon found out that he was in the British version of the marines and was in town for just a few days. I couldn't fucking handle it. It was all too much. I felt possessed and lost all control of my voice, like Sigourney Weaver at the end of *Ghostbusters*. I was in heat, as they say. Who says this? I don't know. Shut up and keep reading about my getting pummeled by this British superhero. We took off and I pretended to be really scared of flying. There was zero turbulence, yet I still found reasons to grab his arm and bury my face in his shoulder, inhaling his scent. I was blatantly throwing myself at him and we both laughed at how aggressive I was being. My clitoris was thumping like the Tell-Tale Heart and I kept thinking of the 98 Degrees song "Give Me Just One Night (Una Noche)." Even though I was slightly famous at the time, he'd never heard of me, which was another major plus. I told him I had a show that night and that maybe I would see him after. We exchanged emails and I prayed to every god that it would happen.

I've been in this kind of situation a couple other times where I could have had a one-night stand and I just couldn't go through with it. Once or twice, my instincts told me no. It didn't feel safe. But mostly I have decided against it just out of pure laziness. I will think of the practical things, like, *When can I leave so I can eat pasta? We are not dating, so I can't do domestic things like brush my teeth and wash my face and put on my eye mask and earplugs. It's supposed to be hot and sexy, but I look like a blond Shrek in the a.m. What will the morning be like? What will we say? Will I order him an Uber? What if he says something hurtful or he tries to have sex with me in the morning when we both know my vagina will smell like a bowl of ramen?* I'm just too pragmatic and lazy for one-night stands. I consider consequences and I don't drink like I did in college.

All that being said, the Sam situation felt different. He was such a turn-on and a fantasy. Even the accent made him seem unreal. It didn't hurt that he'd be returning to his foreign home shortly after the sun rose the next day. After we parted ways in the airport, I went to do my show, and the whole time I couldn't help but hold my breath hoping that I would hear from him. Sure enough, when the show was over, I had an email from him asking me how it had gone. I joked that I had gotten discovered and was going to make it in this business.

He wrote back: "Who discovered you?"

I wrote: "A magician. I'm going to be his assistant." Which I thought was pretty funny.

He wrote: "Is he gonna saw you in half?"

I answered: "I was hoping you would."

BAM! That is the most sexually aggressive yet true thing I've ever written. And it worked.

We made plans to meet up at the dance club in the lobby of my hotel. We had half a beer, we danced to Ice Cube telling us we could do it if we put our back into it, and we left. Walking through the bright lobby and into the low lighting of the elevator was a lot of reality for this sexy affair we were both trying to have. The things that were going through my mind on the elevator were as follows: *Fuck me fuck me fuck me fuck me fuck me.*

I really needed a boost of sexual confidence during that time of my life. I'd recently learned that a guy I'd been in love with and had dated in the past was gay. Even though it had been a while since we had dated, it still broke my heart when he came out to me. And it made me begin to question myself. This person who made me feel beautiful and sexy for so long was attracted to men. I thought, *Am I like a man?* When you get older and wiser, you get your confidence from within, not from the person you are having sex with. But finding out someone I'd dated was gay at that moment in my life was giving me a hard time. I was having trouble feeling like a sexual being and was wondering about my own worth.

Enter Sam—this beautiful, masculine fantasy man who wanted to help Stella get her groove back. The elevator to my room could not travel fast enough.

We got to my very corporate-looking room and wasted no time.

I dropped my bag and we stripped down to our underwear and got into bed. There was no question of what we were doing there. We both had the same goal in mind: to devour each other. *Ewwwwww*, I know, sorry. But it's true. Everything felt right. Kissing him felt right. His body felt right. We went for it. I can't *Fifty Shades* out right now and write a sensual paragraph, so I'll just tell you some facts. We were both very giving (head). We both couldn't believe it was happening (we both came a lot). He was so appreciative and excited (we high-fived at one point). Which felt amazing (the sex, not the high five). Coming off the depressing discovery that a guy I'd had a lot of sex with was attracted to men, it felt incredible to have this heavenly being take me in his arms and make me feel both wanted and beautiful. The sex was perfect. He was perfect. We were both in ecstasy, enjoying and relishing every smell, sound, and touch.

When we were finally finished, I said it was such a pleasure meeting him and wished him good luck in all his endeavors. He couldn't believe I didn't want him to stay. He couldn't believe it so much that he stayed and we had sex at least three more times, with little affectionate breaks in between, telling stories and laughing and holding each other.

I did eventually tell him it was time to go. I was apparently fine having sex with a stranger, but sleeping next to him was just too intimate. He tried to make future plans and I let him know that I wanted this to be a one-time thing. I said it was perfect and that I would never have a one-night stand again because it would pale in comparison. We kissed good-bye, and I went to sleep with the biggest smile on my face, thinking, *Thank you*.

I do realize that one of the best nights of my life was just a one-night stand in Tampa. But I felt like Marlene Dietrich in *Morocco*. Let the record show I am not proposing that everyone limit themselves to just *one* one-night stand. Oh no no no, on the contrary, some of us might be better off if we had *only* one-night stands for the rest of our lives. But for me, this encounter just fell in my lap when I wasn't feeling so attractive to men. Or sexual in general. I was wanting some reassurance, and a night of unexpected sex with a built, British red-head was the Z-Pak I needed to kick the leftover mucus. (Is there an unsexier metaphor? No. Also I feel like that antibiotic never works.)

We all know one-night stands aren't cure-alls for broken hearts and low self-esteem. That shit can backfire hard. We've all tried some form of remedy by way of sex and wound up feeling even more alone and running back to whatever dickface we'd just found the strength to leave. But some-times one-night stands can fix a specific problem. And even better, sometimes when you're try-ing to fix a problem with sex, you find that sex is just its own reward. No lessons to be learned. No agenda other than fun. And sometimes tons of well-deserved orgasms from a guy looking at you like you're lunch right when you fucking need it is just what the doctor ordered. Can we make a day National Redhead Day? This man deserves a parade or something.

He reached out to me a couple more times when he was back in the US but I stayed true to wanting to keep sacred what strangely felt like the purest night of my life. And it still is.

I AM AN INTROVERT

I am an introvert. I know—you're thinking, *What the fuck, Amy? You just told us you hooked up with a stranger in Tampa, and now you're claiming to be shy? You're not shy, you're a loud, boozy animal!* Okay, fair enough. Sometimes that's true. But I am, without a doubt, a classic textbook introvert.

In case you don't know what that word means, I will fill you in quickly. If you *do* know what it means, then skip ahead to the chapter about where to find the best gloryholes in Beijing. Just kidding. I don't have that info. Also, just fucking read my description of an introvert. Why are you in such a rush to skip ahead, you pervert?

Being an introvert doesn't mean you're shy. It means you enjoy being alone. Not just enjoy it—you need it. If you're a true introvert, other people are basically energy vampires. You don't hate them; you just have to be strategic about when you expose yourself to them—like the sun. They give you life, sure, but they can also burn you and you will get that wrinkly Long Island cleavage I've always been afraid of getting and that I know I now have. For me, meditation and headphones on the subway have been my sunscreen, protecting me from the hell that is other people.

There's a *National Geographic* photo I love of a young brown bear. He's sitting peacefully against a tree near the border of Finland and Russia. The caption reads something like, "The cubs played feverishly all day, and then one of them left the group for a few minutes to relax on his own and enjoy the quiet." This was very meaningful to me because that's what I do! Except in my case, the bear gets ripped away from his chill spot by the tree, and several people paint his face and curl his fur and put him in a dress so he can be pushed onstage to ride one of those tiny bicycles in the circus. I'm not saying he doesn't enjoy making people laugh, but still, it's hard out there for a fuzzy little introvert.

I know some people who've written books have struggled through it, and you can feel them ripping themselves apart on every page. But for me, writing this book has been one of the great pleasures of my life. Sitting and writing and talking to no one is how I wish I could spend the better part of every day. In fact, it might be surprising for you to learn that most of my days are spent alone, unless I am on set, which is crazy draining for an introvert. As soon as lunchtime arrives, I skip the food service tables and rush to my trailer or a quiet corner and I meditate. I need to completely shut off. This time spent silently is like food to me. I also eat a lot of food. But if I'm not shooting something, I like to be alone all day. Maybe an hour lunch with a friend, but that's it.

When you're a performer—especially a female one—everyone assumes you enjoy being "on" all the time. That couldn't be further from the truth for me or any of the people I am close to. The unintentional training I received when I was little was that because I was a girl *and* an actor, I *must* love being pleasant, and making everyone smile and feel comfortable all the time. I think all little girls are trained this way, even those who aren't entertainers like I was. Women are always expected to be the gracious hostess, quick with an anecdote and a sprinkling of laughter at others' stories. We are always the ones who have to smooth over all the awkward moments in life with soul-crushing pleasantries. We are basically unpaid geishas. But when we do not fulfill this expectation (because we are introverted), people assume we must be either depressed or a cunt. Maybe I'm a cunt anyway, but it's not because I don't want to blink and smile at someone as they tell me they ran cross-country in middle school.

I was living with my boyfriend Rick during the time I started having this realization about myself. But even as a child, I had always known something was up. I didn't like to play for as long as the other kids, and I absolutely always bailed on slumber parties. But as an adult, my mom wasn't around to come pick me up in the middle of the night anymore, and I began to see things more clearly. You could say Rick was the first adult relationship I had, and for the first time, I was playing house with someone, mimicking the way married people dutifully fulfill each other's friend-and-family obligations. I remember going to his family's house for the holidays and realizing I would need to take frequent breaks from the lovely group of people we were hanging out with all day. Every ninety minutes or so, I would retreat to his room or go for a walk. I wasn't made to feel bad about this, but everyone was clearly clocking it. Once, Rick took me to his friend's wedding. After about two hours of small talk and formalities, I went to hide in the bathroom. I had nothing left to give or say, and I felt the unbearable sensation that I was treading water.

It wasn't until I became best friends with some fellow comics and performers that I realized being an introvert wasn't a character flaw. Even when we all go on vacations or on the road together, we take little breaks in our own rooms and then text each other to check in. This quality is tricky when your job actually requires you to constantly travel and interact with new faces, new towns, and new audiences. You cross paths with lots of people in this line of work, and you feel shitty if you don't give away some of your energy and conversation to every driver, hotel front-desk clerk, promoter, backstage crew member, member of the audience, waiter, and so on. And I do mean "give away." Energy is finite between recharges. That shit runs out. It's not that I don't respect these people working hard at their jobs (which are all jobs I have done, by the way, because I have done every job in the world other than being a doula. More on that later). I know they mean well, and I know there are many people out there who, unlike me, want to tell their cabdrivers all about how their flight was (flights are always fine) and what the weather was like in New York (cold or hot—who gives a fuck?). How many hotel room keys do you want? (A hundred and nine.) I'm just not one of those people, and I don't want to waste their time and energy (or mine) with mindless small talk. Every time a driver picks you up from the airport, they ask why you're in town and what you do for a living. When I was a rookie, I used to tell them the straight answer, but I learned my lesson because this kind of thing would happen every time:

"Oh, you're a comedian?"

"Have I seen you before?"

"Are you on YouTube?"

"Oh, my cousin's a comedian. His name is Rudy Fuckface. Do you know him? Google him."

"Have you ever met Carrotbottom?"

"You know who's funny? Jeff Dunham."

"You should do a show about cabdrivers."

"Oh, I could tell you some funny material for your act."

"Weren't you in that one movie?"

"You weren't? Are you sure?"

"I don't usually like female comics."

That one really gets me. It's not like anyone would so casually say, "I don't usually like black people." Either way, it's offensive to say this to a female comic. And let me guess, you've only ever seen one female comic in your life and it was in the eighties and guess what? You probably fucking loved her.

So to avoid this kind of conversation, for a while I changed my story and told them I was a schoolteacher. But they still had too many follow-up questions for me, and so I started saying, "I tell stories for a living." This was just creepy enough for them to cut the small talk.

I can stand onstage all night talking to thousands of people about my most vulnerable and private feelings—like my thoughts on the last guy who was inside me, or the fact that I eat like the glutton in the movie *Se7en* when I'm drunk. But I really don't do as well at parties or gatherings where I feel like I am obligated to be more "social." Usually I will find a corner to hide in and immediately begin haunting it like the girl from *The Ring*, just hoping no one will want to come talk to me. But in the right time and place, I can be pretty pleasant. For example, I've had several nice exchanges with nude elderly women in gym locker rooms. Even if they are blow-drying their hair with their gray tornadoesque bush out, I will engage.

It is probably no surprise that sometimes I prefer social media to human interaction. This is probably an introvert thing as well. Social media is just more efficient, like online dating. Everything can be quick and painless, and when you find out that someone is crazy or not funny, you can promptly tap out of the conversation. Even the photos a person chooses to post on Instagram can help save you a lot of time. I once ended a potentially romantic relationship because the dude posted a picture of his friend's dog's funeral. Like literally the dog's body being lowered into the ground in a garbage bag. Saying he was honored to be a part of the day. Not even his own dog!

In my opinion, what a person posts on Instagram should be humanizing and accurate. Not that a dog funeral isn't those things. But his post made it clear he thrived on sadness and enjoyed being a part of drama to make him feel alive and important. My favorite pictures to post are of my sister picking up piles of her dog's shit when we go on walks. Why not be real and show all of yourself? One of the first times that I was paparazzied, they caught me stand-up paddleboarding in Hawaii. I didn't even recognize myself. I saw the shots in magazines and thought, *Oh, cool, Alfred Hitchcock is alive and loves water sports*. But nope, it was me. When my friend told me they were online, she broke it to me as if both of my parents had died in a fire. But I proudly posted the worst picture on Instagram right away, because I thought it was hilarious. I will make fun of myself a lot in this book, but understand I feel good, healthy, strong, and fuckable. I'm not the hottest chick in the room. I would be like the third-hottest bartender at a Dave & Buster's in Cincinnati. Another time, when a paparazzo photographed me committing the unspeakable act of eating a sandwich, I immediately posted a correction as to the type of meat it was (they said ham, but it was prosciutto).

On the other hand, there are those men and women we all know (celebrities or regular people) who only post amazing shots of their abs or photos where they look accidentally gorgeous, known as #humblebrags (RIP @twittels, who coined that perfect term). No, and pass to those people. I don't even want to know someone who isn't barely hanging on by a thread. Social media is a great tool for all of us introverts and decent people alike as it speeds up the time between thinking someone is great and realizing they're the worst. I don't know how introverts survived without the Internet. Or with the Internet. Actually, I don't know how we survive at all. It feels impossible.

Now that I know I'm an introvert, I can better manage this quality and actually start to see it as a positive. For example, it's a known fact that a lot of CEOs are introverts, and being in charge is a comfortable position for me too, whatever I'm working on. I surround myself with smart, talented people, let them do their thing, listen to their ideas, and figure out the strongest ways to collaborate with them to make the best possible final product. I write all my own jokes when it comes to my stand-up, but anything else I've created has been thanks to the collaboration of small groups of funny people working alone together, which is my favorite way to get things done. It should come as no surprise that a lot of writers are introverts, so on my TV show, the writing staff is happy to work together side by side for short stints and then disappear off individually into our productive little introvert pods at home to get shit done. We are mainly a group of cave dwellers who can only socialize for limited amounts of time. On any given day with the writing staff, the schedule usually looks something like this:

Noon:	Staff arrives at the office.
12:15:	The group orders lunch. We all want soup, but the soup delivery has taken up to two hours, so we get Bareburger. Kyle Dunnigan always takes the longest because he is gluten-and-dairy-free and we all need to hear about it forever. (This year he stopped being G-and-D-free and we are all furious he quit after we had to listen to him talk about it for so long.)
12:16–12:59:	Staff discusses and laments how long it's taking for lunch to arrive.
1:00–1:15:	We consume our lunch and talk about *The Bachelor*.

1:15–1:30:	Bathroom breaks all around. Kurt Metzger tells a story about a weird girl he went down on.
1:30–2:00:	Discuss scene ideas or talk shit about people and watch YouTube videos together.
2:00–3:00:	Discuss what snack we should have. I pee for the hundredth time.
3:00–4:00:	We punch up scripts.
4:00–7:00:	Everyone writes in the safe shelter of their own homes.

It's hard to be in the company of others for very long while being creative, and I don't know how the writers of the late-night shows do it: together all day, churning out jokes and scenes. I feel lucky to have a huge group of people who let each other do their own thing, and the process of writing alone together is the best. My sister, Kim, and I often sit side by side on the couch, writing the same movie together quietly without speaking—not just for hours, but for days. We will say about two sentences to each other and they are always about food.

So in closing, I'd like to pay tribute to the introverts' secret weapon—one of our greatest coping mechanisms for handling social situations. The Irish good-bye is something I've perfected over the years. No offense to the Irish with that term. You guys are geniuses for coming up with this patented method of getting the hell out of Dodge without having to explain why. Even if I'm drunk, I can slip out of any event, very subtle and ninjalike, and with no warning—a classic introvert move I rely upon heavily. I'm like Omar from *The Wire*. Except no. *"Amy, I didn't see you leave last night . . . you didn't say good-bye!"* You bet your sweet ass I didn't. If I say good-bye to you, it is completely by accident and because you were right in the doorway as I tried to plow through it.

I wish I could Irish-good-bye my way out of this chapter because, true to form, I'm exhausted from writing about myself for this long. But first, before I ghost you like a pro, I want to remind you to stop judging a loud, often tactless, volatile, blond book by its cover. (Except for this book, because the cover is nice and the inside is nice, too.) Just because my job requires me to make fun of myself into a microphone and wear my heart on my sleeve for hire doesn't mean I can't be an introvert as well. Believe it or not, I do have a complex inner life just like you, and I enjoy being alone. I need it. And I've never been happier than I was when I finally figured this out about myself. So if you're an introvert like me, especially a female introvert, or a person who is expected to give away your energy to everyone else on the reg, I want to encourage you to find time to be alone. Don't be afraid to excuse yourself. Recharge for as long as you need. Lean up against a tree and take a break from the other bears. I'll be there too, but I promise not to bother you.

ON BEING NEW MONEY

The term "nouveau riche" is a fancy way of saying you're a rich person who acquired your wealth on your own. You didn't inherit it all from your great-grandfather. You worked for it. Either that or you bought that lottery ticket fair and square. But I actually prefer the term "New Money" because it's a way of saying, "Yes, I am trash and I'm embracing it!"

I am New Money.

I feel lucky to live in America—where people will treat someone like me (trash) as if they come from bloodlines with Benjamins streaming through them. In England, they are not as impressed with people who have made their own dough within their lifetime. New Money is considered gaudy there. But in America New Money is celebrated more than Old, because it was earned in some way or another. We use our new money for stupid shit like spa treatments where eels eat the dead skin off of our toes or baby seal fat is injected into our assholes so we look young again. (A lot of marine life is utilized for some reason.) People applaud us. Go ahead, start a charity and give back a little and no one in the States gives a hot damn how you got it. You were knocked up by a basketball player and took him for all you could? Great, here is your own television show. You made a sex tape with a mediocre rapper? Here is the key to a billion-dollar corporation. Or in my case, hey, you told dick jokes to drunk people in small rooms at places called the Giggle Bone and the Banana Hammock? Would you like a movie deal?!

Looking back, I realize this is technically my second time to fall into the New Money category. My parents were living the textbook New Money lifestyle during my childhood . . . until they slipped into the No Money lifestyle just in time for my delicate preteen years. But I'm getting ahead of myself.

I was born a precious little half Jew in Lenox Hill Hospital on the Upper East Side and sailed the five blocks home to our huge duplex apartment in a limo. Dad's idea. To unbury the lede, my parents were rich. They were rolling in it. I mean, I thought they were. They'd take a private jet to the Bahamas at a moment's notice, and they thought the high life was going to last forever. It didn't.

My dad owned a company called Lewis of London, a baby furniture business that imported cribs and such from Italy. I don't remember why they named it "Lewis of London" but if they were looking for a fancy name that only New Money people would use in order to make something sound high-end and international, they knocked it out of the park. At the time, no one else was selling fine foreign baby furniture, so rich Manhattan parents sought out my father's store, where they could pick up the fanciest tiny infant prisons that money could buy.

I had some extravagant, rich-person things as a little kid. We moved out of the city to a nice suburb on Long Island when I was five, where we would eat lobster once a week and smoked fish for Sunday breakfast. Or as we called it, Jewing out hard! On lobster nights, Mom would bring the live ones home from the grocery store and put them on the kitchen floor for my brother, sister, and me to play with. At the time, I thought it was just a fun thing we did before boiling the tasty crustaceans, but in retrospect, I realize that we were playing with our future food in a Little-Mermaid-eating-Sebastian way that was very uncool. Couldn't they have just gotten us a pet goldfish? All the other kids were outside riding bikes and we were making our lobsters race each other like gladiators. Sick. Either way, when I remember what it was like to grow up in a wealthy household, the food we ate stands out the most. Come to think of it, that's mostly what I remember about any event or moment in life—the food that was there. A couple years ago, before I had "real" money, I asked Judd Apatow if it was fun being rich, and he explained to me that once you become rich you find out all the good things in life are free. He said you can buy a house, good sushi, and CDs, but that's about it. Still, as someone who waited a lot of tables and ate off people's plates on the way back to the kitchen, fancy sushi sounded pretty good to me.

Anyway, Lewis of London cornered the market—until other stores started selling European baby furniture and my parents lost it all. Which happened, incidentally, during the onset of my father's multiple sclerosis. Cool timing, Universe!!! I don't remember how it felt to lose everything, but I do remember men coming to take my dad's car when I was ten. I watched him standing expressionless in the driveway as it was pulled away. My mom claims she didn't know what was happening financially, but if this were an episode of MTV's *True Life: Squandering That Chedda* they would say, "She blew his millions on furs and homes." And if it were a Lifetime movie, they would say, "She was a victim whose life changed drastically in a split second." I don't know which is true. Probably neither. All I know is that my mom stayed in the house denying reality like it was her job when those men came to take away the black Porsche convertible.

I didn't generally notice the loss, but I did notice a change in the quality of my birthday parties. That's probably where I felt the biggest shift in my family's financial situation. When I turned nine and we still had money, my parents threw me a "farm party" at our beautiful home on Surrey

Lane, a quiet street in Rockville Centre. Early that morning, a box with holes in it was placed in the garage. When I removed the lid, a gaggle of baby ducks looked up at me. I thought I'd died and gone to heaven. I remember believing in my heart that I was the little girl in *Charlotte's Web*. I was so in love with those little creatures that I could have sat there and petted them all day, and died happy.

Since we could afford the whole kit and caboodle, real-life farmers carted real-life farm animals to our house in shifts throughout the day. Bring on the donkeys! We had a pony; we had goats; we had chickens. If you're a kid from Iowa and you're reading this, you're like, who cares? A couple of animals in your yard sounds like a Tuesday. But trust me, if you're from New York and you have a cow in your driveway, you're rich—and the most popular kid in school for a year. All of my little friends dressed up in overalls and played in a pile of hay and went fucking crazy. It's gross when you see it for what it really was: a bunch of well-off kids whose idea of a great time was to slum it like poor farm children. I've also been to a food-fight birthday party. Can you imagine starving kids in Syria watching us waste food like that? It makes me shudder.

Don't worry, the irony came back to bite me in the ass soon after. Life got less and less comfortable for us after my parents lost all their money. We began moving into smaller and smaller homes until it felt like we were all sleeping in a pile—and not a fun pile like the monsters in *Where the Wild Things Are*. A sad, poor pile like the grandparents in *Charlie and the Chocolate Factory*. (*Amy, do you ever reference adult books?* No!) By the time I was in college, my mom had moved us into a basement apartment where my sister, Kim, who is four years younger than me, had the one bedroom, and I had to share a bed with my mom. (Quick tip: Do not try to ditch a cab when you are blackout drunk and then get in bed naked with your mother. The cabdriver will follow you home and knock on your door, and then your mother will have to apologize to him and give him cash while you lie giggling and nude under the sheets, where you are experiencing the bed spins . . . I heard from a friend.)

But to be honest, I never felt poor, even when we were. I always had enough money for lunch and to go on field trips with my class. I was always well provided for. We would go to the occasional Broadway show or take a road trip to somewhere with trees and a lake or pond, or a sizable puddle when the going got really tough. We were living above our means, just not *Real Housewives of New Jersey* level. It was more like the staff at Lisa Vanderpump's restaurant. (Yes, I only speak in Bravo metaphors; thank God for Andy Cohen.) Luckily, all of my friends dressed bad and never had any interest in designer clothes or other material things. I've never worn jewelry (or spelled "jewelry" correctly on a first attempt) or name brands. My friends cared a little more than me but it wasn't too noticeable. We would buy shirts from Bebe, but we could only afford the actual T-shirts that read "Bebe." Those shirts were always on sale—and for good reason.

I drove a shitty car, but at least I had a car. Twizzie was a very used station wagon that smelled like a stable but could turn on a dime. I loved doing donuts in that car and would drive as many people home from school as I could fit. I would shout, "Pick 'em up!" (I think it was a *Dumb and Dumber* reference) as I made the parking lot rounds. If Twizzie went above thirty miles per hour everyone in the car felt like they were holding Shake Weights. But, still, it was a car! I didn't feel like a low-income kid. I remember loving my prom dress so much that I wore it to the prom twice—when I went junior year and also for my own prom, senior year. I can't remember ever wishing for something that I couldn't afford. I was very lucky.

It wasn't until college that I began to take note of the fact that I had to work a little harder than the average student to get by. I was living on my meal plan, stealing food from the student union, and scamming drinks off guys when necessary—which wasn't easy because freshman year, I looked like a blond Babadook. I got a job teaching group exercise classes at my college and those classes were my main source of *legal* income. (I sold a little weed and shoplifted from department stores too . . . oops. Shhh. That doesn't leave this book.) Anyway, I was the worst drug dealer ever. I would run out of baggies and have to use entire Hefty garbage bags for the smallest amount of weed. I'd give a gift along with it, like a baked potato or whatever I had lying around the apartment. And every summer when I came home from college, my sister and I would bartend at the only bar in Long Beach, where we served beer and wine and food fried within an inch of its gross life. We would work sixteen-hour days, returning home covered in ten layers of film from the fryer, our feet swelling out of our sensible shoes and aprons filled with dollars. We'd lay our tips out on the bed and count them, some days totaling as much as five hundred bucks, and we thought we were sultans. We'd fall asleep smiling and wake up at eight a.m. to do it again the next day.

When I graduated college I was B to the R to the O to the K to the E, broke broke. Vanilla Ice broke, before HGTV Ice. I made enough money waiting tables to pay rent and eat nothing but cheap dumplings every day for breakfast, lunch, and dinner. And snack. And brunch. I lived in a closet-sized studio apartment with a Craigslist roommate. One night a bunch of comics were going to get sushi and I couldn't go because I'd spent my last few dollars paying for my five minutes of stage time that night (an investment well worth it, since I bombed in front of all seven disgruntled stand-ups in the audience). Sushi in New York costs more than a blood diamond, so it was out of the question for me. But one of the comics, Lorie S., kindly bought me a California roll. I was so grateful and felt really embarrassed that I needed her to get it for me.

But I worked really hard, and soon enough, instead of buying stage time at open mics and going home hungry, I started making a couple hundred dollars a weekend doing stand-up. And then about four years ago, I started making a couple thousand a weekend. The first very very big check I got was for a college performance where I was paid $800 for one hour. I ran around my apartment screaming for joy.

When I made my first real chunk of change doing the *Last Comic Standing* tour, I took Kim to Europe. Instead of sharing a cot in a filthy youth hostel, we got to stay in real hotel rooms with private bathrooms and everything. They weren't fancy, but we felt like the Rockefellers. Or if you're a millennial, the CEO of Roc-A-Fella Records.

But the thing about Old Money (Rockefellers) vs. New Money (Roc-A-Fellas) is that both still have M-O-N-E-Y. I don't care if the Old Money folks look down on me for being New Money. I will happily clink glasses with them sitting up front on an airplane. What an amazing privilege it is to fly first class! I don't take that for granted. I still recall the first time I stepped foot on a private jet. The first time for anything having to do with money is the best. I was doing a show headlined by Louis CK, Sarah Silverman, and Aziz he-doesn't-need-a-last-name. The show was only in Connecticut so the trip home wasn't far, but when Louis asked if I wanted a lift I said, "Fuck yeah!" People with money feel guilty about having it in front of people who don't, and they don't want to say the words that make others hate them. He didn't say, "Amy, would you like to fly on a private jet I have paid for to travel the mere twenty minutes it takes to get home?" No. He said, "Do you want a lift?" as if we were in an old movie and I was a distressed damsel waiting for a streetcar on a rainy night.

It is awful how wonderful it is to fly private. Just disgusting. I recommend you treat this paragraph like a Choose Your Own Adventure book and skip ahead, so you don't hate me and your life. When you fly private, a car drives you right up to the runway at the exact time your flight takes off. You want to take off at 9:00 p.m., your car drops you there at 8:55 p.m.! No standing in a crowded terminal (which is the right word for that, because it feels like death), no fluorescent-ass airport lighting, no long bathroom lines, no waiting in line for security with frantic people who left too late for their flight. No endlessly long lines to pay ten dollars for a water and gum you don't even like, because they didn't have your favorite. You just get out of your car and walk onto the plane, and you're in the air in about fifteen minutes. There is a car waiting at the other end, right when you get off the plane; they hand you your bag and you go on your merry motherfucking way. I have been on a couple of jets that were fancy hip-hop-video-looking ones and some that were old and dirty. But it doesn't matter.

You are alone on there!!!! All of this is to say I feel crazy lucky to be in a position to even set foot on a private jet. I appreciate every second of it. Just like a New Money person should.

I stay in nice hotels, I Uber instead of hailing a taxi . . . even during pricing surges. I can get expensive meals when I want and that's what I do for myself. I'm not going to bullshit you: it feels great to know I could send my niece to any school she wants even though she is already a genius at two and will get a full ride for her grades or a scholarship when she becomes a Division I volleyball player. It's relaxing to know I can pay for my dad to be in a better facility and make sure he sees the best MS specialist in America. I also know how unfair it is that not everyone can do these things. I'm New Money, not an asshole. That's a lie. I haven't lied to you yet in this book, and I don't want to start now. I am an asshole.

The best part about having money is that you get to be an asshole and burn money on stupid shit. If one of my friends is working at a comedy club, I will sometimes pay to have their greenroom filled to the brim with ridiculous bouquets of flowers, like a hip-hop artist's funeral, with wreaths and the whole nine. One of the writers on our TV show made the mistake of telling me he had booked a very small guest role on the TV show *Veep*. Naturally, I had an insane amount of roses delivered to his dressing room to weird out the rest of the cast and embarrass him. I can afford to buy expensive fake astronaut suits in the gift shop at the Museum of Natural History for my sister and me so we can walk around in them all day just to be dickheads and never wear them again (see picture at the end of this chapter, on page 42). I can hire a private chef to cook for me and my family, without needing it to be a special occasion.

My agent is my friend and he is a young guy who is incredibly shy and does not like attention called to him. Unfortunately, I think it's hilarious to humiliate him, so I have, on several occasions, hired a clown to show up at his office while he is in a meeting and make him balloon animals and sing to him. I've rented Ferraris just to drive them for an hour with friends. I've chartered a boat simply because it's sunny outside. I am like a rapper, but a manageable one. I don't buy the Ferrari or the boat; I rent them and purchase all the insurance. I don't load up on Cristal for the ride. I buy a moderately priced sparkling wine and I only drink half a glass because it gives me a headache and I have writing to do. I'm like a conservative, reasonable rookie athlete. Or a lottery winner with a financial adviser and a sick sense of humor. I am NEWWWW Money.

It's weird to be treated differently all of a sudden just because you have been on TV or have some cash. I am not special just because I'm famous right now. I won't be famous forever—not even much longer actually, which is fine with me because it doesn't feel good to have people be nicer to you because of your money. My favorite people in the world still give me shit and treat me like the Long Island trash receptacle that I am. I want to be treated the same way I treat people. One thing I will say for myself is that I am cool about money. Anyone who comes out of the rags-to-riches experience and isn't cool about money is a douchebag. I try to remember where I came from. I remember when a 30 percent tip changed my day, or sometimes even my week. I remember when I had to sell my clothes to secondhand stores so I could do an open mic. I remember when I almost donated my eggs because I didn't know what else to do to make a buck (and besides, I'm Jewish and my eggs go for double the price!). I remember when I went to the Penny Arcade coin-counting machine at TD Bank so I could take my boyfriend out to dinner at TGI Fridays for his birthday.

And now I can take my girlfriends on vacation and buy a California roll for everyone! I've definitely spread the wealth—whether through leaving good tips or helping out worthy causes, friends, and family. This should be standard practice for wealthy people. I get paid a lot for what I do. That is the nature of show business. If you are someone who can sell tickets and get people to see you live, you are overpaid. So there is no excuse not to hook people up. When I left the bartenders a $1,000 tip at the Broadway musical *Hamilton*, I found it odd that it became a viral news story. Doesn't this sort of thing happen fairly often at

THE most popular musical in a city where tons of rich people live? If I make a bonus at shows, I pass it on to my openers and to the people who did my hair and makeup. I've given most of my amazing best friends six-figure checks to make their lives a little easier, and I donated the majority of my salary for the fourth season of my TV show to the crew, all of whom have worked with *Inside Amy Schumer* anywhere between two and four years. Every dollar I made shooting the movie *Thank You for Your Service* went to the families of PTSD victims and charities for military families.

It's fun to give money away! I still remember the first time like it was yesterday because it was something I had always dreamed of doing. After getting paid a large sum, I wrote my sister a check for ten thousand dollars and handed it to her in my living room. She looked down at it and said, "Shut the fuck up. No. No. Really? No." She was excited about the money, but mostly she was just so happy for me, knowing how great it must have felt to be able to share. We walked around Chelsea Piers looking at the check and smiling. We ate lobster rolls and cake bites and felt like we were floating. It was one of the best feelings I've ever had in my life. But more than being fun, giving is important! However, my business managers have told me to slow my roll, and my sister has warned me several times not to Giving Tree myself to the point where I am a stump with everyone's names carved onto me. But I'm happier being generous, because even though I know what it feels like to have a surplus of money, I haven't forgotten what it feels like to truly need it. People have had it way worse than me, of course, but I know what it is to depend completely on yourself in life.

THE YEAR AFTER my parents lost it all, my birthday party was much different than the barnyard fantasy experience I had during the rich years. The theme was the Lionel Richie song "Dancing on the Ceiling." My dad put a light fixture on the rug in the middle of the living room and the seven kids in attendance danced around it as the song played, over and over again. My dad filmed it with his camera upside down, and then we all watched the recording and ate pizza.

I actually remember it being a great time. It was, and still is, a great song, and the kids didn't care. We didn't need a bounce castle or someone dressed as Rainbow Brite to have a good time—give us some pizza and a disco ball, and there's a party. I didn't even realize we were out of money; I just thought my parents were confused about my level of affection for Lionel Richie.

Today, I'm just as happy as I was when I was waiting tables at a diner or collecting unemployment after getting fired. I don't believe that money changes your level of happiness. But things do get easier, and I feel great in the moments when I can help someone. I still mostly stay home and order

Chinese food or sushi. I still get drunk and binge-eat late at night. But now it's just on more expensive wine instead of the boxes of Carlo Rossi that got me through more than half of my life. I'm glad I struggled. I think I'd be an asshole if my money were anything other than the "new" kind. And for the record, when my niece asks me for a car in thirteen years, I will say "Of course" and treat her to a very shiny station wagon that turns on a dime and shakes what its mama gave it any time it goes over thirty miles per hour when she's going to buy her friends forties.

AN INTRODUCTION
TO MY STUFFED ANIMALS

For some reason I've always been drawn to these old, nightmarish stuffed animals. This started early on in my childhood. I never really liked the new, plush, cute animals—the kind with rainbows and hearts that they always market to little girls. You would never see my favorites crowded together in a toy store display. No. I liked these horrifying, broke-down creatures from yesteryear.

I'd like to introduce you to them—in no particular order. (I don't want them to think I have any favorites. Even though, of course, I do.) At some point, I plan to put out a request on Twitter where I ask people to post photos of their childhood stuffed animals that they still have and love. Let me clarify that if you still sleep with these animals, and you are a woman in your midthirties, you are weird. I absolutely do NOT do that every night. I don't. So shut up.

I got Mouser when I was about ten years old

at my friend's garage sale on Long Island. I had helped set up the goods they were selling, and I was eyeing him all morning. He just had a good vibe and we clicked. There was debate about whether he is a mouse or a bear, but I always felt he is clearly a mouse. Another confusing fact about his identity is that he is made of felt and velour but he is somehow covered in rust.

Bunny came into my life when I was about seven years old. She was the only one among my stuffed animals who was very new and freshly store-bought when I got her. This particular puppet style of flat rabbit was kind of hot at the time. Despite her being the most corporate of the gang with her mass appeal, I love Bunny, no question. I am calling Bunny a girl but I just now realized that I never actually assigned a gender to any of my stuffed friends.

I got Panda when I was eight years old. She too was kind of on the new side, but because she is so soft, she's gotten the most play out of me. I tattered her up right quick. Again, never thought of Panda as a girl or a guy. Just a panda.

I saw Penny at an antique store when I was seven. We have shared the most forbidden love story of all. I loved her so much, so fast. While my mom shopped around, I held on to this little felt panda puppet with a hard head full of straw and soulful googly eyes. I was heartbroken when my mom refused to buy her for me because she cost forty dollars. But a couple weeks later, we were reunited when my mom surprised me by bringing her home to me. Upon seeing her, I yelled, "Penny!!" My mom was very moved that I'd named a creature who wasn't yet mine. I once lost Penny for a year, only to find out she was at this chick Rachel's house. Rachel said she thought I'd given her Penny, and I explained to her that she was nuts because I would never part with precious little Penny. This second reunion with Penny was especially sweet. I think Penny is a girl but that never defined her. She's a little warrior.

The MVP has gotta be the lady in the photo at the end of this chapter: Pokey. Pokey was my mom's when she was a little girl so I've had her since I was born. She has, without fail, scared the shit out of every single boyfriend I've brought around. When I was a little girl, I was not invited to sleepover parties unless I promised to leave Pokey at home. She's been described as the bride of Chucky and also a nightmare machine. But I don't see her that way. I love her and still put her arm around my neck when I need comfort, just like I did when I was a little girl. Also I'm not sure Pokey is a chick but I do know that I have stained her with enough tears to change her color. She— or he, or it—has gotten me through it all. Pokey is filled with the same hard straw material as Penny's head, and despite my very fluid interpretations of her gender, I did choose to have her re-covered in pink fabric and white lace when I took her to the doll doctor (which is a thing). I have never been one to pay much attention to gender identification.

We had—well, we *still* have—a cat named Penelope who lives with my mom, but she has both paws in the grave at this point. I named her Penelope before we learned she was actually a boy, but we didn't change her name and we still refer to her as a "her" to this day.

Other stuffed animals have come and gone over the years. I have a two-headed bear that I never named. It was a gift from an ex-boyfriend. It was a pretty perfect gift. Soft and disturbing, which is how I would describe myself. I still have it. It's too perfect, which is also how he would describe himself. I've gotten a lot of stuffed animals from boyfriends over the years. I'm someone who likes to erase all record of an ex as soon as we break up. I try to *Eternal Sunshine* them from my life. I erase all pictures from my cell phone and throw away all gifts. I save printed pictures, but in a box in the closet.

The same ex who gave me the two-headed bear gave me a huge—and I mean huge—stuffed gorilla for Valentine's Day. We named him Carlos. And don't look into that for some racial undertones. I just liked the name Carlos. We'd joke about how he got me huge gifts even though I had a tiny apartment. He'd buy me giant things that didn't fit in it, sometimes on purpose. Once he got me a huge plant, more like a tree, which made my apartment look like a place Jane Goodall would want to hang out. I had to drag it to the backyard area, which in

New York City is really just a frightening alley for rats to frolic in and eat whatever you're storing out there—in my case, boogie boards.

The last stuffed toy I got from a boyfriend is a little stuffed horse. When my two-year-old niece first saw him, she started to call him "Neigh," which is the sound a horse makes, in case you grew up in a city. She now sleeps with Neigh and I have to play the waiting game until she moves on from him, but they've been going strong for a while now. I hope she isn't like that with dudes when she grows up. Or chicks. Or maybe she won't identify as female. Whatever she does will be fine. Or he. Damn, it's hard to write a book and not get yelled at.

I know you just started reading this book so you are still getting to know me, and maybe you are questioning my commitment to these animals. You think I'm writing a fanciful flight about these odd and amusing creatures. But I am 100 percent genuine in my devotion to them. Where does my obsession with them end? Not in a disgusting New York City garbage can where I once made a boyfriend rescue them after we discovered the movers had made a terrible mistake and thrown them all away. (To be fair to the movers, Pokey does look like she belongs in a dark alley in a war-torn village and not in a nice grown-ass woman's bedroom.) You might be thinking of asking me, *Amy, did you commission Tilda Swinton's life partner, Sandro, to paint a portrait of your stuffed animals to commemo-*

rate them forever and ever? No, that would be taking it too far—oh wait, no, I mean fuck YES I did that.

They're worth it. Each one of them is a ratty, pilled pile of fabric sewn together precariously, but I love them more than most of my family.

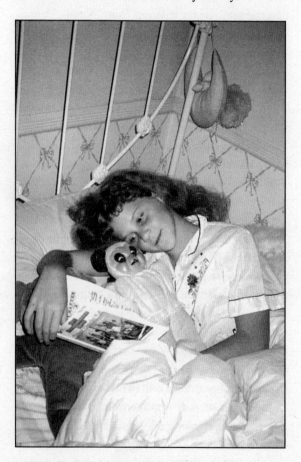

DAD

———

When I was fourteen my dad shit himself at an amusement park.

It all went down one fine summer morning when he took Kim and me to Adventureland, which is exactly what it sounds like: an amusement park filled with adventure, as long as you've never been on an actual adventure or to an actual amusement park. I'd fantasized about the trip the whole week, dreaming about my two favorite rides: the pirate ship and the swings. Granted, they were two of the tamer rides at the park, but for me, they were at the absolute outer limit of my comfort zone. I liked the rides that gave you that feeling of weightlessness that shot from your stomach right down to your vagina when the ride dropped, but I'd never enjoyed a ride that went upside down or spun around until I puked, and I still don't. I guess you could say I have a low tolerance for fear in general.

The movie *Clue* terrified me beyond belief as a child. I slept with a pillow on my back because the chef in that movie was stabbed in the back with a huge kitchen knife. *Not gonna happen to this gal; just try to get a knife through this pillow*, I thought. As if a murderer would enter my bedroom at night intent on stabbing me in the back, see that there was a pillow there, and cancel his plans. I used a similar tactic after hearing about (but not seeing) the movie *Misery*. I slept with pillows covering my legs in case Kathy Bates got a late-night urge to drive out to Long Island, break into my home, and beat my legs with a mallet. Maybe this is why I always slept with (still sleep with) all my scary-looking horror-show stuffed animals. For protection.

Suffice it to say, I was a major scaredy-cat. In fourth grade, I had a talk with the school psychologist about all the things that actively terrified me. I wasn't sent to see him by a concerned teacher, I actually *asked* to see him. I was probably the only nine-year-old in history who requested time with a shrink. After our session, he handed my mom a list of all my fears. This list included earthquakes and tapeworms, which didn't usually come up much where I lived, but my brother was learning about them in school and he couldn't resist the urge to convince me I was nothing more than a sitting duck who was 100 percent going to get eaten alive from the inside by a worm. Highest (and most memorable) on the list, however, was the specific fear that I'd accidentally churn myself into butter. This was inspired by a creepy antique children's book called *Little Black Sambo*, which is one of those stories from the simpler, more racist times of yore when people wrote frightening, insulting tales to help children fall asleep at night. It was highly popular back in the day and has since been rightly banned or taken out of circulation. But my mom had a copy lying around. It's about a boy who goes on an adventure and ends up getting chased by tigers, who circle and circle around a tree so fast that they churn themselves into a pool of butter, which the boy then takes home for his mother to use to make pancakes. Like ya do. Anyway, I was always riddled with fear that I'd somehow be transformed into melted butter, which now doesn't really sound like that much of a bummer. It sounds more like how I'd like to spend my last twenty-four hours on this earth.

Anywhoozle, the morning my dad was going to take us to Adventureland, I woke up and got dressed in denim shorts that stopped just above the knee (crazy flattering) and a long T-shirt with the Tasmanian Devil on it, to let people know what was up. The shirt had to be knotted at the side because it was the early nineties and that's how you rocked out then.

It was not usual for my dad to take us on fun outings, but our parents had recently divorced, so we'd started spending solo time with him. This way, we could sneak in some fun, and he could sneak in feeling like a parent. He picked us up in his little red convertible around ten a.m. (even after he lost everything, he still always drove a convertible). I sat in the front because the back was too windy, and I convinced Kim that she'd like it better. It was about a forty-minute drive from our house, but it felt like four hundred because of the anticipation: the dozen or so rides, the limitless Sour Powers, and the arcade games just inside the park!

My dad always made me feel super loved and did the best he possibly could, but when I was a kid, his identity confused me. He wasn't the golf-playing, beer-drinking family man I saw on TV or in my friends' kitchens. He wasn't so easily labeled—or so easily understood. When he was younger, he'd been a wealthy bachelor living in 1970s New York City—when it was also in its prime. He'd shared a penthouse with his best friend, Josh, who was a well-known actor at the time. He did drugs and slept with girls and enjoyed every moment of his life. When he met my mom, he said good-bye to that lifestyle. Kind of.

Throughout my childhood, he was always in shape—tanned and well-dressed. He was an international businessman, frequently traveling to France, Italy, Prague, and I'd know he'd returned home from a trip before I saw or heard him as his smell was so potent and gorgeous. I thought it was a mixture of expensive European cologne, a faint smell of cigarettes, and something else I didn't yet recognize but later discovered was alcohol.

I never knew my dad to be a big drinker. I never saw him and thought he was even a little buzzed. If you don't know the signs, then they can't be there. I remember coming home from school and seeing him passed out naked on the floor, but not putting two and two together. I remember that he once apologized to me for missing a volleyball game that he was at, but I just thought, *Oh, forgetful Dad!* I knew he smelled like scotch, but I thought nothing of it. (To this day when a guy I'm with is really hungover or drunk, the smell reminds me of my dad, as I warmly cuddle him closer. When I tell the guy, he laughs, thinking I'm joking.)

I only later found out that my dad was as serious an alcoholic as they came. He needed to go to detox several times when we were children. To his credit, he was clever with his addiction. He only drank when he traveled or when we slept, so . . . all the time and every night. The only thing that slowed down his drinking was multiple sclerosis.

He was diagnosed when I was about ten and was soon in the hospital for a while since the disease hit like a tidal wave. It started with a tingle in his feet and fingers and grew to complete numbness and pain in his legs. When he finally got out of the hospital, he kind of went back to normal. I didn't think about his illness and no one brought it up again. I loved my dad, but like any self-obsessed teen, I wasn't worried with his mortality. Even though I saw him lying in the hospital bed in pain, I still thought of him as invincible. The morning he picked us up to go to Adventureland, I had pirate ship rides on the brain and can't say I was too concerned about his health.

When we pulled up to the gates of the park, we

ran to the high-flying swings and got in line. It was
a little chilly, so it wasn't too busy, which meant
that we got to go on the ride two or three times
in a row before moving on. I loved those swings
because I could pretend I was fearless and twist my
chair around and around before they shot up in the
air to begin the ride, spinning me high in the sky.

I wanted to beeline to the pirate ship, but Kim
wanted to go on the big scary roller coaster. We had
all day, so I said fine, even though roller coasters
brought me zero joy. Being jolted around and the
yelling and the possibility of dying didn't—and
still doesn't—do it for me. I hated creeping up the
hill at a painfully slow pace only to shoot down and
hear the screams of all the people filled with regret
for coming aboard. But Kim liked them. And I
liked Kim. And since I was the big sister, I wanted
her to always think I was brave, so I pretended it
was no big deal and got in line.

But to be honest, I also wanted to wow my
dad. He knew I was a complete chickenshit, and
I thought he might notice and say something like
"Hey, Amy . . . you going on that ride was very
cool and interesting." He loved things like skydiving, which I eventually did when I was older,
also to try to impress him, even though I hated
every single second of it. So there we stood in a
long line that felt like it was moving too fast. I
hunched over a bit, hoping I wouldn't meet the
height requirement for the ride, but no such luck.
I continued to hope that the roller coaster would

close down for the day right before we got up to the front, or that there would be a lockdown on the park for a missing kid. There were thousands of kids there. Couldn't just one of them get lost? But alas, no, we were next.

"Do you want to sit in the front car?" the six-year-old-looking kid operating the ride asked us.

"YES!" Kim yelled.

I looked at my dad, who was giving me a most-likely-sarcastic thumbs-up. "Yeah," I added, even though Kim had already hopped in the front.

"I'll be watching you girls!" he said ecstatically.

We waved to my dad as we started creeping up Suicide Mountain, or whatever the roller coaster was called.

I don't remember much of the next two minutes, but finally the car stopped and I opened my eyes. The only silver lining was that I didn't get physically hurt, and it was a great way to practice dissociating—something my siblings and I all perfected by our early teen years. We climbed off, and Kim was thrilled. She'd had the time of her life.

I can't speak for the other maniacs on that ride, but for me, the roller coaster was traumatic. When I walked down that ramp I felt as though the president should have been at the bottom waiting to give me a medal for valor. But there was no medal; just my dad, smiling at us.

"There's no line!" Kim shouted. "Let's go again!"

And so we went, and we went and we went. Each time my dad cheered us on from the bottom.

We must have ridden that thing five times when we reached the end of the ride and he wasn't there.

"Where's Dad?" Kim asked.

I told her, "He's probably getting us candy or something."

While we waited for him, we rode the ride again and again and again. After the twelfth go I was feeling real ready to get on that pirate ship, which was the main adventure I wanted to have in this land. Kim was raring to go again, but I had to stop. I thought it might be nice to take a break and maybe have kids someday, and I was sure Dad would meet us when he was done doing . . . *What was he doing?*

At that point in time, I hadn't yet realized how funny my dad is. Most of the things he did or said flew right over my head, and everyone else's for that matter. His sense of humor was so dry that days would pass before people realized he'd insulted them. He threw out perfect one-liners under his breath while talking to waiters or bankers or my mom—and no one heard them but me. Once my grandma was talking to him, and she said, "If I die . . . ," and he corrected her slyly: "*When* . . . " He was even dark with us as children. I remember walking into the kitchen one time and seeing him pretending that I had just caught him in the act of putting our dog, Muffin, in the microwave. He had a way about him that made it seem like nothing could ruffle his feathers or surprise him.

So that day while Kim and I sat on a bench and

waited for my father, I saw a new side of him. We waited and waited. I put stupid braids in Kim's hair and made her give me a hand massage until he finally reappeared. When he walked up to us, the first thing I noticed was his expression; he was panicked and defeated at the same time. The second thing I noticed was that he didn't have pants on.

Kim didn't observe any of this because she immediately asked, "Can we get fudge?!"

"Sure," my dad answered.

He and I looked at each other. I was speechless. His T-shirt, which was soaking wet along the bottom half, was long enough to cover his underwear, but his pants were long gone.

"We need to go, Aim," he told me very calmly.

I thought about asking something reasonable, like "Where are your pants, Dad?" But he looked in my eyes and communicated that I shouldn't ask any questions. I went into the country-store-themed shop and got Kim her fudge, and then we all walked briskly to the car. I didn't look to see if anyone was staring. I only watched ten-year-old Kim, who was fully enthralled by every bite of her treat. *Does she really not see that he's pantsless? I know it's called Adventureland but I don't think those adventures involve men over forty dressing like Winnie the Pooh after a wet T-shirt contest.*

We'd just gotten very close to the car when a breeze hit and sent the smell my way. It was shit. Human shit.

It was then I realized, *Oh, my dad shit his pants.*

Okay. I quickly leveraged this opportunity to look like a selfless and charitable sister. "You can get shotgun this time, Kimmy!" I was quick on my feet.

"Really?!" she answered. She was so excited to get this privilege that it kind of broke my heart. Amusement park fudge AND shotgun? She couldn't believe her luck. Little did she know she wouldn't be able to enjoy eating that fudge for much longer, or possibly ever again.

We climbed in the car, me in the back, Kim up front with my dad. As he put down the top, I looked in the side mirror and saw Kim's nostrils start to flare. She'd picked up the scent. The most silent car ride of my life began. The fudge sat in Kim's lap for the rest of the ride and her head slowly crept further and further in the direction away from my dad. The entire top was down on the car, but she still felt the need to hang her little head out the side. She looked like a golden retriever by the time my dad pulled up to our house to drop us off.

I was so impressed with her for not saying anything. *What a good girl*, I thought. She kissed my dad on the cheek and thanked him and ran into the house, her face the same exact hue as Kermit the Frog. I hopped out and held my breath to kiss him. I started to walk up our driveway when he called to me.

"Aim!"

I turned and answered, "Yeah?"

He took a breath and said, "Please don't tell your mom." I nodded.

The saddest realization I've had in my life is that my parents are people. Sad, human people. I aged a decade in that moment.

THE SECOND TIME my dad shit himself in my presence, I didn't have a roller coaster to keep me from witnessing it. It was right in front of me. Well, more to the side of me.

It was four years later, the summer before I left for college, right before I got on a plane to Montana to stay with my older brother, Jason, for a couple weeks. I worshipped Jason and was always trying to hang out with him. He is almost four years older than me, and as far as I was concerned, he should have won *People* magazine's most intriguing person of the year, every year. He was a basketball prodigy in his early teens but suddenly quit in high school because he didn't want to live up to other people's expectations anymore. He was curious about things like time and space, and genuinely considered living in a cave for months and being nocturnal. He became an accomplished musician without telling anyone. He didn't go to his senior year of high school, choosing instead to earn the credits needed for graduation by driving cross-country and writing about it—somehow convincing the principal of our high school and our mother that this was a great idea. I know this is sounding like that Dos Equis ad that glorifies the eccentric old guy with a beard, but the point is I have been crazy about Jason since I was born and I always wanted to be a part of whatever unusual existence he was living. So I went to hang out with him any chance I had.

At this particular time, my dad was on a kick of wanting to do "dad stuff" for me, so he asked if he could drive me to the airport. When you have MS "dad stuff" becomes playing bingo or giving you rides places. It was midafternoon when he picked me up to head to JFK.

When we got there, I pulled my giant suitcase out of the trunk of his car and navigated the airport entrance without his help. This must have looked strange to other people, seeing this strapping man watch his eighteen-year-old daughter lift and tote her giant suitcase all by herself, but they didn't know he was sick. I didn't really understand the symptoms of the disease, but I did know that it slowed him down, that even if he looked normal he could still be in a lot of pain, unable to do the small physical acts he used to do with ease.

My dad accompanied me as I juggled my bags and checked in, and everything seemed fine. It was pre-9/11 so he could walk me to the gate, and that's exactly what he wanted to do. He kept saying, "I'm going to walk you to the gate." I think it was a big deal for him, because he never did stuff like that for me. That was a mom-type job. But I was glad for his company, because even though my list of fears had definitely gotten smaller by this point in my life, I was still pretty terrified of flying.

We both went through security, shoes on—the

good ol' days—and started walking down the long hall to my gate. That particular terminal was under heavy construction at the time, so we had to be careful where we walked. We still had a ways to go when my dad took a sharp right turn and beelined it to the side of the hall. I stopped walking and turned to see what he was doing. He shot me a pained look, pulled his pants down, and peed shit out of his ass for about thirty seconds. Thirty seconds is an eternity, by the way, when you're watching your dad volcanically erupt from his behind. Think about it now. One Mississippi. That's just one.

People quickly walked past, horrified. One woman shielded her child's eyes. They stared. I yelled at one chick passing by, "WHAT?! Keep it moving!"

After he had finished, my dad stood up straight and said, "Aim, do you have any shorts in your bag?"

I opened my suitcase and grabbed a pair of lacrosse shorts. I handed them over, thinking, *Damn, those were my favorite*. He threw his pants in the trash and put the shorts on. I went in for a top-body hug good-bye. I didn't cry, I didn't laugh, I just smiled and said, "I love you, Dad. I won't tell Mom."

I started to walk away from the whole scene when I heard, "I said I'd walk you to the gate!"

I turned around to see if he was joking; he was not. To the gate we walked. I was mouth breathing and shooting dirty looks at anyone who dared to stare at him. Once we got to the very last gate in the goddamn terminal, at the end of a very long hall, he kissed me good-bye and left.

Normally when I would board a plane, the first thing I would do was worry about how scary take-off would be and try to think of ways to distract myself from the anxiety. But that day, I sat on the plane thinking about nothing. My mind went blank. It was too painful. I didn't think about my fearless father, who was dealing with a mysterious disease. He used to breeze through the airport in a cloud of expensive cologne and flashy watches, and now he'd been transformed into this anonymous, helpless guy who lost control of his bowels in the airport while his teenage daughter watched. He didn't wince or let me see him sweat even once. I mean, he was drenched in sweat. Physically he was being taken over by MS, yet on the inside he was still as brazen as ever. But I didn't think about any of that. I just stared out the window for five hours, fully numb, until I got off the plane in Montana and hugged my brother longer than he would have liked.

I tried to talk about these two shitting incidents onstage. So many parts of these stories are so disturbing that they make me laugh—because it's too much to digest any other way. The image of Kim's head leaning out of the car, the image of me standing next to my pantsless father and the trolley that carted people around Adventureland. I look at the saddest things in life and laugh at how awful they are, because they are hilarious and it's all we can do with moments that are painful. My dad is the same way. He's always laughed at the things that are too dark for other people to laugh at. Even now, when his memory and mental functioning have been severely impaired by his MS, I'll tell him his mind is a pile of scrambled eggs and he will still laugh hysterically and say, "Too true, too true!"

My dad never shows any sign that he pities himself. He never has. He's not afraid to look dead-on at the grim facts of his life. I hope I've inherited this quality of his. I've only seen him cry once about his disease, and that was very recently—when he learned he'd be getting stem cell treatments that would help him feel a lot better, and maybe even help him walk again. That day, he sobbed like a baby. But never before.

I have wonderful early memories of spending time with him at the beach. We were beach bums, and he was a sun worshipper. If it was January and the sun was shining, he'd douse himself in baby oil and sit outside in a lawn chair. He was tan year-round. And if it was summer, we'd get in the ocean early in the morning and get out after the sun went down. We'd body-surf together; that was our thing. All I wanted to do was take a wave in further than him, but it never happened. I even cheated, standing up and running a little to catch up, but no, he always won.

The most joy I remember feeling as a kid was when a storm was coming and the waves were big. Other people were scared and stayed out of the water, but not us. Not even when the ocean was angry and pulling us sideways. We would have to get out and walk half a football field on the beach before it swept us all the way down the shore again. We swam out against the current and caught the best waves of the day. Nothing kept us out—not rain, not my mom yelling, nothing. I can still picture him looking young and healthy and strong, with his bronzed skin and his black hair soaking. For some reason, I wasn't afraid. Maybe it was because I was with him. Next to him, I was invincible.

EXCERPT FROM MY JOURNAL IN 1994 (AGE THIRTEEN) WITH FOOTNOTES FROM 2016

I've decided to get a journal because some things you just can't say out loud.[1] I'm 13 years old, and I have several problems. My brother Jason is a senior in high school. He's my half brother, meaning we have the same mother, but his dad died when he was 11. When Jason was two years old our mom married my dad. My dad didn't like my brother, and as a matter of fact, he wished Jason wasn't a part of our family.[2] I never noticed, but my Dad actually never went on our "family trips."[3] My mom just recently pointed all of this out to me. She said she tried to keep everyone happy by having my dad go in one car and me and my brother and sister go in the other car with her.[4]

---

1 I obviously don't subscribe to this advice anymore, as someone who onstage has gone into great detail about an encounter with an unexpected uncircumcised penis.

2 Yikes, was that true? There is a lot of heavy brainwashing from good ol' mom in this entry. I don't think my dad particularly cared for my brother, but it wasn't personal. He just only liked children that at one point were shot out from his own penis.

3 I don't know why "family trips" is in quotes. They were just family trips; this sounds like my mom was using us to mule drugs. We would go to Florida or Lake George or our farmhouse. I never once held a balloon filled with heroin.

4 You know that old saying . . . the family that drives separately, crumbles and shatters soon after.

Jason's dad was a very big part of his life. My mom informed me that when he died, my dad made no effort to become Jason's stepfather.[5] They seemed to be acquaintances. This left my mom a single parent, basically, with no help from my father. I'm so glad she pointed this out to me, because I never knew. She allowed Jason to withdraw from our family,[6] which is no longer a family.

My sister Kim is nine years old and in fourth grade. She is very mature for her age. I think she's so mature because I don't permit her to act her age. In her grade there are a few girls who are total &*&*.[7] They treat her like dirt. It doesn't help that Kim is extremely sensitive. These girls do horrible things to her, like one day they were all sitting at the lunch table, and when Kim sat down, they all got up and left. When my mom told me about it, tears started streaming down my cheeks before she even finished her sentence. My heart broke for Kim. So I hopped on my bike and road straight to those #\$#\$'s[8] houses and yelled at them. And told them to leave my sister alone OR ELSE![9]

---

5 This was true, but maybe pointing this out to a tween isn't the best move from a parent.

6 As I previously mentioned, Jason talked his way out of his senior year of high school and got to leave home and roam the country.

7 If I wrote this now I would use the word "cunts."

8 CUNTS!

9 We recently Googled the girl who was the meanest to my sister. We found her on Facebook. She's now a Pilates instructor, of course, and if I had her current address, I'd ride my bike to her house again and tell her she's still a worthless mean girl in my mind.

Kim sometimes acts really phony.[10] *She'll act so innocent and fragile,*[11] *and I'll get really mad at her and treat
her like crap. My mom tells her to just express herself when
someone at school hurts her feelings. I say, "No way. You
have to be tough and don't show them they hurt you."*[12]

*About 8 weeks ago I found out that my parents were
getting a divorce.*[13] *My dad travels a lot, so I wasn't
majorly depressed. My sister was, though. After the
first five years that my parents were married my mom
realized she wasn't in love and never had been.*[14] *But
she stayed with my dad another five years because of me
and Jay and Kim, and also because my dad developed
a condition with -osis at the end of the word.*[15] *Anyone
who knows my mom will tell you she's the nicest person
you'll ever meet.*[16] *But they're getting a divorce.*

*I'm going to see a psychologist this Thursday. I
don't want to, but I know it's necessary.*[17]

---

10 Wow, I was just saying how great she was.

11 Innocent and fragile? Dude, she was nine . . . What did I
expect her to act like? Slutty and hardened?

12 I stand by this. Never let those cunts see you sweat, which
is good advice and a good name for an eighties hip-hop album.

13 Whaaaaat? But Mom kept us all happy by having us drive in
separate cars!

14 Again, damn, Mom, lot to lay on a kid who's still in middle
school, but okay.

15 It was multiple sclerosis. You couldn't look stuff up on your
phone back then, so I just left it at -osis . . . makes sense.

16 "Brainnnnnwasssshhhhh, at the brainwash yeah" (singing this
to the tune of "Car Wash" . . .).

17 I still say this exact same thing every single week.

I have another problem: my friends. Lauren, Becky, and Kate. I guess you can say we're the athletic, smart, pretty girls of our grade.[18] Becky is sort of slow; she has a moon shaped face with light freckles and pin straight, shoulder length, dirty blonde hair. She's as tall as me but a little slimmer. She thinks she's totally gorgeous and wishes she was Lauren. She's also a snob.[19] Then there's Jen; she's excellent at soccer and totally dedicated, but she's also a ditz and always the last to know what we're talking about. She's 5 foot 3ish and has mousy brown hair and looks very Irish. Everyone does, I guess.[20]

I can't believe I haven't mentioned my other best friend, Mark. His hair is chin length and he's always showered and clean. He's a really good soccer player, and he's an excellent drummer. I met him in 5th grade. He started a band this summer, and I was interested in being the lead singer. When it was just me and Mark in the band I was fine, but when it became a real thing I backed away. I strive to be more like Mark.[21] I think I care too much about how people feel about me. Mark isn't like that at all. If I wasn't friends with him, I wouldn't be half as happy. Now that I think about it, he may be my only real friend.[22]

Now about boys.[23] *There are several boys I like, but*

---

18 Guess I wasn't afraid of feelin' myself.

19 Never too young to talk shit about your friends.

20 Jen is a nurse with three kids now, and we're still close.

21 I was in love with him.

22 Mark is now the drummer in the band Taking Back Sunday.

23 Sorry, Mark!

the two I'm concentrated on are Kevin Williams and Joshua Walsch. Kevin is shy, funny, and cool. He has shaggy brown hair and is over six feet tall. He has gorgeous blue cat eyes and a mouth like the joker. I told him that once in biology and he smirked and said he knew. Joshua is a year younger than me, but he's so sweet and adorable. He has black hair and a smaller frame than me, but he's strong and has porcelain skin covered in freckles. He looks like he just hopped off the boat from Ireland.[24]

Both boys have little speech impediments, I've noticed. Joshua has a speech impediment that makes him sound like the Kennedys. The real ones![25] And Kevin has a gap in his front teeth and a lisp. Uhhh soo cute.[26]

I've gotten to first base, which is French Kissing, but I think I'm ready for 2nd.[27]

---

24 I was real obsessed with the Irish. Pretty sure I'd either just done a book report on them or watched *Far and Away* at a slumber party.

25 As opposed to those hack, bullshit, fake Kennedys?

26 I have always been turned on by a good impediment, like a baby arm or a stutter.

27 I wasn't.

OFFICIALLY A WOMAN

Everyone says you become a woman when you start your period or lose your virginity. In Judaism, you're deemed a woman when you have your bat mitzvah. I of course saw this ceremony as an opportunity not only to chant my Torah portion but also to make my big stage debut in the temple. I'd been doing musicals since I was five, and I was ready to steal the show. *I'm gonna show these Jews what I'm made of*, I thought in an unracist way. All eyes were on me—just the way I liked it—as I looked out into the crowd from the bimah. My mom was crying tears of joy next to my dad, who was absolutely bursting with pride. I wouldn't have been surprised if they gave me a standing O before I finished. I was nailing it.

I sang those Hebrew words like the little half-Jew angel that I was—without the slightest idea what I was saying. I could have been chanting a call to action to continue apartheid. In Hebrew school they taught us two things: how to read Hebrew and how to read Hebrew. A year before my bat mitzvah I was in class with my teacher, Mr. Fischer, a frightening, expressionless man, the kind who would look the same sleeping or in an earthquake. I was sitting in the first row, and Mr. Fischer called on me to read aloud from the Torah. After about three minutes, I stopped and asked, "What does this mean?" For the first time ever, he showed emotion. He slammed his catcher's-mitt-like hand onto his desk right next to my head and shouted, "Go to the principal's office!" I never asked again.

I'm sure this wasn't the first time I got in trouble for asking a question, and it certainly wasn't the last. In school we were encouraged to ask questions, but sometimes when we did, we were accused of being provocative or rude. Now that I'm out of school and there's no threat of a principal's office looming down the hall, I ask whatever the fuck questions I want. It feels pretty good. Pretty womanly, too.

But none of that mattered on my big day. I didn't care what I was singing; I just wanted to blow everyone's socks off. I belted out the last couple lines of my portion—move over, cast of *Fiddler on the Roof*, your jobs are all in jeopardy—and on my final note, I let loose with all my might. That was when my dream turned into my nightmare. My voice cracked. I William Hunged my last note. My heart started to pound too quickly, and I could feel my face turning into a beet the way it loved to do. Silence filled the room, and I thought I might cry.

Then came the first laugh. Then another. And

the rest. I looked out at the people in the seats, and they were all laughing—and looking at me with adoration. I saw Kim nervously giggling, waiting to see how I'd react. I realized that even though it was an accident, I'd made everyone happy, and I wanted to let Kim know that it was okay to laugh, so I joined in. I laughed hard. I was laughing at myself. We were all laughing together—a real laugh that went on for a while.

I'm pretty sure that's why I officially became a woman that day. Not because of the dumb ancient ceremony where children are gifted bonds they can't cash until they're twenty-five (by which time they have lost them). No, I became a woman because I turned a solemn, quiet room into a place filled with unexpected laughter. I became a woman because I did, for the first time, what I was supposed to be doing for the rest of my life. I may not have had that exact thought in the moment, but in retrospect it is so clear to me.

There are lots of "firsts" like this in life, little flashpoints here and there when you're unknowingly becoming a woman. And it's not the clichéd shit, like when you have your first kiss or drive your first car. You become a woman the first time you stand up for yourself when they get your order wrong at a diner, or when you first realize your parents are full of shit. You become a woman the first time you get fitted for a bra and realize you've been wearing a very wrong size your whole fucking life. You become a woman the first time you fart in front of a boyfriend. The first time your heart breaks. The first time you break someone else's heart. The first time someone you love dies. The first time you lie and make yourself look bad so a friend you love can look better. And less dramatic things are meaningful too, like the first time a guy tries to put a finger in your ass. The first time you express the reality that you don't want that finger in your ass. That you really don't want anything in your ass at all. Or to have any creative, adventurous sex for that matter. That you just want to be fucked missionary sometimes and without any nonsense. You will remember all these moments later as the moments that made you the woman you are. Everyone tells you it happens when you get your first period, but really it happens when you insert your first tampon and teach your best friend to do the same.

Speaking of menstrual blood, let's get back to becoming a woman in the temple. After I brought the house down by dropping the ball on my Torah portion, it was time for the rabbi to walk over and speak to me in front of everyone—not unlike a sermon, but tailored to me. I'd been told that most people hated this kind of attention, but I thought, *Bring it on. Let the compliments begin.*

Rabbi Shlomo was a tall man, and he had to reach down to put his hands on both of my shoulders. I gazed up at him and prepared to look humble. He began, "Amy . . . ," and that's the last thing I heard. His breath was so bad, I literally couldn't listen to a word. It took all my strength not to pass out from the stench he was sending my way. I figured out quickly that I needed to gasp for breath while he was inhaling. He was giving me heartfelt words of wisdom and I was doing Lamaze. *What did he eat for breakfast?* I thought. *An adult diaper? A cadaver?*

The speech went on for hours. It was probably only five minutes, but when you're in the panic room of someone's dragon mouth the clock really stops. Just as I was getting dizzy from lack of oxygen, I could tell from his body language that he was wrapping it up. Everyone applauded. I turned away, filled my lungs with fresh air, and smiled out into oblivion. It was official: I was a woman.

Now I could have a short luncheon with smoked fish and bagels and take my closest friends to Medieval Times in New Jersey. Just as God and Golda Meir intended.

CAMP ANCHOR

When I was fourteen, I volunteered at a camp for people with special needs. Camp Anchor is still around today; it's an amazing program that now serves more than seven hundred campers a year. People volunteer there because you can help those in need, it's good for your soul, and it enriches your life. I did it because the boys were doing it, and I wanted to have a soccer player's tongue in my mouth before I died.

I would like to say that I went into it wanting to help others. But let's be real—I was a teenager who only cared about herself. Adolescence is full of awkwardness and insecurity for most people. But in my case it was also full of grand delusions. Besides wanting boys to like me, I also wanted to embody all the impossible combinations: I wanted to be both beautiful and kind, smart and selfless. My mom was a teacher for the deaf, so I'd been around kids with special needs for as long as I could remember. I thought it would be easy, and I knew how to talk to these children like adults. I'd show them love and respect and be giving of myself. I pictured teaching a little girl how to swim and was already patting myself on the back for being such a great person: Saint Amy. People would line up around the block just so I'd smile at them and once in a while give them a hug, like I was a Buddhist street monk, and they'd be eternally blessed. But mostly I was excited to ride the bus and try to fit in with the cute guys.

A lot of the cool older boys from my high school volunteered at Camp Anchor, but I only had eyes for Tyler Cheney. He had soulful brown eyes and a mess of curly hair. He was a great soccer player but also loved Phish and the Grateful Dead. (Wow— could there be any limits to how diverse this guy's interests were?) I loved making Tyler laugh, which wasn't hard to do because he was a complete stoner and his double-digit IQ wasn't what made him attractive. For most of my life I have had the habit of being attracted to hot guys with the intelligence of a jack-o'-lantern and a distended belly. I always loved a belly. Tyler was no different. All I would have to do to make him laugh was quote the movie *Tommy Boy*. I knew it by heart, so he basically thought I was George Carlin. I think he's in finance now and has a hedge fund or something else I can't understand. (How come stupid people can still make money like that? I don't know what a hedge fund is. I want a hedgehog fund. They are so cute and I think I need one. But I would probably kill it by accident. I can't even keep a plant alive. Okay, never mind.)

Tyler sat in front of me in Spanish class and I'd stare at the back of his curly head, trying to will him to turn around and declare his love for me, something that never even came close to happening. But when I heard he was going to volunteer at Camp Anchor, well, guess what, Tyler Cheney? So was I. I'd save the shit out of some kids to be close to him.

On our first day at Camp Anchor, we waited for the bus to pick us up at an elementary school parking lot. I remember I'd laid out my first-day-of-work outfit on my bed the night before. *Wait until Tyler sees me in this*, I thought. A Twitter-blue T-shirt. My flannel plaid blue-and-green boxer shorts that had PENN STATE on them (and not even on the butt; this was a few years before the marketing geniuses decided to put their paws right on the spot where every dude's and most curious women's eyes go right away). I pulled up those shorts, did a half turn in the mirror, and hoped deeply and sadly that this would be the outfit I'd be wearing when Tyler realized I could be good for him. I knew I had a long way to go, because so far I was still just the oily-faced girl whose idea of seduction was to whisper impersonations of America's favorite sweaty three-hundred-pound male comic in his ear. But maybe camp was the place where he would see me in a new light. *If I could just make myself become more his type*, I thought. I tied up my hair in one of those ballerina buns and took a hair dryer to my bangs, but within ten seconds they blew up in the summer humidity so that I bore a striking resemblance to Sammy Hagar.

I sat one row away from Tyler on the bus and was already sweating through my carefully selected outfit, sticking to the green pleather seats, which were torn up and graffitied by badasses whose parents were failing. I listened to Roxette on my Walkman and tried to seem distant and interesting, like Brenda on *Beverly Hills, 90210*, whom I've modeled myself on for most of my life. She was the queen of the impossible combinations. She seemed to have been born with an innocence (me) yet she oozed sex appeal (totally me) and she would fit right in doing something as pure as a sing-along, but only if it ended with her getting railed from behind by Dylan under the bleachers. Sweet, with a dark, dirty edge, just like fourteen-year-old me. Except none of that, and I'd never even been fingered and was deeply heinous looking at the time. But I wanted so badly to make the shoe fit, to be the kind of impossible person Brenda was. Anyway, when the bus pulled up to camp, I took a break from envisioning myself as the center of attention at the Peach Pit, peeled my legs off the seat, and got off the bus. We walked to registration en masse, while I was channeling *We're gonna be a cool, fun group all summer, right, you guys? I'm one of the guys, but you have feelings for me. You will give yourself over to me around the Fourth of July, RIGHT, TYLER?*—type energy.

As I approached the registration desk where we were going to find out what group we were assigned to, I had only two wishes: 1) that Tyler and I would be assigned to the same group, and 2) that I'd get the cutest littlest kids—the five-to-eight-year-old girls, called the "Junior 3s." The groups were divided by sex and age, and I'd seen the Junior 3s listed in the brochure when I was considering volunteering. I wanted to be their cool big sister who'd impact their lives forever. They were adorable, and I pictured us doing the annual talent show and laughing and hugging. I'd give them each a piggyback ride and Tyler would say, "Wow, you must be sore . . . need a massage?" And I'd say, "Sure, maybe later. I just have to make sure everyone gets a turn first." Like a hero. And then I'd give him a massage and slip and fall on his penis and get pregnant and trap him and be on the first season of *Teen Mom*.

"Senior Ten!" announced the elderly woman who I thought was a man until she barked at me.

"Excuse me?" I barked back.

"You will be working with Senior Ten—that is women thirty-five and up. There is your group," she said, pointing to a herd of ladies who looked more *Golden Girls* than little girls.

I was thrown off. "I didn't know there were campers older than me," I demurred.

The woman, who resembled my grandpa when he let his hair grow a little too long, gave me an expressionless nonreply.

"What a fun surprise," I said.

I was a flake, and she could smell it on me. I'd come to Camp Anchor to flirt with boys and put something on my college applications, and she knew it. She saw right through my Chia Pet bangs into my shallow heart and frowned. She handed me my paperwork and sent me on my way.

I slowly approached another volunteer, a beautiful Latina girl from a couple towns over. "Hi, I'm Carli!" she said, beaming goodness. She was here for the right reasons, I thought. She was a beautiful, pure-souled girl, and I was a pug-nosed disaster. She was a Brenda with a twist. Even more gorgeous, sexy without seeming slutty, and charitable on top of it all. That kind of perfection didn't yet make me furious. It just made me want to be exactly like her. Then there was Dave Mack, a gorgeous guy whom I would have immediately fallen in deep West Beverly High love with except for the fact that I could see he'd already set his sights on Carli. *Man, maybe if I had gotten here first I'd have gotten him*, I lied to myself. But he was smart and could see that Carli was a living angel with perfect olive skin and a sweet little tush.

Our group leader, Joanne, was a pretty woman with frizzy blond hair, a pronounced Italian-looking nose, a fanny pack, and a great rack. She was the only one of us who got paid, though I can't imagine it was a lot. She was a kind, strong woman who'd been around the block with these ladies. She was no-nonsense, but she'd still laugh with the rest of us when ridiculousness occurred. Which was often.

Every day, I'd put so much mental energy into wanting to be appealing to Tyler—or wanting to be as flawless as Carli. But the Senior 10 chicks who I was now spending all my time with had much better strategies. They generally didn't waste energy hiding who they were or faking who they weren't. There was Mona, who was always wearing a baseball hat and a huge muscle T-shirt with Mickey Mouse on it. She was strong and masculine, and her smile would light up a room. Mona had Down syndrome, as did her best friend, Lucy, who had a short, boyish haircut and knock-knock jokes for days. I almost never understood the punch lines, but she was so delighted by reciting them you couldn't help but laugh right along with her.

Another camper, Debbie, was openly flirtatious and boy crazy. She kept her hair braided perfectly so she felt pretty. Plump and youthful, she was like a Juliet looking for her Romeo. She had Down syndrome, too. Blanche had a long, thin, freckled face. She didn't mind being mean and made it clear early on that she didn't like me one bit. I respected that and stayed out of her way. No energy wasted between us faking it.

Enid was schizophrenic and reminded me of Woody Allen in terms of her voice and her physical movements. She had short red hair with tight curls and was very neurotic. She'd often pace around and talk to herself. Once, I nudged her to tell her it was time for lunch, and she replied, "Don't interrupt me, can't you see I'm having a conversation?" Well, damn, she was right. I didn't let it happen again. She couldn't stomach small talk but was kind enough to engage in some good debates with me. She was so bright that I'd forget about her ailments. Much like a stoic big sister, Enid would sometimes refuse to have anything to do with me, but other days we were thick as thieves. By the end of the summer, I was closest with her.

One sunny day it was my job to hang with a camper named Beatrice, a sweet sixty-year-old woman who spoke like Gollum from *The Lord of the Rings* and had an even bigger crush on Dave than I did. Dave and Beatrice were sweet on each other. At all the dancing events it was understood that no one danced with Dave but Big B. She was only four feet tall but weighed about two hundred pounds, and though her words were, in general, indeterminable, listening to her speak was a treat. She'd mumble something that sounded like it would only make sense in the Shire, and laugh wildly to herself and slap her knee.

On this particular day we had a huge game of Marco Polo planned for the campers in the pool. Nothing says summer like a game centered around a Venetian merchant sailor who may or may not have traveled through Asia in the 1200s to 1300s. I was fully prepared to win the game: I was younger and faster than my Senior 10s and I knew I could dominate that pool. I was extra motivated knowing that being in bathing suits always made the campers grabby with one another's bodies. Especially mine. They thought it was funny to grab my breasts, and if one of them caught up to me, my boobs would be squeezed like lemons at a lemonade stand. Not that I don't like affection, but they grabbed hard and I bruise like a peach. But before the game started, Joanne asked me to take Beatrice to the bathroom and wait for her while she put on her bathing suit.

I brought her into the muggy bathroom and while she was in the stall changing, I looked at myself in the foggy mirror. I didn't recognize myself. My body was in the adolescent state where I would get frequent growing pains in my legs. Exactly every other day I looked either long and lanky or chubby and potatolike. The only constant at the time was the difference in the size of my breasts. My right one was very much in the lead. The left wouldn't catch up for years and never fully has. The mirror got foggier as I stood and stood and waited and waited.

"Beatrice?!"

She made a Nell-like grumble from within the stall. "*Whloppppr.*"

"Bea, what's goin' on, sister? Let's go, we're gonna miss the game."

After several minutes the door was flung open and out came Beatrice ready for the chlorine in her bathing suit and Teva sandals. There was just one problem: her bathing suit was on backward. Her scoop-back one-piece was facing very much the wrong way, which meant that I was getting a full-frontal view of what used to be Beatrice's breasts. They were long and old; at the time, I'd never seen anything hang on for dear life like this before. They looked like those fake snakes that pop out of trick cans of peanuts. Her cans were attached to her chest and those snakes were loose, skin-colored, and almost to the floor. She looked around the bathroom, anywhere but at me. I looked right at her. I was mesmerized: here I'd been afraid of one of the campers grabbing my breasts, and I was now faced with hers. I could tell that she had absolutely no clue about the wardrobe malfunction and she made a beeline for the door.

"Whoa whoa whoa!" I yelled, trying to block her.

She knew something was off, but she was fired up about the pool. "Poo poo," she said, meaning "pool." I think.

"You need to turn your suit around. It's on backward, honey."

She looked at me with anger in her always-red eyes. I could see that she was ready to go and wasn't going to let me stop her. She was not interested in turning that suit around; it was game time.

I body-blocked the exit, led her gently but forcibly back into the stall, and did what needed to be done. I took those bathing-suit straps in my hands and yanked them down. It was a struggle. The suit was so tight I had to drop down to my knees and use my body weight to get it off her. There we were, Beatrice nude, staring and blinking, and me trying to grip and pull at the spandex swimwear, my face inches away from her vagina and breasts, which at this point were very much in the same general area. Her soft, stretched-out nips rested on my sunburned shoulders while I twisted her suit around and told her to step back into it. She ignored me. She was probably daydreaming about her and Dave summering on Martha's Vineyard next year. Undeterred, I picked up her white and soft-as-porcelain-looking foot and placed it in one leg hole, did the same with the other leg, and then, with all of my might, pulled that tiny suit over her pear-shaped body.

I was dripping with sweat by the time we were finished, and the bathroom could have doubled as a steam room. We walked out hand in hand to the pool. Finally, someone at this camp wanted to hold my hand. I think she knew I needed it. Almost whistling, she led me to the pool, but I was too exhausted and freaked out to join the Marco Polo game. Instead, I sat on a deck chair, staring off into space without moving, as Beatrice splashed around with the other ladies. One of them probably grabbed my breast, but I felt nothing for the next forty-eight hours.

Coming face-to-face with B's unmentionables wasn't even the most memorable moment in the Camp Anchor bathroom. That one is reserved for Sally. She was a Senior 10 who had some sort of aging disorder. Even though she was forty years old, she had the body of a seven-year-old and the face of a much older woman. She had Peter Pan—short black hair with some grays mixed in, tons of freckles, a furrowed brow, and a harsh look in her black eyes. She was very thin, spoke like a child, and always kept to herself. To get her jazzed about any group activity was beyond impossible. I remember approaching her once and, mustering up some false enthusiasm, telling her, "Sally, we're going to the arts-and-crafts tent to make picture frames now!" She stared into my eyes and looked through my soul. She didn't care. She knew I didn't care. She knew I knew she didn't care. In that moment we nodded and made a silent contract to keep it more real with each other.

One day in the last week of camp, there was a fun hangout planned for all the volunteers at the end of the day. I was wearing cut-off denim shorts with my uniform T-shirt sleeves rolled up. I'd planned a special outfit because I had confirmed that Tyler would definitely be there (I knew because I'd asked him and all his friends three hundred times). I'd noticed earlier that I was the only person not wearing Converse sneakers (like a dolt), so I'd bought a pair that were blue and white and almost identical to Carli's. She'd noticed, and instead of being annoyed, she'd said, "Cool! We have the same shoes!" Did this girl's perfection ever stop? Could you drop the ball just once, Carli? A queef . . . something . . . anything to let me know you're human and not an American Girl doll with perfect titties?

By that point in the summer I was pretty sure she and Dave were an item; they found excuses to touch each other and giggle when they were away from the pack. That night, Dave was whispering something into Carli's ear, and I was left alone with my new sneakers and socks that were too big for them, standing around a piano with the girls in the music tent, failing to learn the words to "We Didn't Start the Fire." I would have done anything to trade places with Carli. The shoes weren't cutting it. She was like Cinderella and I was one of the stepsisters trying to force the glass slipper on my foot so the prince would marry me. Suddenly, out of nowhere, Sally tugged on my sleeve and pointed to the bathroom. She was a woman of few words and she obviously had to go. Members of Senior 10 were always to be accompanied to the bathroom, and on this occasion Sally designated me the lucky escort. Truth be told, I was honored that she chose me to walk her. We headed over to the bathroom together in silence. By that time we were like coworkers. She was about twenty years older than me and had laid it on the line: no pleasantries, bitch. Which I completely appreciated.

We stood in line for the cramped four-stall bathroom where we'd stood dozens of times before, and when she was on deck, she again pulled on my sleeve and I looked down at her (she was no more than three feet tall). She was gazing up at me very intensely, like she was casting a spell of some sort. But you can't yell at one of your campers, "Are you casting a spell on me?!" So instead I asked, "What's up, Sal?" She didn't answer, and she didn't need to. I looked down at the floor and noticed there was liquid shit running down not one but both of her legs and onto her feet, and onto my very new shoes. I resisted the urge to scream my way out of the bathroom and run to the nearest lake. Instead, I kept staring into her black eyes until she was finished. She seemed to want to hold eye contact in this moment and by God, I gave that to her.

After it was over, I focused on mouth breathing while I threw my Converse sneakers in the garbage. The jig was up. I would never be Carli. I put Sally in a stall and told her, "It's okay, Sally, everything is fine." But she wasn't worried. She was kind of looking at me like, *Well, what now, skank?* And my answer to that was . . .

"JOANNE!!!!"

That's how I spent my last memorable moment at Camp Anchor—standing barefoot in human excrement, calling for help. Joanne did come and bail me out, but when camp ended a few days later, I rode home alone in the back of the bus. Word had traveled that I had been knee-deep in doo-doo, and believe it or not, people weren't falling over themselves to hang out with old shoeless Schums. I never got to spend time with the other volunteers that night, and I still didn't know a single line to "We Didn't Start the Fire." I never came anywhere close to making out with Tyler or Dave. Back at school that fall, Tyler dated this unbelievably beautiful blonde named Stacey. They were our school's Brad and Angelina. Had there been a tabloid magazine about them, I would have subscribed. They kind of looked like siblings, which didn't bother me, but in retrospect it is very creepy and also explains why I am drawn to *Game of Thrones*.

Anyway, I got a lot more than I bargained for that summer. I didn't achieve my goal of getting the boy I liked to fall for me. I was running out of Chris Farley jokes for Tyler, and Dave barely even knew I was alive. But I got so much more than knowing that a few teenage stoners I was crushing on could get semihard around me. I got to spend time with the women of Senior 10. I went through war with those chicks. We did it all together, and I would be honored to be in the trenches again with any of those gals. Except for Martha, the oldest one in the group. She dressed like Marilyn Monroe and smelled like a bag of dicks left out in the sun for a year. I would still fight on her side, but I would have to be a sniper stationed far away or something.

Twenty years later, I still keep their faces and names in my heart. They are people and they have feelings—and bodies—like everyone else. And sometimes those bodies produce a ton of poop and you have to stand in it, and sometimes you have to scoop their boobies back into their very backward bathing suits. And they didn't give a fuck about any of that. And it made me feel the same. For a teenager like me, learning to give zero fucks was nothing short of revelatory.

People often romanticize children or adults with special needs, as if they are innocent-yet-wise creatures who can humble us all into becoming better humans. First of all, nobody can be innocent and wise at the same time. That's another one of those impossible combinations. It's as unachievable and improbable as Brenda. Or Carli. And secondly, I'm not suggesting the ladies of Camp Anchor were either one of those things in particular. But they owned their own flaws, and I am grateful I got to meet them when I was only fourteen. I left camp knowing a bunch of women who weren't afraid to claim the guy they wanted to dance with; they didn't change a thing for the men they loved. They weren't ashamed of their bodily functions and they didn't lie to themselves or others. They had no patience for small talk or false pretenses. They would laugh when they wanted to like there was no tomorrow, and cry their eyes out when they felt like it. Basically, I had finally found my people.

HOW I LOST MY VIRGINITY

I always fantasized about losing my virginity the way I think most girls envision their weddings: being surrounded by my friends and family, with a clergyman present. JKJK. But seriously, I've never been a girl who dreamed about her future wedding. Nothing about the white dress or the way I'd walk down the aisle. That was just never in my fantasy Rolodex. I'm not sure why it wasn't. But for many years, I *did* think about the moment I'd lose the big V. I imagined looking the man I loved right in the eyes and kissing him and smiling and intertwining our fingers and then two becoming one and the whole thing being slow and beautiful. Lots of soft whispers of love and its feeling like a levee of good feelings was breaking, orgasms, and happy tears. I thought we'd both be virgins until the moment we took a deep breath and then we . . . weren't, and then we'd cry and hold each other all night. I thought we'd laugh about what a big deal it was that we'd just finally done it, and spend the next day together holding hands and walking around in our own little world experiencing a new kind of calm and bliss until we could hide away again together and repeat our perfect lovemaking, and all would be right in the world. But that is not what happened. I didn't get to have that moment.

About a year before it actually happened, I'd wanted to lose my virginity to a guy named Mike. He wasn't *officially* my boyfriend, but I was crazy about him, and we'd dated off and on since I was thirteen. At age sixteen, I'd felt ready. I went to my mom and my friend Christine and told them: "I think I'm ready and I want to have sex with Mike." Looking back, I realize that going to your mother for a pep talk about losing your virginity in high school is odd. But I was raised with no boundaries, so at the time it felt like the thing to do. I talked to my mom a lot about sex stuff, actually. Whenever I'd have a question, my mom and I would go to Bigelow's clam bar and I'd ask away, all while downing a bowl of New England clam chowder. I'd make her laugh slurping the soup up and asking obscene questions. In retrospect, obviously none of this was okay or appropriate. But it definitely helped make me who I am. During this particular sex talk, however, my mom and Christine both said, "No, don't do it—you need to wait and make it special." My mom pointed out how awful I'd feel if he made out with someone else the next weekend. I thought about it and she was right. I wasn't a hardened groupie following my favorite band on the road. I was a teenager. So I listened to them and held on to my hymen for another year.

Right around that time, I started dating a guy named Jeff. He was a classically handsome, popular guy. But there was something different about him too. He was angrier than most teenage boys, and a little misunderstood. I ignored the signs that he was probably a bit unstable. Signs like when they gave him a fish fillet at McDonald's instead of a Big Mac, he became so furious that he cried. Truly lost it. Real tears of rage. Like the kind of tears guys are only supposed to get when they watch a movie that touches on their dad issues. (So, most movies.) Isn't it funny that they say most girls have daddy issues, when really, every dude does? But this dude had daddy, mommy, doggy, and fish fillet issues. I just thought, *Well, he can't help it. But I understand him. I'm here for him.* Even though we were both generally well liked, when we were together it was us vs. the world.

I've only recently broken my pattern of being drawn to the "you're the only one who gets me" guy. Which is a bad guy to be drawn to, and it's not a coincidence if everyone—including all your friends and family and your dog—dislikes him. But Jeff was charming, and he loved me, and I him. He was the Bieber to my Selena—except that he had no money and neither of us was particularly talented at the time.

We'd somehow gotten into the habit of watching *Monday Night Raw*, which is a televised wrestling show where there is a bad guy in tight shorts who talks smack to a good guy in different tight shorts, and they both get very emotionally invested and show great feats of strength for a few minutes before one guy's arm is lifted in the air by a bald ref with a belly. I didn't enjoy it, because although I'm now friends with some wrestlers and even dated one, it's just not my bag. I appreciate the athleticism and the theater of it all, but . . . it just doesn't do it for me.

I did enjoy that Jeff and I had our own tradition and that we'd sneak forties of beer into my room and make out a little. I lived for these nights. Everything was so new to me. I'd just had my first orgasm a month before—on my own of course. I'd taught myself how to masturbate while watching the movie *Mannequin*. I'm not particularly turned on by that movie (no judgments if you are), but I was watching it alone on the couch one day and I just put my hand down my pants and rubbed the very top of my vagina and finally came. I was so pumped. It was like a new toy. I tried to do it again right away. I soon learned you have to wait about half an hour. I really hope girls are having orgasms. Just in case they're not, you should lick your finger and rub where your vagina comes to a point at the top in a circular motion until you have an orgasm. Show the guy you're with how to do it so you don't resent him for being the only one who is coming. You're welcome, and you deserve it! Also, let him go down on you. Don't be embarrassed. Live your life.

Where was I? Anyway, at this point, I think I'd come close to having an orgasm with Mike, but it turns out I'd been confused by the sensation and thought I had to pee. (Anyone with me here? No? Okay.) I'd excuse myself and go to the bathroom and wipe up all the moisture, which I thought was humiliating. It was later explained to me that that wetness was good. *Thank God*, I thought, since all those trips to the bathroom were getting suspicious.

But at that point I hadn't done a whole lot, sex-wise, with Jeff. We'd gotten to third base, as they say, and I'd tried to jerk him off many times. But it never worked, and it became the cause of major frustration on both our parts. I was getting Michelle Obama arms, but no other good was coming of it. I think he had religious guilt about all sex stuff and couldn't mentally get there. Or maybe I sucked at it. Either way, this seemed to either enrage him or embarrass him. I understand how that could be difficult for a guy, and he was my boyfriend, whom I really loved, so one time I told him to jerk off in front of me so he could get over the embarrassment. I acted supportive of his tugging on himself to completion even though I was kind of grossed out by it. But the plan worked. It helped him loosen up and I was (finally) able to help him reach orgasm. This was important to me because I wanted to have sex with him, but not until we'd rounded third base appropriately. I don't know why I got that in my head. Perhaps because in high school we talk so much about getting to different bases, it seemed everything should go in order.

The way it was for me growing up was that the guys were always trying to see what they could "get from us" sexually. We girls were basically conditioned to think we should hold out or we'd be labeled a slut. I wanted to wait to go "all the way" because I just wasn't ready. I wanted a little bit of a lead-up to having sex. Step by step.

After the successful jerk-off *Monday Night Raw* evening, Jeff and I continued to hang out and watch wrestling every week. Mankind and Stone Cold Steve Austin pretended to beat each other up, and we drank beer. One night, as we lay on my bed with the lights off watching wrestling, I was zoning out. The combination of the time of night, the content of the show, and the beer had me in and out of sleep. At one point, I was lying on my back, not paying attention, and suddenly felt Jeff fingering me. We hadn't been fooling around at all, so it seemed strange to go right to that. It started to hurt, which hadn't ever been the case before, so I looked down and realized he had put his penis in me. He was not fingering me. He was penetrating me. Without asking first, without kissing me, without so much as looking me in the eyes—or even confirming if I was awake. When I startled and looked down, he immediately removed himself from me and yelled quickly, "I thought you knew!" This seemed very strange to me, for him to protest so adamantly with such a prepared, defensive line—even though I hadn't yet said a word. I looked down and saw some blood on my bed. I was confused and hurt. He left soon after, and I rolled over and cried.

The next day he apologized. He was very upset, saying how awful he felt and that he wanted to harm himself for what he'd done. I did my best to comfort him, and I was genuinely worried about him. I wanted him to feel better. I was so confused. I was confused as to why he would have done this to me in this way, but the most dominant feeling I felt was that the guy I was in love with was upset and I wanted to help him. I put my head on his chest and told him it was okay. *I* comforted *him*. Let me repeat: *I comforted him*.

I was still bleeding a little and feeling sore and terribly confused. What had happened was settling in, and I was getting sick to my stomach thinking about it. It made no sense. I was his girlfriend; we'd had conversations about sex and were very open when talking things through like that. I'd just helped *him* figure out how to have an orgasm in front of me. I remember being the more sexual of the two of us. If he'd asked me to have sex that night, I think I would have said yes. I didn't understand why he approached it the way he did. Did he feel like he needed to literally "sneak it in"? He had so much guilt attached to sexual activity, I recall, and lots of fear. Maybe he thought it would be a guiltless, shameless way to do it. Maybe, like the jerking-off sessions, it was easier for him to do it if I wasn't an active participant. I don't know. But he'd made the decision without me. It wasn't about *us*, it was about *him*. I felt sad and betrayed. I thought he really cared about me, but this didn't feel like something someone who cared about you would do. But I still wanted us to be okay.

The strangest part is that even though Jeff apologized and told me how bad it had made *him* feel, I don't remember ever really taking him to task about how it made *me* feel. I did what most girls do and continued on. I didn't know enough about it. I didn't know that it is incredibly common for sex to be nonconsensual. Sexual assault is so widespread, in fact, that we now have big campaigns aimed at teaching boys and young men what it means to get consent.

But I was seventeen years old and I wanted my boyfriend to like me. I still wanted to be with him and I was. We kept right on dating and started having sex regularly a couple months later. The second time we did it, I tried to pretend it was the first time. I even went in my mom's room after and told her I'd lost my virginity. But it was a lie, and I'd also be lying now if I said it didn't feel like my whole experience was ruined. My trust had been shattered—not just my trust in him but, in a lot of ways, my trust in anyone. My fantasy of a beautiful intimate memorable moment between two people had been taken from me in a flash. He took it. I didn't know it then, but I know now that it toughened me up in an irreversible way. For many years, when it came to sex, I didn't get the luxury of just being myself. Half of the time I was too defensive and guarded, assuming the guy wanted to hurt me or take too much. The rest of the time, I was too flippant—almost to the point of being dissociative, as if the act of sex didn't matter much to me. I'd tell myself I could have sex with any guy I wanted, even if I didn't care about him. Neither one of these versions of me was real.

Today, I wish I could say that sex is finally free of this kind of self-consciousness and self-protection for me. But it's not. Until I'm in a committed relationship, I'm on my guard hard. I want to be the one making all the choices. I have to be with someone for a while and truly trust them before sex is fully fun and carefree. And then, I love it. I'm definitely a very sexual chick. But my first experience didn't really set me up for a happy-go-lucky journey to get to where I am today. Women, like men, deserve to enjoy sex and to figure it out on their own terms.

So many girls have nights like my "first time"— or worse. Some girls wake up to a friend or boyfriend having sex with them. Some girls are violently attacked in public or in their own homes. One out of every six women is raped. Of that, 44 percent of those women are under eighteen.

Any time someone comes forward about being sexually assaulted in some way, there are so many opinions about it. People will have opinions about this chapter. Some might say it wasn't a big deal. Or that it was all my fault since I was drinking, he was my boyfriend, and I was lying right there next to him.

Isn't it sad that when a girl says she was sexually assaulted, our first instinct is to think she's probably lying? Statistics and facts tell us the exact opposite. We demand "perfect victims" who better not have been drinking or hanging out at a party in a short skirt or revealing dress or have ever been known to enjoy sex.

The facts in my situation are pretty clear to me still: He was inside of me in a way I hadn't consented to.

Many girls remain silent about their experiences. And that is their choice. I'm opening up about my "first time" because I don't want it to happen to your daughter or sister or friend someday. I want to use my voice to tell people to make sure they have consent before they have sex with someone. I hope all parents talk to their kids about consent, and when you do, please, please don't make the mistake my mother made. Don't do it over a bowl of clam chowder. Because that is just gross and creepy.

I wish I'd have talked to a parent or adult at the time to sort out my feelings of confusion and betrayal. I wish I'd have stood up for myself more and told Jeff that what he did was wrong. It shouldn't have gone this way. I don't want someone reading this to think, *My son isn't rageful and doesn't cry furious tears over a breaded fish sandwich, so he probably understands that he needs to get consent before putting his penis in a girl*. But this happens so frequently that clearly we need to talk about it. Everyone should understand that there are no excuses for nonconsensual sex. People who commit sexual assault should have to pay the consequences for their actions. I used to do some stand-up about this confusing area. I'd call it "grape," as in "gray-area rape." It's not some crackhead who popped out of the bushes in Central Park and raped me. I wasn't screaming no. He didn't keep forcibly pumping away until he finished. He was only inside me for a short time. But it isn't right that it happened that way. Virginity shouldn't be something you "lose" or "give." Sex is something you share. My first time didn't need to be perfect, but I would have liked to have known it was going to happen. Or have been part of the decision. Instead, he just helped himself to my virginity—and I was never the same.

THINGS YOU DON'T KNOW ABOUT ME

Constructing a list of things you don't know about me is pretty difficult, because I'm an open book. But here's my attempt:

1. I have a bad scar on my left leg from a surfing accident I was in as a teenager. I think it's cool but I know deep down it's gross.

2. I speak sign language. I'm not crazy fluent, but I can communicate pretty well. I've learned the hard way that not all deaf people want to talk to you just because you can sign.

3. I am terrified of spiders, and ferrets make me puke.

4. I am not allergic to any foods, but eggplant hurts my mouth.

5. I have an innie, not an outie (talking about my vagina).

6. The birth control I use is the NuvaRing. (I've never been paid to endorse the NuvaRing, but I believe I should be. Same goes for Rombauer chardonnay.)

7. I have never been pregnant, but I look like I have.

8. I have never had anal sex. (I would be willing, but they say you can't eat for a couple hours beforehand, and I don't see that happening.)

9. No one has ever come on my face (but I think everywhere else has been covered).

10. My favorite food is pasta with Parmesan and I like to eat it as I'm falling asleep.

11. I have been skydiving but I didn't like it because you have to JUMP OUT OF A FUCKING AIRPLANE.

12. I don't go to temple anymore, but I like that I'm Jewish, and I enjoy the grossest Jewish food, like whitefish salad and gefilte fish.

13. I like my feet and my ears. I know my mouth is really small, but I like it, and it has gotten me out of going down on several people.

14. My favorite living actors are Samantha Morton and Mark Rylance.

15. I like smoking pot and I like smoking pot.

16. I have eaten mushrooms a couple times (funnnnnnnnn).

17. I have never done ecstasy, cocaine, or acid. But I feel like I'm already on all of those things.

18. I love Ani DiFranco. You are going to get sick of hearing about this because she comes up a lot in this book. I've been going to her concerts since I was thirteen. I don't want to meet her ever. I'd start crying and ruin her day.

19. I can't stand Rod Stewart's voice.

20. And the seventh thing you don't know about me is that I'm really good with numbers.

21. My sister tested my IQ when she was getting her master's degree in school psychology and I tested as a genius in half the categories and nearly cognitively impaired in the other half.

22. To date, I've slept with twenty-eight people. I can't remember all of their names, but I remember the nicknames I gave them (Third Ball, Pit Bull Guy, Cousin Steve—JKJKJKJK).

23. I faked falling in a dirt pile to get out of running a mile in gym class. I lay in the dirt until someone found me.

24. My favorite poet is Anne Sexton and my favorite poem is "Admonitions to a Special Person."

25. The thing I own the most of is wine, but please send more.

26. I've read the book *Tortilla Flat* ten times for some reason. I've watched *The Royal Tenenbaums* one hundred times.

27. My favorite scene in a movie is when Billy Crudup meets Samantha Morton's character at the daytime house party in *Jesus' Son* and she's dancing to the song "Sweet Pea."

28. At parties, you can usually find me . . . at home. I hate parties.

29. The thing that's on my mind the most is my family.

30. I have a thing for guys with a gap between their teeth.

31. My paternal great-grandmother was a bootlegger in NYC.

32. I'm not sure when I've laughed the hardest in my life, but I am sure that I was with my sister when it happened.

33. The best thing I've ever bought was a comfy bed.

34. The two things I always decline, every single time they are offered to me, are cocaine and ham.

35. I mostly hate being in museums, except for the American Museum of Natural History. I like the dinosaurs and animal tableaus, and they sell astronaut ice cream at the gift shop.

36. My favorite place I've traveled to in the US is New Orleans. The music, food, and people are the best. My favorite place I've been outside the country is Altea, a little fishing village in Spain.

37. I hate horror movies because I get so scared, but I always forget and watch them by accident. I come up with an excuse about why my sister has to sleep in the same room as me. She's nice about it but knows it's because I am a deep loser.

38. I don't know if I want kids. Maybe not.

39. One of my favorite things to do is go dancing with Amber Tamblyn and twerk to the best of my abilities.

40. I've never hooked up with a girl, except on camera for my TV show, but it seems fun. This is unrelated to #39.

41. I meditate twice a day for twenty minutes each time. It helps clear my mind and get rid of stress, and it gives me energy.

42. My sister and I went to Oktoberfest in Munich once and snuck into the tents and had one of the best times of our lives.

43. I am a pathological liar.

44. Just kidding.

CAN'T KNOCK THE HUSTLE

I've been a hustler my whole life. I know you're thinking, *Check yourself, Amy, you are not Jay Z.* But it's true. You can't be a comic and make complete strangers laugh without a strong hustle. Mine has always been solid. Since day one. There is evidence of this as early as my first few months of life. Like most newborn babies, I didn't welcome sleep, and I certainly didn't want to be left alone in a room to sleep by myself. So I figured out how to trick my mother into sleeping on the floor next to me. I cried like hell and didn't let up until she was by my side exactly where I wanted her to be. I'm sure my dad wasn't too keen on this idea, but for months, I kept up this impressive scam, dictating the sleeping arrangements for people who were decades older than me. Suckers!

My hustle has often involved food, because, much like household pets or toddlers, I am food-motivated, which is a handy thing to know about me. I was talking my way into the food I wanted from a very young age. When I was two, I figured out how to break open the kitchen cabinet and eat Cheerios. At six, I lied to my kindhearted grandfather's face, telling him that my mom had given me permission to have another yogurt when she hadn't. I let him take the fall for me, and it was never really the same between us. Even now, I still do this. Just last week, when I was leaving Kim's apartment at one a.m. after a TV night, she caught me sneaking a bag of microwave popcorn from her pantry to take home with me.

When you're a kid, the hustle is oh so necessary. You have so little control over what you get to do: what you eat, what you wear, where you go, who or what you play with. It's a nightmare. So I got started pretty young working on my tactics for negotiating with adults. I came on pretty strong at my friends' houses because their parents weren't used to my methods and strategies. I'd look them in the eyes, serious as a heart attack, and call them by their first names as a negotiation tactic. "Look, Laura, your beautiful daughter and I are going to follow our cake with a bowl of ice cream now. Would you like to scoop it for us, or should I?" Like Laura, most parents were caught off guard, laughed nervously, and said, "Ha ha ha . . . My name is Mrs. Booker, Amy." To which I would reply, "I know your last name, Laura. Now, can you get me a step stool so I can dig around in your freezer for our second dessert?"

Sometimes I'd see that my attempts to close a

deal made the adult laugh. And making adults laugh was the most power I could ever have—it made me feel like I was one of them, holding some of the reins they always held, especially with male figures of authority, who always seemed to be throwing the book at me one way or another. Whether it was teachers catching me talking in class or cops catching me with beer in my backpack on the beach, it always felt like my only way to get home free was to make everyone laugh. It always dismantled the power structure within seconds. Being funny was my ultimate hustle! Once when my high school teacher Mr. Simons wouldn't let me leave class to go to the bathroom (okay, it was actually to walk the halls and meet up with my boyfriend, and Mr. Simons was fully onto me), I said very loudly in front of the whole class: "That's cool, Mr. Simons. I'll just stay here, even though I can feel my period blood leaking out of my vagina and about to seep through my pants and onto my chair." Mr. Simons turned red, everyone else laughed, and I strutted right on out of the classroom.

Besides making large audiences laugh at my jokes, I'd say my biggest hustle in life was shoplifting as a teenager. It's not something I'm proud of—in fact it was a spectacular failure in the end. But I probably wouldn't take it back, because even though this is going to sound weird, I learned a lot from executing the old five-finger discount like it was my job. It was all part of my process of honing my instincts, learning how to take what

I deserved in life. Don't get me wrong, I do not condone shoplifting. One of the things I learned from the whole experience was NOT TO SHOP-LIFT. And I'm aware that when people give you sage advice to grab life by the balls and take what you deserve, they usually mean you should ask for a hard-earned promotion or carve out a little "me time" for yourself, not rob a well-known department store blind. But when I was a teenager, I took that idea literally.

I started out stealing pieces of candy here and there, nothing too serious. When I hear other people talk about their adventures in shoplifting (it's pretty common among teenage girls), they usually recount how they stole something like a cheap pair of dangly earrings or a magazine, and they always attach tons of guilt to it. But I didn't have those feelings because I was targeting the big chain stores. I never took anything from a mom-and-pop shop or an actual person. (To this day, I still hesitate to tell people that I have a record for shoplifting because when something comes up missing I know they'll suspect me. But never have I ever stolen anything from a person. Except food. From Kim's kitchen.)

By high school, my friends and I had graduated to stealing bathing suits from stores in the mall because they didn't have sensors on them and they were easy to take. We'd also steal makeup from drugstores. We didn't take these things because we were in need of them; we didn't wear makeup and we rarely went swimming. We took them because stealing makes a teenager feel cool and powerful. Even white girls in the suburbs want to be badasses. And if that meant robbing J.Crew of a gingham one-piece, so be it. I guess you could say I worked my way into being an angsty teen one stolen shimmery grapefruit-flavored lip gloss at a time.

The first time I got caught was when I was fourteen years old and had traveled to Sacramento with my club volleyball team for a tournament. Being in club volleyball meant that when the regular volleyball season at my high school ended, I'd then compete on teams with kids from other schools. Meaning, I never, ever stopped playing volleyball. It certainly shaped my work ethic (and kept a good thirty pounds off me), but it did mean missing a lot of fun weekend shit so that I could sweat it out in a poorly lit gym, eating pasta salad and catching moments of sleep in between games. Even now, I find myself feeling sleepy and craving pasta salad whenever I'm in a large school gymnasium. Or regular gymnasium. Or library. Or home. Or now.

This is how most of my weekends in high school went:

- Get picked up on Saturday morning at five a.m. and drive two to five hours to a tournament.

- Arrive and suit up to play until you're eliminated.

- Understand that if, God forbid, you make it to the final match, you'll play for up to twelve hours, then take home a little plastic trophy that you will have to pack and move into every new apartment you find yourself in until you throw it away begrudgingly at the age of twenty-four.

Come to think of it, it's not unlike film/TV production, except your parents are with you all day and there are no union rules, so you have to play and play until your little knee pads give out or you bleed through. You consume whatever the parents brought to try to one-up each other. Health wasn't really a thing back then, so we'd eat big chicken-cutlet sandwiches and pasta minutes before having to hurl our bodies back out on the court.

But back to shoplifting in Sacramento. My teammates and I were out exploring the town. We landed in a place called Old Sacramento, which was full of shops selling shitty novelty items for tourists: shot glasses, coffee mugs, T-shirts that said the name of the city and also hilarious phrases like "I'm not gay but my boyfriend is." I'd already been stealing for a couple months, and I'd built up quite the reputation with my regular friends at my school. But since this was the club volleyball league, these girls didn't know me as well and didn't realize what a total badass I was. I couldn't wait to show them.

I wanted to be popular with the three coolest

girls on the team, so I called them over and told them how I'd learned to steal. They were really impressed with how easy I made it sound, and we started racking up the most sought-after items in the stores: tie-dye half shirts that said "Co-ed naked lacrosse," snow globes, and of course the coveted "1 tequila, 2 tequila, 3 tequila, FLOOR" shot glasses. (Who writes this stuff? Is it Mark Twain himself?)

About six of us were in on the scam to rob Old Sacramento. After it was over, I walked into my hotel room and emptied my treasures onto the bed. I looked at all of the bounty. In retrospect, not one thing would have cost more than $1.99 to purchase. Not on my watch! 'Cause my watch is free!

It just so happened that my mom was chaperoning this particular tournament, and she arrived at the hotel that night. When she got in, she hugged me and told me she had some disturbing news. She seemed really disgusted that some of my teammates had been caught shoplifting and were taken to the police station. I played innocent, partially because I couldn't bear to disappoint her, but also because I was terrified I'd be caught and my new prize possessions (especially the hat with fake dreads built into it) would have to be returned.

In the morning I saw the three chicks whom I'd gotten into this mess, and I found out they were going to be benched for the tournament. They'd been up all night, crying. They looked at me like, *How could you do this to us, Amy?* I could see the anger on their faces. They hated me. My whole plan to get them to like me had backfired worse than I could've imagined.

In reality, the charge wasn't even going to show up on their permanent records because they were all minors, but still, they were mad. Honestly, I was a little mad at them, too, for sucking so bad at shoplifting. *These fucking rookies*, I thought. *I should never have taken them under my experienced lawbreaking wing.* Then I thought about it some more and remembered the Sisterhood of the Traveling Volleyball Spandex, and I decided that the right thing to do, both for these other gals and for myself, would be to admit that I'd stolen, too. Is there such a thing as a hustler with a conscience?

Predictably, I got benched for the tournament. I stood on the sideline with my knee pads around my ankles, fighting off dirty looks from the girls I'd so desperately wanted approval from. I'd flown all the way to Sacramento from New York to play zero volleyball and get some shitty shot glasses that I wouldn't be able to fill with anything other than water for another seven years. I guess I got what I deserved. You can't buy or steal popularity and affection; you have to earn those things the old-fashioned way, not the Old Sacramento way. I think I learned a valuable lesson about teamwork, sisterhood, and friendship that weekend. But unfortunately, I didn't quite learn not to shoplift yet. For that, I would need a felony on my record.

It all went down at a serious department store.

Let's call it Schloomingdale's. My stealing had gotten out of hand. This was when my family had slipped from New Money to No Money and we could no longer afford to buy the kinds of nonessential things in life you feel you must have as a teenager. So I employed all my well-honed hustling skills to get what Kim and I "needed." This was a win-win because Kim got to fulfill her quota of teen rebellion and I got to own a white jumpsuit! We started doing it more and more. And it had the side benefit of making us feel invincible and powerful. I don't think my stint with stealing expensive clothing is amusing or sympathetic in any way, but it isn't surprising, either. When you're a teenage girl, especially one with a broken family and no money, you're newly and fully aware of just how mind-blowingly little you matter in the world. And even worse, I was just starting to feel myself creeping closer and closer to that angry edge—that place most women arrive at in college or maybe during their first job—where you realize not only do you matter very little *right now*, but this moment in time is probably the *most* you will *ever* matter. It's all downhill from here. You're eighteen years old, and this is your last chance to TAKE WHAT YOU CAN GET. I know none of this is an excuse for shoplifting. I really don't think it's a cute thing to do, but it's also not shocking that it made us feel as powerful and invincible as it did.

After doing it several times, we felt we were running a great scam. We'd take two of the same item into the dressing room, and then we'd put one in a bag or under our clothes and the other one out on the rack.

"How'd it go in there?" the salesgirl would ask me.

"Not well," I'd reply, trying to display the self-hatred most women feel when leaving a dressing room. But really I'd be celebrating what a genius I was for my incredible "take two, steal one" plan. My genius was brutally halted the day my sister and I were put in the back of a cop car.

We were in the Roosevelt Field mall on Long Island—a typical mall, maybe on the fancier side as far as malls go. Over the years a Gucci had appeared, and a Valentino. But that side of the marble halls always seemed especially empty, so Kim and I chose to hang on to the more lively, shittier side. Give me a Hot Topic and an Auntie Anne's pretzel. That was more our vibe.

So Kim and I were walking past Schloomingdale's when she said, "We should go in. It's sooooo easy to take whatever you want from there. Especially underwear!" I should have thought, *This is a bad idea. You've never scouted this place out, and you don't want to end up in jail.* But instead what I thought was, *Oooooh, I need underwear!*

So we did it. We really did it. We went on a total bat-shit, no-holds-barred spree. We did not stop at underwear. We took jackets, scarves . . . What's this? Dolce & Gabbana has a new perfume? Leopard-print onesies? Don't mind if I do. Cashmere tops? Seven jeans? Well, I think I deserve to own those! Kim had been eyeing a tank top with a bejeweled dollar sign, and why shouldn't she have pajama pants with white doily cuffs to go with it? And if she didn't take that strapless teal bra now, she would never again have a chance to own one. Today was the day! And the pièce de résistance? A leather fedora! We took it all into the dressing room.

I remember squeezing myself into a pair of too-small Guess jeans while I lovingly fondled a Juicy Couture jumpsuit. *I'll save this for special occasions*, I thought. We were high from the adrenaline as we manically, meticulously took the tags off each item. I took the perfume out of the box and stashed it in my coat pocket. *Good thinking, you brilliant girl*, I thought, patting myself on the back. We put all the tags from all the items we were about to be the new proud owners of into the empty perfume box, and we loaded up. We smiled at each other, hugged, took a deep breath, and out the door we went.

We passed a pretty girl with shoulder-length brown hair and dark eyes who'd been lurking in the hallway. *She's cute*, I thought, *but bad energy*. Kim and I walked toward the Bloomingd—whoops, that was a close one—exit that led out into the rest of the mall. We held hands, vibing on the same chemicals in our bloodstreams that are enjoyed by gambling addicts, Formula One racers, and Tom Cruise as we took the plunge past the sensors. They didn't chime. We'd done it. Success. My heart was racing, but I wasn't sweating or doing anything that could be a tell (by this time we were pros). What a perfect excursion. To top it all off we had tickets to see our favorite singer, Ani DiFranco, that night. Which of my new outfits would I wear? *Definitely gonna debut that leather fedora!*

And then . . .

We were swarmed by five people dressed in civilian clothes. It was the girl from the dressing rooms and a guy I'd smiled at while walking around the store. A whole bunch of plants. It was like the scene in *Blow* where the waiters all turn out to be working for the DEA. They circled us, yelling, "Stop right there!" But they didn't touch us. (I later found out that they're not allowed to lay a hand on you; to this day I still regret not running. Had I known they wouldn't have been able to touch us if we ran, I would have Forrest Gumped right the hell out of that mall and not looked back until I reached the ocean or Robin Wright.)

They kept us there in that strange holding pattern until the store detectives came out and got us. They walked us back to a little room in the bowels of the store. Picturing that moment now still gives me the worst pit in my stomach. I went into protective big-sister mode with Kim and was worried about how she would handle this, but more than anything, I was embarrassed. We were caught. We couldn't leave the little room. I couldn't save my sister. I couldn't joke my way out of this. We just had to give in.

The five store detectives crowded into the room. They laughed and celebrated their victory and taunted us a little. It was humiliating. Kim was not looking good. She'd always been my cute little partner in crime, but I knew she'd take this harder than I would. She'd recently acquired the tried-and-true yet mildly disturbing family coping mechanism of dealing with stress and anxiety by dissociating. She was dangerously good at it. She'd basically detach from her immediate surroundings and revert to a kind of catatonic state. I could see she was drifting off, and I was losing her. I had to do something.

That's when my *real* hustle kicked in. I did the one thing I can almost always do to make things better: I made her laugh. As the detectives laid out our clothing on the floor so they could assess the charge, I came alive. I pointed to a pair of flannel plaid pants Kim had stolen. "Where were you gonna wear those, Kim? Did you join a country club I don't know about?" I went into insult comedy. I roasted her choices as a thief. I comforted her with cracks about her taste. She laughed. She stayed present in her body.

"Grand larceny!" the pretty brunette exclaimed, and the detectives high-fived one another. My guess was the bigger the charge, the bigger the bonus. The door flung open and a middle-aged guy with a torso bigger than seemed right for his pit bull face walked in. His hair was graying on the sides but not the top. He was radiating smugness like someone who works at the Apple Genius Bar on the day of a product release.

"So, you thought you'd come in here and steal from my store?"

Kim's eyes were starting to waver, and I could tell she was about to head into a black hole. Before he could get to his next megalomaniacal question I jumped in . . .

"Well, Mr. Bloomingdale" (the cat's out of the little brown bag), "it is such an honor to meet you, first of all. Second of all, do you live in the store?"

Kim blurted out a laugh and then stifled herself.

Needless to say, my jokes didn't save us. I don't blame Mr. Bloomingdale for not appreciating my sense of humor. We got the maximum charge. We were taken to the mall police station, which is a thing, in the back of an unmarked cop car. The cops who drove us were nice; they blasted Pink Floyd's "Comfortably Numb," and I was mostly relieved that Kim wasn't numb anymore, that I could make her laugh even though we were on our way to the clink. We sat there looking at each other and holding hands. It was the end of November, so one of the cops' frozen Thanksgiving turkey was resting between us on the seat. At the station, they took our fingerprints and mug shots, then we sat on a bench while they tried calling our mom. No answer. Thank God.

"Well, sir, actually, our dad is more our care-taker." HUGE LIE. They called our dad and left a message. I explained that he probably wouldn't call back for hours, and that our mother was kind of an absentee figure in our lives. HUGE LIE.

I felt in that moment that it was up to me to be my own guardian. My parents couldn't help me. And I also felt an unmistakable sense of resolve that I had to take care of Kim and get her through this. I blurted out to the cops that I had stolen everything. It was all me. They were all my items. The mall cop told us that because Kim was a minor it wouldn't be a big deal if the charge were on her record. I then took back everything I'd previously stated and tried to pin it all on her.

When it was all said and done, our punishment ended up being community service, but it wasn't too bad. We even made it to see Ani DiFranco at the Beacon Theatre that night, singing at the top of our lungs, celebrating our freedom. What better way to commemorate our last days as rebels than spending an evening screaming out the lyrics of the singer who was basically every eighteen-year-old white girl's Joan of Arc? I remember, during her song "Swan Dive," Kim and I belting out the lyrics *"I don't care if they eat me alive. I've got better things to do than survive!"* and it felt more exhilarating than wearing all the stolen tube tops in the world.

And in the end, getting caught at Bloomingdale's really corrected my game. After all, the hustle I'm honing isn't about shoplifting or lying or winning friends with horrible heists gone wrong. And it's definitely not about grabbing what belongs to someone else just to make myself feel more powerful. It's about being my own best advocate and knowing how to take what I deserve in life without bringing anyone else down. It's about making my sister laugh when we are both in deep shit. Now that I'm all grown up and no longer driving up the price of bad tchotchkes in Old Sacramento, I've graduated on to the next-level hustle—making people laugh. It's something I'm still perfecting: skirting the rules, writing jokes about life's mountains of bullshit—all to make people smile and feel better. There's no sleight of hand or trickery involved. It's hard work—without shortcuts. Making an audience laugh is much more difficult than sneaking out of Bloomingdale's with a fedora under your shirt that only Ving Rhames can pull off, but it's still a hustle I just can't quit.

Dear Journal,

It's a Monday and I'm still home. This break has been a lot of fun. It's been more of a learning experience than anything else. It's time for me to reflect on this past month.[1]

Last Tuesday-Wednesday, some of us went to Gormans.[2] It was fun. We had good conversations and we danced.[3] Thursday we went to Roulettes. It was a lot of fun. We all got to a good level of drunk[4] and danced like we had never danced before.[5] We were dancing like lesbians. It was so fun.[6] Every guy there would

---

1 Very deep, Amy. Are you reflecting on a goodwill trip to Guatemala? Or your time volunteering at a shelter? No, you are reflecting on all the bars you went to. What an insightful mind. Proceed.

2 A bar that allowed underage kids to drink.

3 I would imagine the conversations went like this: "I like your shirt, where's it from?" "Armani Exchange." "Oh, that's why it says 'Armani Exchange' on it." "Good catching up with you."

4 Most likely blackout.

5 I will never be able to express how grateful I am that there is no footage of this.

6 I want to apologize to all lesbians. There is no way lesbians dance the way we were dancing. We must have been incorporating the age-old technique of trying to get the guys to notice us by

have died for any one of us.[7] *Right before I left, I ran into Nick.*[8] *I was so glad to see him. He really was exactly what I wanted right then. A guy to be really interested in me and that I would like to mess around with. He was extremely friendly. I told him to call me. He called me the next day and asked me to come to a Long Beach bar. I said maybe, but I would have to see.*[9]

I saw the movie Girl Interrupted *with my friends.*[10] *It was really good. Saturday night I had over a bunch of girls, three of which go to college with Jess Sap. We got pretty drunk and went to meet up with Nick. He was so happy to see me.*[11] *He bought us drinks all night.*[12] *We didn't pay for a thing.*[13] *I looked amaz-*

---

pretending we were on the precipice of letting the music (most likely "Come On Eileen") take over our souls and make us forget what we knew our sexuality to be and just start licking each other right there on the dance floor of that shitty bar.

7 Inflated sense of self, Amy? I would like to edit together a video of how I saw myself that night and then what was actually happening. I blame MTV's show *The Grind* for making everyone think they were Daisy Fuentes.

8 He was a very hot and strong dude. I remember him looking like Superman or Chris Klein.

9 Yeah fucking right. I'm sure I started getting ready right then for an entire twenty-four hours.

10 It was basically a documentary about all of us, except we were less hot.

11 Red flag.

12 Redder flag.

13 Reddest flag.

ing.[14] *I wore this tube shirt from Zara that ties in the back.*[15] *He said the sweetest things to me.*[16] *When the bar closed we all went back to my house. Everyone else left and Nick and I went into my room. We hooked up for like three hours.*[17]

I liked how he kissed but he was very aggressive and rough. He kept trying to "shock" me which is sticking one finger up my ass and one up my vagina.[18] *I had to be on my guard. It felt different, not too bad. I just didn't want him doing that.*[19] *I never let any of my boyfriends do that so why should this guy?*[20] *He*

---

14 I am dying laughing knowing what I looked like at this age. The only amazing thing about how I looked was that people were able to identify me as female.

15 I remember this shirt. It was made of wool and thin brown leather straps with three ties in the back. It was insanely itchy and gave me a rash all over my body. It looked like what a poor commoner who gets raped by a soldier on *Game of Thrones* would wear. It was too short, so my belly stuck out, and I had no waist and was shaped very much like an old-timey radio, which I must have wanted to accentuate.

16 Of course he did; I had a target on my head, or my lower back, I should say.

17 This now sounds like a nightmare to me, just an exhausting bacteria exchange. Pass.

18 Thank you, Dr. Schumer, very sexy. I really spared no details, I guess. But what great writing. Don't you feel like you're in the room with me? It's like we are all sitting on his finger as he is trying to put it in my butthole.

19 It's always been my least-favorite way to have my temperature taken.

20 That's good logic, right? No one I loved or trusted got the

kept trying to make me touch myself.[21] *I was making jokes like "I don't think we're at that stage in our
relationship."*[22] *The oddest thing that he did was after
he had gone down on me I went down on him for a
minute and he was trying to finger me with his toes.*[23] *I
was like "no thanks" and he actually asked why.*[24] *He
also kept biting my nipples really hard.*[25] *It made me
so mad the next day because they were really irritated.
So was my vagina from him fingering me so hard.*[26]

*He spent the night. I asked if he liked his own space
when he slept. He said yes. I jumped up naked and
slept in my mom's room.*[27] *I woke up a couple hours*

---

honor of touching the inside of my butthole. *You must be knighted
by the queen before entering a digit into my buttocks* was my phi-
losophy, I guess.

21 Lazy.

22 I think this behavior is probably more typical now with the
generation raised on porn, but at the time it was pretty out-there
in my eyes.

23 Or as they called it in ancient China, toeing.

24 I would like to present this guy with the medal for brass balls.
Why?! You want to know why I don't want your toes in me?!
Maybe because that's fucking gross and my pussy is not your own
personal moccasin. So until Crocs comes up with a new model
called the five-toe vagina shoe, please keep your feet exactly one
leg's length away from my lady part!

25 Guys who do this should be the last residents at Guantánamo.

26 If you're trying to make a girl remember you, maybe just
write her a poem.

27 Hahahaha. She wasn't home of course. I repeat, she was
NOT in the bed. But I love that at eighteen that was already my
steeze to skip the snuggling after hooking up.

later and drove him home. I had Kim come with me.[28]
He kissed me good-bye on the cheek and told me to
call. Later we spoke on the phone and he said that he
felt like I just wanted to get him out of my house. He
was so right.[29]

The next night nothing went on. This week I worked
at Forever 21 in the mall. They have me at cashier now
so it's more entertaining.[30]

---

28 Jesus Christ, Amy, your poor sister! "Hey, want to take a ride
across Long Island with this guy who used me as a puppet all
night?" She was fourteen!

29 Wow, he was so in touch with what women want.

30 I stand by being excited about this promotion! Little did I
know I would be wearing their clothes well into my midthirties.

FAKED IT 'TIL I MADE IT

There is nothing better than being your own boss. Well, there is, actually: not having to work at all. That is way better. But I've worked so many jobs over the years, and have experienced all of the unique and specific humiliations that came along with each one. And even when I was doing something for hire that involved zero dignity, I still always liked the feeling of doing something useful. Even as a kid, I just wanted to show everyone I could pull my own weight (which was never less than 150 pounds, even in middle school). For as long as I can remember, I was seeking employment. I felt so stifled and useless during childhood. I wanted to contribute. Lemonade stands weren't cutting it. I hated that I was too young to get a job or join a gym. It's amazing these things I was so dead set on having are now two of the worst features of my adult life. But back in the day, I wanted in. I wanted the satisfaction of making my own money and being proactive.

Before I got paid as a performer, most of my paying gigs were pretty unglamorous, regular, shitty, low-paying jobs. I worked in at least a dozen bars or restaurants in Manhattan alone, and when I was in college I worked as a house painter for a while. Every weekend at six a.m., I'd be up on a ladder with a roller and brushes, painting the inside of someone's house, a Chinese restaurant, or a school. But I liked all those jobs. Even at a job I hated, I always loved the feeling I'd get when I was done. The beer at the end of a shift, or the feeling of looking at the clock and seeing it change to the minute you can leave, is so freeing. That moment you're allowed to walk out the door is an experience that cannot be replicated. I honestly feel for people who've never had to work, because they will never know that feeling. The people born rich, with their Gatsby-like days spent lying around fanning themselves, wondering if they should go into town. They'll never know the sheer elation you feel when the manager of a steakhouse tells you, "You're cut after you finish your side work!" What a feeling, to furiously roll silverware into napkins and then take that first step outside, breathing the air, knowing that you're now on your own time. Heaven.

My very first job was being a baby model, because I was an exceptionally cute baby. JKJKJKJK. I was a very average-looking infant. By "average," I mean I resembled a pug more than a baby. But my parents needed someone to model the baby furni-

ture they sold. As my parents, they believed I was
adorable—that, and they knew I would work for
free. I posed in a bunch of the cribs, and I was on
the cover of their catalog (it's probably why the
company went bankrupt). It was the beginning and
end of my print modeling career. I've been meaning to get back into it.

My parents continued to take advantage of my
work ethic when they made me model stuff from
their second store, Calling All Girls, which sold
gifts, clothes, and haunted-looking dolls for girls.
It was only a good idea compared to their initial
business plan, which was to sell shoes. ("Schumer's
Shoes"; this would have ruined my life as a tween.)
The slogan my mom devised for Calling All Girls
was "No Boys Allowed!" It should have been "No
Customers Allowed!" because literally no one ever
shopped there. Not a smart marketing technique to
immediately shun 50 percent of the population. But
anyway, "No Boys Allowed" was plastered on buttons and T-shirts that Kim and I constantly wore as
little walking billboards for our parents. I guess this
slogan was supposed to amp up the marketing to the
"fairer sex." But even more than being pro-girl, it
was just straight-up anti-boy. Or it could have been
read the wrong way, like "No boys allowed, but
MEN ARE WELCOME!" There were so many
wrong turns to be made with this slogan. And so
few ways to go right. I was an eleven-year-old
inviting men to approach me. I looked like a walking *To Catch a Predator* ad. Chris Hansen should

have paid me, not my parents. Either way, I guess "No Boys Allowed" was supposed to be my mom's not-so-subtle way of telling us that men were bad. I never bought it, but you could say the writing was on the wall, and on the shirt and the button, for that matter.

With the new store, I was not asked to be a print model, I was asked (or rather told) that I'd be spending my weekends at the Javits Center—a huge convention center that held trade shows on the weekends. My parents would showcase their inventory by using Kim and me as display items. We wore "No Boys Allowed" shirts with a picture of a lock and key on them. And the shirts came with a key you would wear around your neck. In retrospect, this was all a little disturbing. I guess my mom thought it was cute for us to be prissy little bitches who "locked" boys out and dangled the key to our goods in front of them. And the unintentional message had a vague anti-rape implication. I mean, there are some countries where little girls are sold into sex slavery and their virginity is purchased, and there I was at the age of eleven, with my seven-year-old sister by my side, literally wearing a key around my neck and a big message that said, "YOU DON'T HAVE ACCESS TO THIS." Anyway, Kim and I would stand there in our booth for hours and hours and help sell—I'm sure—zero more shirts for my parents' store. I don't remember what I was paid, but I liked the idea that I was a model.

Making me her show pony really backfired on my mom, because when I entered my early teen years, I started demanding a weekly blowout for my frizzy, curly hair. Most twelve-year-old girls were not getting blowouts on the reg, but my town hated Jews and I wanted to hide my little fro, so I began to plot how I could get more blowouts. They were not cheap, so I got the idea that I'd sweep up hair at the salon after school if, in return, they'd blow-dry my hair once a week. I don't remember how long I kept up this arrangement, but it seemed very worth it at the time. I guess the salon, much like my parents, wasn't worried about child labor laws. I loved the work too. I was part of a team, and I felt useful, but the shop wasn't that busy. I'd sit anxiously and watch the stylists clipping hair, waiting for any of it to fall on the floor. When it did, I'd rush over to it, like an annoying human Zamboni or Olympic curler. I was too eager, people complained, and I was let go.

It was the first in a long line of completely justifiable firings in my life. I was so eager to work that I'd "fake it 'til I maked it" even if I was completely unqualified to do a job. And then I would end up getting fired when my inexperience was revealed. The second time I got fired was when I lied in an interview at a different salon and got a job as a shampoo girl. I thought I was doing well until I completely blew it with my first bald customer. This man only had hair in a small patch in the center of the front of his head and a thin strip along the bottom in the back, like a clown. No offense to this specific brand of male-pattern baldness, but it's accurate to say that this dude had textbook Bozo hair. I started washing his hair—just his hair, and not the sizable amount of bald scalp. He shouted at me with a lisp, "Wash my whole head pleathe!" I said, "No! Whenever I wash the parts without hair, the water bounces back and sprays me in the face!" He marched right up to the owner, and within minutes I was fired.

I really appreciated the bosses who deliberately overlooked my lack of skills and hired me based on my confidence and bravado alone. I worked at a well-known steakhouse in Grand Central Terminal—a really expensive, white-tablecloth place that catered to fast-talking businesspeople, commuters, and tourists. I was completely unqualified to work there and had no fancy-dining experience, but I lied and said I did. I didn't make it past the first interview, but as I was leaving, I overheard someone who was there for a second interview, which gave me the idea to just show up the next day and repeat what I'd heard. *Fake it 'til you make it!* I thought. The next day, I showed up and confidently said, "Hi, I have a second interview with Frank."

They looked me up and down, confused, but I sat and waited for whoever Frank was. The general manager came out and asked me some questions. The one I remember is, What is the main ingredient in tequila? I answered, "Triple sec?" He told me I was very wrong and that it was agave and hired me anyway. I still don't know why. Maybe my delusional confidence was mesmerizing.

For most of my nine months working there, I was the only woman. It was an all-male staff full of career steak waiters. I had to wear a jacket and tie. The jacket was white, so the dust from Grand Central would settle on me and turn the jacket gray by the end of my shift and make me scratch my face until I looked like I had leprosy. I was too young and blotchy to work there, but I faked it 'til I maked it and eventually got pretty good at it. My sales were among the top there. I'd offer things that weren't on the menu, like a surf and turf, which just meant I'd charge them for a lobster and a filet. I was indeed an asshole.

There were other times I showed up unqualified and ended up doing a great job. Like the time in college when I taught aerobics—or as they called it, "group exercise"—to chicks like me who'd doubled down on the freshman fifteen. I did actually have a certification to teach kickboxing, and I was able to leverage that into a job teaching a lot of other stuff I had never even tried before, like yoga, Pilates, spin, step, and dance. Before you go down the path of thinking I wouldn't be your first pick for a fitness instructor, let me inform you that my classes were very well attended and fun. I'd have the girls yell out the names of their ex-boyfriends or whoever they were mad at while they threw kicks and punches. I gained some fans who'd follow me from class to class. What I lacked in physique and expertise, I completely made up for with my likability and motivational yelling.

There was one job that I couldn't really physically fake. But I tried anyway. I was twenty-one years old, living on the West Coast with Dan, who did not turn out to be the greatest boyfriend (more on that later). Maybe my unhappy home life with him inspired me to make the strange choice to work as a pedicab driver. For those of you who don't know what a pedicab is, it's basically like a horse-drawn carriage, except a person on a bike is acting as the horse. I don't know what got into my head that made me think this was a good idea. All you technically needed to qualify was a bike, and the pedicab company would rent you the cart for twenty bucks a day. They'd help you hook up the cart to your bike, and then it was up to you to pedal around town and find human beings to haul. There was a main street on a huge hill, and I'd ride to the top of the hill and hope people would want to pay me for a ride down it. Of course, that never happened. I'd sit there and wait for about an hour and then ride down to the bottom, where, naturally, people would always flag me for a lift. I wasn't in great shape, so I'd get about halfway up the hill and feel I was about to roll backward—cart, passengers, and all. I'd come to a halt and yell, "Everybody out!" The passengers would have to help me push my cart up the hill. Due to some weird city ordinance, you weren't allowed to quote passengers a fare. You were just supposed to let them pay what they wanted. Can you imagine if prostitutes had to follow this law too? *"That was pretty good, here's a shiny nickel."* Fuck that! I gave them my price like a nice little prostitute.

I did that job for a few months. I lost about three pounds and that was it. More than I lost teaching aerobics, but still, you'd think I would have lost more weight. But I was so hungry at the end of every shift that I'd binge-eat and then drink myself into a blackout so I could forget about having to work the next day. But something I did enjoy about that job was the nice camaraderie among all the pedicab drivers. We'd meet up in one spot in town, park our carts, smoke cigarettes, and talk about how rough our job was.

The ultimate faking-it situation on my résumé was the time I worked at a lesbian bar. All the female bartenders and I would go out and get really drunk before a shift, because despite what I imagined it would be like, bartending for ALL women was a fucking nightmare. The only thing worse than the drunk drama and the indecisive ordering was the fact that no one ever hit on me. All the other bartenders were straight, but I would look over an hour into our shift and they'd be cheating on their boyfriends, making out with female custom-ers. At the end of the night, the bartenders were even drunker than they had been at the beginning of the night, so counting up the money and tips was impossible. Plus, they made us dance on the bar.

It was humiliating. I'm not a good bar dancer. I'd wear a pair of pink underwear that read I LOVE ME and I'd lift my skirt to display this message, and sway around laughing. I ended up getting fired from that job—not for my gross dancing or my raging heterosexuality, but for closing early without permission. One night, I shut the place down at seven p.m. just because I felt like it.

I was always doing whatever I felt like doing at work. Sometimes it's too hard to hide your feelings just because you're on somebody else's dime. Like at one restaurant I worked in, I decided to stop speaking to the clientele because they were so yuppie and rude. I was done with them. But waiting tables kind of requires you to talk to customers, so I got demoted to being the service bartender, standing in one place and only making drinks for servers to carry out to the floor. And now that I'm the boss and can be openly honest about my feelings at work, I try to set a good example for my staff to let them know they are welcome to do the same. Everyone is free to feel their feelings on the set of my TV show. Sometimes when I am extra emotional due to it being that time of the month, I just get on the loudspeaker and announce to all the cast and crew that I have my period. You should be able to be yourself and keep it real at work, no matter what you're feeling.

Once when I worked at a little bodega by the train stop when I was fifteen, I felt my body telling me to eat a lot of the store's hot dogs. So I did.

Which doesn't seem that strange except that I was always working a five a.m. shift before school. I was truly ill equipped for that job because even though I was supposed to ring up hot dogs, coffee, snacks, and newspapers, I had no clue how to make change. The coffee would cost $1.85 and they would hand me a five-dollar bill. I'd respond by just staring at the bill, hoping that through black magic the right amount of change would just float out of my hand and into theirs. I'm a great salesman, but numbers hold me back. I consoled myself by eating a lot more hot dogs. They were so good there. My paycheck was a lot lower than I wanted it to be because they were charging me for my enormous hot dog intake.

My bosses were these two late-forties Indian guys who ~~thought~~ knew I was an idiot. They'd make themselves feel good by belittling me. They'd stand next to each other behind the counter and trash me. I didn't blame them, because I was a terrible employee. I quit when summer came around, and shortly after that, the shop closed down for good. Mine was an honest and simple job, and I think if I weren't on this career path, I'd like to go back to eating hot dogs all day. And I'm grateful to those two guys because even though they made fun of me every second I was there, they never fired me.

One of the things I've learned as a boss myself now is to have high expectations of people, but also to keep it realistic. You can't expect someone to work past their potential. If you've hired someone with the mathematical aptitude of a pet rock, and she eats all your hot dogs and doesn't know how to make change, try to figure out how and where she shines, and let her excel in that area instead. I try to be patient and forgiving with the people I hire, just as they are with me. Mutual respect. But when I realize they don't have what it takes, I do the kind thing and let them go. I always think of that goldfish quote often attributed to Einstein: "Everybody is a genius. But if you judge a fish by its ability to climb a tree, it will live its whole life believing that it is stupid." Let that goldfish go someplace where it can join a school—and then hire an actual climber instead.

I still love hot dogs and lesbians as much as the next guy, but it was such a great relief when I could finally quit working for other people and focus on working for myself instead. Nothing feels better than running the show on my own now. I'm guessing almost every person reading this knows how much personal dignity you sign over when you work for someone you don't like or for a company you don't care about. But I still have to give it up to all the horrible bosses I worked for in the service industry, because most of what I know as a boss today has come from those experiences. And from learning NOT to ever be like them. All those mean chefs who belittled the waiters, and the sociopathic restaurant managers who led with fear and intimidation, wielding their minuscule amount of power to scare the shit out of any employee who needed a day off for even the most legit of reasons . . . All those assholes really showed me several specific versions of who I didn't want to become if I was ever in charge. So I guess the nine million waitressing and bartending jobs I had really paid off in the end. But it's also nice to learn by positive example now and then. I got more value from just one day on Tina Fey's set and two days on Lena Dunham's than I got from any other long-term job I've had.

Now that I spend most of my time on sets or onstage, I can finally say I love what I do for a living. But still, most days I can't wait until I am done and allowed to go, which is almost never. And despite my poor track record at restaurants, bars, salons, and mailrooms (yes, I once got fired from a mailroom for throwing away the mail), I'm proud to say I've never been fired from a show business job. Once on a small one-episode TV role I was told I'd be canned if I didn't stop ad-libbing inappropriate jokes, but that's the closest I ever came. And now that I'm a boss and it's part of my job to do the hiring and firing, I get what it feels like to have people's fate in your hands. It's not a sensation I enjoy. Turns out being on the other side can also be full of humiliation and hardship. But it still beats working for someone else. And there's no turning back once you get used to running the show.

I GOT MY very first brief taste of being in charge at the age of ten, when I was a basketball referee for a little kids' league. I'd wake up early Saturday mornings and put on my striped shirt and hang the whistle around my neck like a girl boss. Literally. I was still physically a little girl and hadn't even started my period yet. But I was made for that job. It wasn't easy, because the parents were bloodthirsty and insane. The kids were six-year-olds who couldn't even lace up their own shoes, but these parents were calling for technical fouls. I threw my fair share of them out of the game. I'd call traveling on one of the kids and the father would literally get in my face—my ten-year-old, three-foot-eleven face—and yell, "Terrible call!" I'd blow my whistle and point to the door, and the angry adult would leave the room in a huff. It was the most difficult job I've had to date, harder even than hauling three obese men from Green Bay uphill in a pedicab. But somehow I think that job prepared me for everything I do now. It prepared me for being a female boss in an industry that is still mostly run by men. It prepared me for being called fat, ugly, and talentless on the Internet (because, I assure you, every troll online is even more vitriolic and nasty than those adults getting in my face on the basketball court). And it prepared me to get up early, work my ass off, and stand by my calls.

Today I wake up every day, mostly with way too much work on my plate and not enough hours to get it all done. I worry about the people on my payroll, that if I don't do a good job they'll be affected. I try to treat everyone equally (badly).

JK, just equally. I do my best to make decisions that are fair and good for me and everyone else. I'm tired and beaten down a lot of the time. But it still feels so fucking good to know that no matter who or what comes at me, this is my court and I wear the whistle.

EXCERPT FROM MY JOURNAL IN 2001 (AGE TWENTY) WITH FOOTNOTES FROM 2016

I got home around 2:50.[1] Today I went with my mom and Kim to meet Jay at LaGuardia. We got to meet his good friend from his school, Eileen.

Throughout the weekend he made his usual fat jokes about me,[2] and Kim looked so wonderful and thin[3] and I felt so heavy and the mixture of all of that has made me decide to try to develop an eating disorder.[4] Hopefully it will safely work out.[5] I'm sick of feeling confident and then suddenly self-conscious.[6] It's too hard. I have become something I never thought I would. I've never had any real issue with my weight but I'm seeing Dan in three weeks and I'm sick of being looked at as the

---

1 Wow, very precise. What is this, *Law and Order*?

2 I honestly don't remember my brother making fun of my weight at all. I remember him making sure my ego was in check and that I never got too full of myself.

3 I had no idea that she was battling an eating disorder at the time.

4 Cool idea, Aim! Really smart and not dangerous. What an inspiration. By the way, my swing-and-a-miss at an eating disorder lasted under one day. I think I skipped one meal and then decided, *Nope . . . fuck that noise.*

5 Like they always do.

6 Well, get used to it, bitch. It's for the rest of your life.

big girl. I want to feel what it's like to be considered really hot. I hate that that is such a priority to me. But right now it just is.[7]

I can just see myself reading this entry when I'm recovering from the disorder and gaining back the weight, but I have to give it a shot.[8] *I've tried everything else.*[9] *If I don't look much better than now, I will refuse to see Dan. I want to see him and feel thin and beautiful or not see him at all.*[10]

This is such a humiliating thing to actually write down, but I'm sort of depressed and I've worked pretty hard and this is just how I feel. So be it. We'll see what happens.

Luv,

Amy

---

7 I understand what I'm saying here. Feeling this way is a theme in every girl's life, I think, and at that age, you think there's some other version of yourself that is waiting to come out and blow everyone's dick off. I am so glad this is almost fifteen years ago and I know myself and my body now. Sorry, girls this age, but if you can, just skip the self-hatred and the striving to be some other type of girl. Just let that phase pass you by and love yourself how you are. Don't waste any energy on it. If you want to lose a little weight, fine. Make sure you are healthy, but fuck, skip all the rest. You are hot and the person who will love you won't notice ten pounds. I really promise.

8 Not only was I so confident in my ability to develop an efficient eating disorder, but I was also certain I would recover from it. Do you think I get ahead of myself?

9 Except for not drinking like Nic Cage in *Leaving Las Vegas*.

10 This was the boyfriend who made me feel bad about myself and my body so I would have low self-esteem and he wouldn't lose me. More on this prize later.

P.S. I guess Dan has too much power over me. I need something else. I've been seriously thinking about the AmeriCorps=Hell yea.[11] I wish it was now. I should be enjoying college not praying for it to end.[12] What the fuck. I want to go to NYU so bad.[13] Towson sucks, Baltimore is bullshit.[14] Get me the fuck out of here.[15]

A few days later:

Dear Journal,

It's been two weeks since my last confession. Haha.[16] I just read over my previous journal entry. It makes me sick.[17] I don't feel that way at all right now about my body. I like my body.[18] Before hooking up with Dan I

---

11 That is like the Peace Corps but in America, which my brother did. Which I never even came close to doing. I am a flake. Also . . . "Hell yea"??? Yikes.

12 That is not true, that is exactly what I should have been doing. People who enjoy high school or college too much are wack in my humble opinion.

13 I don't remember ever thinking that.

14 I disagree with myself here. Baltimore is not bullshit; I grew to really love it.

15 Many people think I have this unshakable confidence, so I hope this look into my most intimate thoughts will support the idea that loving yourself takes time. Like any healthy relationship, it doesn't happen overnight. And sometimes, it can only come to fruition after several failed attempts at eating disorders.

16 What a hack. I seriously thought I was Woody Allen.

17 My emotional swings in my twenties were like those of someone with multiple personality disorder.

18 Oh okayyyyy, boo boo!

never had a real issue with it.[19] *If he continues to make me feel self-conscious I really don't want to communicate with him anymore.*[20] *I feel pretty good about myself and my weight right now. Anyway, I'm on a plane on my way to visit Dan haha. Again, with a mere mention of a visit, I'm on a plane to go see this little bastard.*[21] *I hope we have so much fun. I just don't want to take this too seriously.*[22] *He is my friend who I love on a deeper level than other friends. The sex certainly completes it but that's just a factor of our friendship.*[23] *I'm excited to see how this weekend goes. It's Thursday right now and I'm staying til Sunday.*[24]

---

19 I was putting the pieces together that this guy was treating me like garbage.

20 Yeah, bitch! I want to jump off the couch and celebrate for this girl—follow this girl, ladies!

21 Turns out I was right. He was a bastard. See chapter titled "The Worst Night of My Life."

22 Hear me now! The "I'm just gonna have fun and not be attached" tactic has never and will never work, sistas. I do not know one girl who wants to get a bunch of different dick. We aren't wired that way, honeys.

23 Damn, you can hear me lying to myself even on the page.

24 Okay, I Googled it and that checks out. It was a Thursday. It was also my brother's birthday. Happy belated, Jay!

BEAUTIFUL AND STRONG

Right before I left for college I was running my high school. I knew where to park, where to get the best chicken cutlet sandwich, and which custodians had pot. People knew me. They liked me. I was an athlete and a good friend and I felt pretty. I felt seen. I had reached my full high school potential. I had an identity. I was looked at as strong, funny, and fair. It was this sweet spot in life when I didn't spend a lot of time questioning my worth. I owned what I had and didn't sweat the rest.

Then I got to college, where the class of freshman girls at my school, Towson University in Maryland, had just been voted *Playboy* magazine's number one hottest in the nation. And not because of me.

All of a sudden being witty and charismatic didn't mean shit. Day after day I could feel the confidence draining from my body. I was *not* what these guys wanted. They wanted thinner, blonder, dumber. My sassy one-liners were only working with the cafeteria employees, whom I was visiting all too frequently, tacking on the freshman thirty, not fifteen, in record-breaking time. No males were noticing me, and, I'm embarrassed to say, it was killing me.

The closest thing to attention I got came from this guy Brett. He was five years older than me and looked like a Hitler Youth. He was also a "super senior," which is a sexy way of saying he should have graduated but needed or wanted another year before entering the real world. He barely ever spoke, which was perfect for all the projecting I had planned for him.

Getting attention from a cute older boy felt like success. I'd get nervous to see him on campus—my heart would race, and I'd smile as he passed and look him in the eyes and feel all the blood rush to my face. I'd spend my time analyzing that interaction and planning my outfit for the next time I saw him. *Should I wear simple clogs or Reef sandals? Will he be at the bar tonight? This calls for a zebra-print mini and a tube top!*

I wanted him to call, but he never called. And then, one day, he called. It was eight a.m. when my dorm room phone rang.

"Amy, sup? It's Brett. Come over."

Holy shit. This is it, I thought. *He woke up thinking about me. He realized we were meant to start a life together—that we should stop all this pretending that we weren't created just to love one another. I wonder where we'll raise our kids? Does he want to raise our family in Baltimore? I'll settle where he's most comfortable. I don't need to raise our kids Jewish, but I certainly won't have them christened.*

I shaved my legs in the sink and splashed some water on my armpits. My roommate stared at me from under her sheets as I rushed around our shitty dorm room, which, in retrospect, was not unlike a prison: neon lighting, randomly assigned roommate, and sealed windows so we didn't have the option to jump to an early graduation.

I ran right over there, ready for our day together. What would we do? It was still early enough to go fishing. Or maybe his mom was in town and they wanted me to join them for breakfast. Knock, knock. I beamed at the door. Knock, knock. *Is he going to carry me over the threshold? I bet he's fixing his hair and telling his mom, "Be cool, this may be the one."* I planned to be very sweet with her but also to assert myself so she didn't think she was completely in charge of all the holiday dinners we'd be spending together. I'd call her by her first name too early so she'd realize she couldn't mess with me. "Rita, *I'm* going to make the green bean casserole this year."

Knock, knock. Knock. Knock. KNOCK! Finally, the door opened. It was Brett, but he wasn't really there. His face was distorted from alcohol consumption and whatever else. His eyes seemed like they'd left his body. They couldn't focus on me. He was standing next to me trying to see me from the side, like a shark.

"Hey!" he yelled, a few notches too loudly, and gave me a painfully hard hug. But I was too busy tilting up my chin, sticking out my boobs, and sucking in my stomach to notice this huge red flag.

He was fucking wasted. I quickly realized that I wasn't the first person he'd thought of that morning. I was the last person he'd thought of the night before, because for Brett, it still *was* the night before. I wondered how many girls didn't answer before he got to fat, freshman me. Was I in his phone as "Schumer"? Probably took him a while to get to "S." But there I was in his room, eighteen years old and wanting to be held and touched and to feel desired. I wanted to be with him, and I imagined us on campus together holding hands, proving that I was lovable and that I couldn't be the troll doll I thought I'd become, because this cool, older guy liked me. I thought, *I'll stay 'til he's sober and we can laugh about the whole thing and realize we really like each other.*

He put on some music and we got into bed. Well, he pushed me on the bed as a sexy maneuver, the move guys so often do to communicate, "Get ready, I'm taking the wheel on this one and I'm going to blow your mind." It's almost never followed up with anything. He smelled like skunked Heineken—well, Heineken, skunk, and Micro-Magic cheeseburgers, which I planned to find and eat in the bathroom once he was asleep. His nine a.m. shadow scratched my face when he came at me (I knew it would look like I had fruit punch mouth for days after this), and his alcohol-swollen kisses made me feel like I was being tongued by someone who'd just been given Novocain.

The music was too loud. I felt faceless and nameless. I was just a warm body, but I felt freezing cold as his fingers poked inside me like he'd lost his keys in there. Then came the sex. I use that word loosely. His penis had all the hardness of an empty banana peel. I knew a few minutes after I walked in that there was no chance of any sort of intercourse. Which was good, because I wasn't ready to actually sleep with him. There was a better chance of a baby climbing Everest than this guy penetrating me.

During this festival of flailing, I looked around the room to try to distract myself, or, God willing, dissociate. The place looked like it had been decorated by an overeager set designer who took the note "temporary and without any substance" too far. I saw a *Scarface* poster, which, of course, was mandatory. Anything else? No. That was it. This Standard White Dude son of an accountant who played more video games and Hacky Sack than I was comfortable with felt the greatest connection with a Cuban refugee drug lord.

He started to go down on me. *That's ambitious,* I thought. Is it still considered getting head if the guy falls asleep after three seconds of moving his tongue like an elderly person eating their last oatmeal? The only wetness coming from between my legs was his drool, because he'd fallen completely asleep and was snoring *into* me. I wanted to scream out for myself: *Get out of here, Amy! You are beautiful, you are smart, and you are worth more than this!* I sighed and heard my own heart break; I was fighting back tears. I could feel I was losing myself to the girl in this bed, almost completely. Then I noticed a change in the music. The song was a bagpipe solo.

"Brett, what is this?" I shook him awake.

"The *Braveheart* soundtrack."

Of course. I should have known. I bet his Mel Gibson poster was in the mail, on its way to hang on the wall proudly next to Al Pacino.

"Can you put something else on please?"

He rose grumpily, fell to the floor, and crawled. I looked at his exposed butt crack, a dark unkempt abyss that I was falling into. I was short of breath. I felt paralyzed. His asshole was a canyon. This was my 127 hours. I needed to chip away at the rock and get out.

Brett stood up and put on a new CD. "*Darling, youuuuu send me.*" He climbed back in bed and tried to mash what was at this point his third ball into my vagina. On his fourth thrust he gave up and fell asleep again on my breasts. His head was heavy and his breath so sour I had to turn my head so my eyes didn't water. But they already were watering, because of this album. These songs.

"Who is this?" I asked. The music was so beautiful. The songs were gutting me. "*Cupid, draw back your bowwww.*" The score he'd attached to our morning could not have been more off. His sloppy attempt at "lovemaking" was more Mel Gibson than William Wallace. And now the most beautiful love songs I'd ever heard rang out as this man-boy lay in my arms after diminishing me to a last attempt at a booty call. I listened, and I cried.

I looked down on myself from the ceiling fan, as if I were my own fairy godmother. I waited until the last perfect note, then slid out from under him and slipped out the door. I closed it behind me, and I was rescued.

I never heard from Brett again, so I never got to thank him for introducing me to my new self and my new love, Sam Cooke.

THIRTEEN YEARS LATER, I still love Sam Cooke, and I still need that fairy godmother from time to time. As a part of my TV show, I have a segment called "Amy Goes Deep" where I interview people who do interesting jobs or have interesting lifestyles. One segment I did that we didn't end up airing was with a professional matchmaker. In addition to letting me ask her questions about her job, she wanted to set me up. Directly after we filmed our conversation, I was going to meet up with the man she'd chosen for me.

It was the most disturbing "Amy Goes Deep" scene I've taped. Keep in mind, I've talked to a climate change denier, a pickup artist, and a diagnosed sociopath. But this woman left the darkest cloud over me. It still makes me feel angry and demoralized. Before we met, she'd sized me up from pictures online and some footage of my performances. She told me very little about the guy she was going to set me up with but emphasized that he was a great catch. She described him as a six-foot-tall, nice-looking guy who worked out. She assured me that he was funny and that he always made people laugh with the insightful things he wrote on Facebook. She went on to instruct me about the benefits of this quality, as if she were speaking to an alien who'd never experienced human emotion before. "When there's great banter, it's really fun and easy—and you feel sexual chemistry happening."

Hearing her "teaching" me—a thirty-four-year-old comic—about sexual attraction and humor in this controlling, prescribed way was making the bile rise in my throat. She asked what icebreaker I'd use to talk to a guy. I asked if she thought I should "push his head down like I was setting off dynamite."

"No," she said, completely humorlessly. "Because the guy is supposed to be the one doing that. You're the woman," she informed me. "You need to be a lady. You need to make it so that he likes you. So that there's a hint of what's to come. I think you just need to sit back and let him take control."

She then informed me that my numerous sex jokes were probably the reason I was still single. How can I say this like a lady? Suck my dick!

If you've seen my show, you know that I expose every part of myself on-screen. I wear unattractive costumes and show my body from all angles. I write about things that I'm truly sensitive about, and I'm often the butt of the joke. But this interview with the matchmaker was, hands down, the most vulnerable I've ever felt. Hearing a dating "expert" inform me why I'm not attractive to men, and then having to put myself out there to meet a man she selected who might actually be interested in me, was very scary.

When the interview finished, I went to a bar to meet the guy, whom I'll call Rex. I'm feeling dizzy even writing this now. I waited at the bar, all of my self-worth leaking out of my sweaty palms, which were gripping a glass of wine like it was the only thing connecting me to the rest of the world. I had a bad feeling. But nothing could have prepared me for who walked in the door.

When I saw Rex, I felt like the *Titanic*, and he was the cluster of icebergs that would finally destroy me. In he walked. He was about fifty-three years old, wearing a denim button-down shirt with a leather vest over it. He was around five foot nine (a solid three inches shorter than the matchmaker's description) and had hair plugs and a significant belly. He was not afraid of exposing his salt-and-pepper chest hair, having left open his top four buttons, which also allowed him to showcase—no joke—a shark-tooth necklace. His own teeth had been freshly whitened and he couldn't wait to

flash them as often as possible, which wasn't difficult because he was so excited about his tan that he
couldn't stop smiling.

I bought him a drink after we hugged hello.
My heart had dropped out of the bottom of my
vagina, and the clock was running the second we
locked eyes. *I am giving this exactly thirty minutes*,
I thought. I focused all my energy on being as
kind as possible. He asked me no questions, which
I appreciated, because I just wasn't in the sharing mood. There was no time anyway because he
needed to tell me about his band that did Bruce or
Billy covers. He talked a lot about the kind of guy
he was, he stared at my tits, and I witnessed the
moment he decided he'd be willing to have sex
with me. I was focusing on my breathing and the
clock. I was smiling and trying to spread joy, but
it was hard because this guy was actually cocky
and a dick. I started to wrap things up at about
twenty-two minutes in. I said I had so much work
to do and how great it was to meet him. He then
said exactly this: "You are really cute. The matchmaker told me you were, quote, 'no model,' but I
think she's wrong." This made my heart, which
had already fallen out of my pussy, proceed to dig
a hole through the Earth's crust, mantle, and core.
Was this supposed to be the great banter the matchmaker foreshadowed? Was the sexual chemistry
right around the corner? I wanted to be sure I'd
heard him correctly.

"What exactly did she say?" I asked.

"Well," Rex proceeded to explain, "I wasn't sure I wanted to go on this date and was nervous about it, and she said, 'Don't worry, she's no model.'"

I pointed out to him how rude it was to relay this information to me. I could have done without hearing her assessment of my appearance. He defended himself by saying that he disagreed with the matchmaker. I started to lay out for him why this was still a shitty thing for him to say to me, but then I thought, *Fuck it, why am I engaging with a dude who was born when Eisenhower was president and who loves wearing dead shark parts close to his heart?* I thanked him for his time, hugged him good-bye, and left decimated. Not for myself, but for all the single women out there trying to date. I wanted to run to the top of the Empire State Building and make an announcement to all of them to let them know they are worth so much more than this. That they don't need to wrangle some warm body to sit next to them just so they aren't alone on holidays. That they should never let a magazine or dating site or matchmaker monster tell them they're in a lower bracket of desirability because of their age or weight or face or sense of humor. That they don't deserve to be manipulated into thinking this is something they should strive for—this decaying turkey of a man who'd been encouraged to believe, like so many other men, that he was a great prize for someone like me. Why should I have worked so hard to keep him interested, as the matchmaker suggested women are supposed to do? He wasn't funny, he wasn't particularly nice, and I've been more interested talking to people's pets.

And as for the matchmaker, she makes her living redefining women's dreams, telling them to lower their expectations. She creates and confirms what she thinks you deserve. If you're "no model" I guess she thinks your best hope is to be matched with a man who has a pulse and a bank account, and that you should be grateful if he musters an erection with your name on it. I walked out of there like the building was on fire and I had started it, thinking, *FUCK THAT!*

I'm not going to lie in that freshman dorm bed or sit in that bar with Rex and his vest ever again. And for anyone who has ever looked for love and found nothing more than a denim-on-denim-on-leather-wearing Hair Club for Men dude, I want to say, *Love yourself!* You don't need a man or a boy or a self-proclaimed love expert to tell you what you're worth. Your power comes from who you are and what you do! You don't need all that noise, that constant hum in the background telling you whether or not you're good enough. All you need is you, your friends, and your family. And you will find the right person for you, if that's what you want—the one who respects your strength and beauty.

Most of the time these days, I feel beautiful and strong. I walk proudly down the streets of Manhattan, that same girl I was during my senior year of high school. The people I love love me. I'm a great sister and friend. I make the funniest people in the country laugh. My vagina has had an impressive guest list—truly an inspiring roster of men. I have fought my way through harsh criticism and death threats, and I am alive. I am fearless. Most of the time. But I can still be reduced to that lonely, vulnerable college freshman pretty quickly. It happened that day with the matchmaker and Rex, and I'm sure it will happen again. I'm not bulletproof, and I'm sure I'm not alone in this. As women, we relive our fears all the time, despite our best efforts to build each other up and truly love ourselves. It happens. And when it does, sometimes Sam Cooke isn't enough, and I can't fairy-godmother my way out of it. Sometimes I want to quit—not performing, but being a woman altogether. I want to throw my hands in the air after reading a mean Twitter comment and say, "All right, you got me. You figured me out. I'm not pretty. I'm not thin. I don't deserve love. I have no right to use my voice. I will start wearing a burka and move to a small town upstate and wait tables at a pancake house."

So much has changed about me since I was that confident, happy girl in high school. In the years since then, I've experienced a lot of desperation and self-doubt, but in a way, I've come full circle. I know my worth. I embrace my power. I say if I'm beautiful. I say if I'm strong. You will not determine my story. I will. I'll speak and share and fuck and love, and I will never apologize for it. I am amazing for you, not because of you. I am not who I sleep with. I am not my weight. I am not my mother. I am myself. And I am all of you.

EXCERPT FROM MY JOURNAL IN 2003 (AGE TWENTY-TWO) WITH FOOTNOTES FROM 2016

Dear Journal,

Well it's always a bad sign when I'm not writing. It really means I have something to hide or that I am not living in reality and I don't want to think about it.[1] *This*[2] *past two months have been no exception. I am now in New York on the train on my way to try and get a fabulous waitressing job in the city.*[3]

I have been living in a world mirroring reality but not quite a part of it.[4] *I graduated from college blah blah blah. What exactly does that mean?*[5] *I think I*

---

1 I like that I believed my journal was this priest I had to confess my sins to. I had this unwritten contract to keep shit real with my journal.

2 It's also a bad sign when a "writer" uses "this" instead of "these" when talking about something plural. Crushing it, Amy!

3 I honestly don't know if I was joking or not with the word "fabulous," but what I learned quickly was that there are no fabulous waitressing jobs, or bartending jobs, or any service industry jobs, except maybe there is a professional head getter. Is that a job? You just lie there and get head? That sounds fabulous.

4 I would love to know what the fuck I am talking about here. I must have been reading a heavy-handed Oprah book club pick.

5 I have a point here. To this day, I maintain that going to college is not essential if you want to be an actor, especially if you

know but I've learned that the present truth becomes the future's nonsense.[6]

The last two months of school were busy but great. The play went pretty well. It could have been 1,000 times better but the director was the worst ever and the cast sucked too.[7]

I am trying to begin my life.[8] *I want everything right now.*[9] *I want to be living in NYC,*[10] *getting paid,*[11] *to act and bartend.*[12] *I've only been home a week and I'm already itching to be raking in cash*

---

truly want to perform. Read some plays and study in an intensive course with the technique that is the most useful for you. I liked the Meisner technique, so I studied that for a couple years after college with William Esper.

6 Slow down, Nietzsche. This is utter garbage. Just babble. I am embarrassed for myself, but that's part of reading from a journal.

7 Pretty harsh, Amy Ford Coppola. What did I expect? It was a state school in Maryland. Did I want Mark Rylance and Meryl Streep to costar with me? We were a bunch of teenagers playing adults. Relax.

8 I remember this feeling so well. Since I was ten I'd wanted to feel like life was really starting and it all wasn't just this prep for it.

9 I did.

10 I do.

11 I do.

12 I like that I was realistic enough to know that I would have to bartend and that I included it in my dream. I upgraded from waitressing to bartending in this one journal entry.

and going on auditions.[13] *I want to start a new page.*[14]

---

13 Little did I know that auditions are what nightmares are made of. You are judged by a roomful of people who have no respect for you as you read for a role you will not get.

14 I would like for you to believe that I was being poetic and metaphorical here, but I literally meant I wanted to start a new page of the journal entry. There was a whole line left, but I drew an arrow because I was sick of looking at that page.

HOW TO BECOME
A STAND-UP COMEDIAN

Stand-up is my favorite thing to do. Well, that's not true. I love to have an orgasm and I love to watch a good movie or read a good book. I love to eat pasta and drink wine. Those things are probably my favorites. But after those things. Oh, wait, sleep, I love to sleep—and I love to be on a boat. I love to play volleyball with my sister and I love to go see a band or musician's concert right when I am at my peak of loving them. Those are all my favorite things to do. But all joking aside, even though I'm not joking, stand-up is such a huge joy for me. Especially now, because even though you get better and better at it, the experience doesn't change. Or at least that's how I feel.

Standing up there, onstage, under the lights, and expressing something you think is funny or important (or both) and being met with laughter, applause, appreciation, and agreement is a feeling I can't describe. I am a human being and I want to be loved, and some nights I just want to sit around watching movies with my family or my boyfriend. But mostly every night for the last thirteen years, I've wanted to get onstage.

My first official gig was at the age of five. I played Gretl in *The Sound of Music*. But I was performing even before that—for as long as I could speak. In my room as a child, the bed was placed on a platform in a nook that was built into the wall. There were curtains around the nook to create a cozy little place to sleep, but I moved the mattress out so the platform could be my stage instead. I'd gather any family members I could find, emerge from behind the curtain, and perform for them on my little stage. The performances consisted mostly of me telling boring, meandering stories about bunnies or cats or worms. They pretended they were interested even though they must have been dying for a meteor to drop on the house.

I always wanted to perform. My dad filmed everything, which constantly annoyed me—even as a toddler. I'd stop my performance and ask him to put down the camera. We have a video of me throwing a tantrum because he wouldn't obey my demands to stop filming. You'd think I would have enjoyed being filmed, but for me, the experience was all about the audience and the live show. Even when I was three.

My first time going onstage to do stand-up was very last-minute. I was twenty-three years old and had been out of college for two years. A woman in an improv group I was in, a comic of about forty-five, had been doing stand-up for a long time. She was like a female Woody Allen without the marrying someone who was once his daughter. I went to see her perform one night, and like every other asshole who goes to comedy clubs, I thought, *I could do this.*

Not long after that fateful night, I discovered Gotham Comedy Club. It was on Twenty-Second Street at the time and seated about 150 people. I went in and found out that if I brought four people to be in the audience (people who would pay the door price and purchase some drinks), I could perform that night. I can't remember who all four of these lucky souls were. One was definitely my mom, and another was my friend Eileen, a jazz drummer, but I don't remember the others. I had a couple hours before I went onstage, during which I brainstormed the six-minute set I'd perform. The show was at five p.m. on a Tuesday. Still light outside. Great time for comedy. There were about twenty-five people in the audience. I unfortunately have a videotape of the whole thing. My hair is very curly and the only thing worse than my outfit was my jokes. I wore a Mormon-looking short-sleeved white button-down with jeans that would have fit the original version of Jared from Subway, and I ranted about skywriting:

"It's so annoying. It always fades, and you can never really read it. If a guy proposed to me that way, I would say NOoooooooo."

And then I added:

"So do me a favor this summer, keep it at eye level!"

That was my clever little sum-up. *Keep it at eye level. Blech.*

I could vomit thinking about how awful my act was. But I wasn't nervous. I had been doing theater since I was five so I didn't have stage fright. I was pretty confident for a newcomer with zero original thoughts and even less timing. People laughed enough. They laughed because I was young and hopeful and they could feel my energy and enthusiasm. They laughed to be nice. All that mattered was that they laughed. I was *in*. Some of the actual comedians there complimented me. They told me I should work at it and that I could get better. Maybe they were trying to sleep with me. Wait, just remembered my outfit. They weren't.

From then on, I did a couple shows a month. Always "bringers," which means you have to bring between eight and twelve people to sit in the audience and buy drinks in exchange for six minutes of stage time. It's a bit of a racket, but everyone gets what they want. Everyone except the audience. I'd usually rely on my family and friends from Long Island and whomever I was waiting tables with at the time to fulfill my audience quota. It was brutal to need something from people all the time. Later on down the line, as soon as I stopped doing bringers, I deleted about a hundred numbers from my cell phone. I was thrilled I wouldn't ever again have to text, "HEY! WANT TO COME TO MY SHOW?" As I have said before, I'm an introvert, and after shows I'd just want to go home and think about my set, but instead, I'd have to go to a bar with everyone who came to support me. Doing a show already takes a lot out of you, but then to have to kind of "work a room" was too much. It seemed easier to give a lap dance to an angry porcupine than to stand around with my restaurant coworkers hearing what they thought of my punch lines.

My first year of stand-up I'd pace in the parking lot outside Gotham before the show. I'd walk back and forth past the valet attendants and go over the set in my head the way an actor goes over a monologue: over and over again. Then, when I was a few minutes away from being called onstage, I'd get diarrhea. Every time. It was almost a ritual. I'd panic at the thought that they'd call my name while I was still in a cold bathroom wiping myself within an inch of my life, but it always timed out well. Somehow, I consistently managed to empty my bowels, wipe, and flush before my name was called. I even had a few extra seconds to stretch like a long-distance runner before I had to go on. Which I always did, until I saw someone shadow-boxing before they went onstage and thought it was so lame that I quit my own ritual of stretching.

Now I can be fully asleep or in the middle of a conversation and walk onstage, but back then it was like sacrificing a lamb with all the creepy superstitions I had. The strangest one was watching myself. You could buy a VHS tape of your performance from a guy at Gotham for fifteen dollars. I didn't have a VCR at home, so I'd bring the tape to a store that rhymes with West Buy and put it in one of their machines so I could watch my set and take notes. People shopping would walk by so confused as to why a girl had brought a video of herself to a store and was writing about it. Or once someone thought I was on a really low-budget TV show that I'd happened to catch the airing of. But I couldn't afford a VCR with all the money I was spending on stage time and rent.

I didn't graduate to open-mic shows for a while. Open mics are a bigger step because they aren't bringers, and a lot of the time the audience consists only of other comedians. I decided a good place to get my feet wet would be up in Harlem on 106th Street at a place called the Underground. I went up with a lot of confidence. I'd been performing for months in front of real audiences with a couple hundred people in them, so I thought I could handle thirty comedians. (I'm singing these three words:) *Noooo I cooooouldn't!* I bombed. Hard. Not one laugh.

There's nothing quite like your first bomb. You can feel it in your bones. First you think there might be something wrong with the sound. But there isn't. It's you. You're the problem. You and your terrible jokes that are not funny. You realize everyone has been lying to you. There are no friends in the audience laughing so as not to hurt your self-esteem. It's a sea of unfriendly faces, people who do the same thing you do, so they don't think you're cute. They think you are boring and that you're wasting their time. And all they are focused on is their own set and how they should be further along in comedy than they are. I was dizzy when I got offstage. I sat back down with a few other comics who smiled at me in a "sorry for your loss" way. I hung my head through the rest of the show and realized I had a lot of work to do. I didn't cry but my confidence was in tiny little pieces shattered all over the dirty Harlem floor. Okay, fine, I cried. And I drank several warm beers.

From there, I began doing a couple of shows a week—an open mic here, a bringer there. I'd finish one set and go home to have dinner with my boyfriend, Rick, with whom I lived very happily in Brooklyn. We were both actors who met waiting tables, meaning we were both auditioning for shitty roles in shitty plays and not getting any parts. I remember thinking it was strange that a lot of other comics I knew would do more than one show a night. I could feel their insatiable hunger for stage time and I pitied them. What were they chasing? As if one more five-minute set at a hair salon (yes, they have shows everywhere) in front of ten other drunk open-mic performers would change anything.

And then it happened to me. I thought of my first good joke. The kind that made me feel I had to get onstage to tell it. It happened on the L train on my way home to Williamsburg around one a.m. I was sitting next to an elderly black woman and we were having a nice conversation. Just chitchat. She was Crypt Keeper old, like a California Raisin. That is not racist. If she had been white she would have looked like a yellow California Raisin. Anywhoozle, out of nowhere she asked me, "Have you heard the good news?" At that moment I saw she had one of those cartoony religious pamphlets and I realized she was trying to save my soul. I let her down easily, explaining that I was Jewish and would not be joining her in the kingdom of heaven. That was that. I thought she was just this sweet woman I was connecting with, but she was using me to get salvation points. Little did she know I was a godless, shifty Jew. I walked home from the subway thinking about the interaction and I wrote a joke. A good joke.

I called my sister early the next morning and woke her up. Kim hates being woken up. But she sleeps with her phone on and I know that, so ring ring ring. "Kim, listen, I have a new joke!" She answered me with a supportive, "Good-bye." But I got her to stay on the phone and listen to my joke, which was:

This old woman on the subway asked me, "Have you heard the good news?" She was trying to save me.

I said, "Ma'am, I'm so sorry. My people are Jewish."

She said, "That's okay, your people just haven't found Jesus yet."

I said, "No, we found him. Maybe you haven't heard the bad news."

I listened into my phone for Kim's response. Like I had so many times before. After about three Mississippis she said, "That's funny. Good-bye." And she hung up. But that was all I needed. I loved my new joke. I tried it that night at an open mic, and it went well. But I started working on it. Maybe if I added a couple of wrong guesses of what I thought the good news was, it could be funnier. I went to another open mic, and then another.

A couple weeks later I wrote a new joke:

My boyfriend is always turning the lights on when we have sex, and I shut them off, and he puts them back on.

The other day, he said, "Why are you so shy? You have a beautiful body."

I said, "You are so cute! You think I don't want you to see me."

I loved that joke. I wanted to run it a million times. And I did. I found out there were some clubs where you could "bark"—which meant standing on a corner and giving out flyers, telling people about a comedy show. "Hey, do you like live comedy?" Have you heard those annoying people when you've visited New York? Well, that was me. In ten-degree weather, I'd be out there on a corner trying to get enough people inside so they would let me go onstage. I needed bodies in there, English-speaking or not.

I had caught the bug. I was totally and completely addicted to stand-up, to getting better at it, and it was working. It turns out if you do a ton of open mics and bringers, and if you bark, and if you produce your own shows, and if you have other comics in your shows, and if they have you in their shows, and if you do it every single night several times, and if you are totally obsessed with it, you will get a little better. "Little" is the key word.

Ultimately, anyone who does stand-up is delusional and masochistic. It takes so much work and so much time to be good. To get real laughs requires years and years. I got better little by little. A comic, Pete Dominick, whom I met doing a bringer at Gotham, pushed me hard to get better. He said, "You need to know the name of every club in New York, and you need to get up whenever you can. It has to be an obsession." He was right. Jessica Kirson was the funniest person I'd ever seen. I used to watch her close out the shows at Gotham. She would kill in a way I still haven't seen anyone else do. The audience was physically exhausted from laughing. When she got offstage, your face hurt. She was the first person to let me open for her on the road. I'd go anywhere for nothing. She would give me fifty bucks to be nice, but I was just thrilled she would take me with her.

Then one day—about two and a half years in—I went to a free seminar for new comics at Gotham Comedy Club, the place where I did my first stand-up set. The owner, Chris Mazzilli, had arranged for an agent and a nationally headlining comic to be there to answer the questions of about one hundred comics in attendance. I was furiously taking notes while Chris was talking about the importance of working hard. I'll never forget when he said to the group of hungry comedians, "A good example of a hardworking comic is Amy Schumer. She doesn't know it yet, but I am recommending her to be a new face at the Montreal comedy festival." This was all news to me. I was thrilled he even knew my name. I almost started crying, because he was the first person of authority to make it clear to me that he felt I had something special.

I had an open-mic show right after at a bar. I stepped outside in the rain to head over and it was like that scene in *Fifty Shades of Grey* after Anastasia meets Christian. Yes, I saw it, and so did you. Except I wasn't feeling this way about a hot guy who was going to be dominating me and fucking me in every hole. I was feeling this way about comedy. I don't remember how that open mic went or if any of my jokes worked that night. I just remember feeling like I was flying, knowing that it didn't matter how that show went. All twenty people in the audience could have stonewalled me; I wouldn't have cared. I had major adrenaline running through my veins, and I believed I had a real chance to make it. I didn't know what that meant, but I could feel something was coming.

Soon after, in 2006, I got a college agent. I'd be paid $100 to open for other comedians at universities— sometimes traveling for eight hours to get to one. My first college show was at Bryn Mawr in Pennsylvania, where I opened for a comic named Kyle Dunnigan. Half the crowd walked out during my set, and the other half walked out during his. Kyle is now, ten years later, one of my very best friends and has been a writer on my TV show for four years. He is one of the funniest people I know.

By the end of 2006 I started headlining colleges. The day I found out I was going to be making $800 for one hour, I was running laps in my Brooklyn apartment, thinking to myself, *Would I be this happy if I ever had a baby?* I think the answer was no. After that, I got to do a seven-minute special on a Comedy Central show called *Live at Gotham*. I killed, and blacked out from excitement. I couldn't believe I was getting to do stand-up on television after only two and a half years.

And then the most unlikely thing of all happened when I auditioned for NBC's program *Last Comic Standing*, an *American Idol*–type reality show for comics that was about to tape its fifth season. I didn't think I had a chance. I thought if I got lucky they might use my audition footage as part of a montage in the first episode, or that maybe I would at least lay the groundwork to make it on the show a few years down the road. That was my real thinking. The audition consisted of doing stand-up in front of three judges. After this first round, about two hundred were cut and some thirty people were invited to perform in the next round, which was an evening show to take place that same night. I called my mom and my boyfriend and they came to the show. At the end of the night, they stood us all in humiliating rows on risers to announce who would receive the "red envelopes," which were tickets to Los Angeles to perform in the semifinals. I stood there, knowing I wouldn't get an envelope and that I would have to stay put while they called all the winners down one by one. My face was turning the color of those envelopes. But then they read my name! My eyes bugged out of my head and I ran forward like a contestant being called down on *The Price Is Right*. They handed me my envelope and I couldn't believe it. I couldn't take my eyes off it. I felt like Charlie with his golden ticket. I looked at my mom and my boyfriend. We were all screaming with shock and excitement.

The two months leading up to the semifinals in LA, I worked out hard every day at the gym and did stand-up every single night. I was out in LA all by myself, staying at a hotel with comedians from all over the country and some from around the world. I was so bright-eyed and bushy-tailed. "The hotel has a pool!" I announced around a lunch table full of comics who had been on the road for as long as I'd been alive. Everyone was very nice to me, despite how annoying I must have been. I was the least experienced of the bunch.

When it came time for the big live taping that would determine which ten comics would compete on the show, I was ready. I wore a V-neck shirt from Express and almost no makeup. Someone told me there would be nine hundred people in the audience. The most I had ever performed for was about two hundred. A producer of the show said, "Amy, eight million people will see this on television." But for some reason that didn't matter to me as much as the nine hundred live people who would be sitting in front of me.

I assumed I would be eliminated, so I just promised myself I'd do the best I could and enjoy every second of it—and I did. At the end, when it came time to announce the top ten people who would be competing, my name was read ninth. "Amy Schumer!" I couldn't fucking believe it! I ran out onstage and waved like I had won a pageant. I cried. All that really happened was I made it onto a reality show, which was pretty much just casting. It's not that I was funnier than the rest of the comics. I was just a good "character" for the show. But I knew none of that at the time and I'm so glad I didn't.

Being on that show was so intense and exciting. Each episode consisted of a different challenge, and strangely, I was the most prepped for these challenges. The other comics were seasoned road dogs who were used to relying on their well-crafted jokes and long stories they told doing sixty to ninety minutes headlining sets on the road. But I only had about fifteen minutes of material, and it all worked in little sound bites—so it was perfect for a reality show. I was up for thinking on my feet, and they weren't.

The final challenge determined the top five comics, who got to go on a national tour together—

which would have been great for anyone's career, mine especially. It was explained to all of us that the challenge was going to consist of making models laugh. We would go room to room, one at a time, and do a joke or two for them. I remember saying, "Aren't you guys tired of only being appreciated for your brains?" They laughed. A bell went off to indicate that I was supposed to go to the next room. In that next room sat a clown. There were no more models to entertain. The production had of course tricked us, and the next rooms consisted of a drill sergeant, a transvestite, and a nun. I told my Jesus/ bad news joke to the nun and she laughed! I did my best but assumed I was going home.

The people from each room voted on their favorite comic, and when we all lined up for the results I was shocked to hear I had won. Thanks to the clown, the nun, the models, and the trans-vestite, I was going on the tour! I was thrilled for about ten seconds, until one of the comics who also wound up in the top five leaned over to me and said, "You don't deserve it." I ran into the bath-room and cried, because at the time, I believed him. I was paranoid that I hadn't actually been the funniest, that maybe the producers rigged the results in order to keep me on the show, since I was the young female comic who was good for their ratings. They wanted to film me while I cried, but I wouldn't come out of the stall. I refused to be a girl on reality TV sobbing and being a victim. I wanted to be strong. Later, when I watched the episode air,

I saw that without question, I'd performed the best. One of the producers, Page Hurwitz, said, "Amy, it wasn't even close. You won." Nothing bad to say about that comic who told me I didn't deserve it, but FUCK THAT GUY, RIGHT?!

I ended up getting eliminated on the next episode, earning myself fourth place on the show, along with the opportunity to tour the country on a giant rock star tour bus with four men in their forties. We performed in forty-two theaters to crowds of about two to four thousand people—the kind of places I'd never performed in before in my life. I bombed pretty much every single night. Forty-two cities, and I think I ate it in about forty of them. I wasn't ready; I didn't have the road work under my belt. You can fake it for seven minutes—even fifteen if you're charismatic enough—but when you're doing nearly a half hour, people are going to see what you're made of, and at that point I was made of less than three years. Not only was I short on material, I wasn't confident about my jokes yet, because I shouldn't have been. I didn't have the experience to sell it up there.

I'd cry in my bunk on the bus. One of the comics said he thought I was talented but wouldn't ever make it as a stand-up. It hurt. Looking back now, I can see clearly how experienced comics can get bitter. It's a tough business, and often things don't work out the way you think they will. But the rage and jealousy comics can feel for others' success is a highly toxic waste of time. I want to go back to those days knowing what I know now and say to that comic, "Focus on your own goals and how to achieve them. No one took your spot, there's room for all of us."

Anyway, the bus and hotel life on that tour was hard for me. I was lonely and not doing well. One night, after a show, I got on an elevator and a little old woman said, "Which floor?" and I didn't know. I started crying because I couldn't remember where I was. This sad moment is something most road comics, and I'm assuming musicians, can relate to. I had no idea how frequently this would happen to me over the years. It happens all the time.

But even though it was difficult, that tour was also my personal comedy boot camp. I'd logged enough hours bombing and sweating onstage that my molecules were permanently altered. Stand-up recalibrates your fear sensors. It thickens your skin in ways that come in handy all the time. Clocking so many hours under all those lights, while people in the crowd are viewing every expression and hearing every inflection, hanging on every word, just waiting to be moved by you (or to boo you) . . . This experience over and over again can only make you stronger. I think for anyone to become good at something, they have to fail a lot too. And they have to be completely unafraid to fail or they'll never make it to the next level. I did so bad for so long in front of so many people on that tour that I stopped caring. I got desensitized to crowds not liking my jokes. I lost the protective shell that holds so many of us back, and I just started going for it. This, in turn, made me *own* the crowd. Once you own your jokes and stand by them, you can relax. Being tentative sours the crowd. They see your fear and then they can't laugh. They want to have fun, not worry about your next move. If they have to cringe or feel bad for you, their experience is ruined and they are taken completely out of the moment. Like when you fart during sex: sure, you can finish and go through the motions, but something has been lost. Once I figured this all out and wasn't seeking the audience's approval anymore, they were free to have a good time, relax, and enjoy.

After the tour, I started headlining on my own for about a year, which is what doing well on a reality show will buy you. And then I went back to featuring, which is the middle spot after the emcee and before the headliner. I was on the road for years with Jim Norton and Dave Attell, two of my all-time favorite comics. And the answer is no, neither of them ever even tried anything with me. I should be insulted, but I'm not. It's the ultimate compliment to have someone take you on the road with them. They're saying, "I think you're funny, and I also can stand to hang out and travel with you." Jimmy and his bodyguard, Club Soda Kenny, and I had a blast on the road. They lived to embarrass me, shouting my name across stores and hotel lobbies, inviting stares from everyone around us— something they knew I hated when I was offstage.

They loved making me blush, which I actually did a lot more of in those days. I am such a loud little sassafras onstage, but in real life I like to keep a very low profile, and those guys took every opportunity to destroy any hope I had of blending in.

In 2012, I went back to headlining on my own in small clubs with under two hundred seats. I would get paid about $2,000 for seven shows. The weekends would go like this:

- Arrive on a Thursday and have an eight p.m. show.

- Get picked up at five thirty a.m. on Friday to do morning radio. Someone affiliated with the club (sometimes a crackhead) drives you from radio station to radio station. Sometimes there are local news shows to do on camera. If you're lucky it's just two of each. But some clubs fuck you in the ass and you have to do so many. And they say it's to get more tickets sold but it doesn't usually translate to that and is really just promotion for the shitty club.

- Arrive back in your hotel room by eleven a.m. (hopefully, if you're strong enough to refuse going out to breakfast or lunch with the crackhead driver or attention-hungry club owner who snuck on the radio appearance with you).

- Grab an apple and peanut butter from the depressing all-day buffet in the lobby, because you've missed breakfast.

- Desperately try to go back to sleep, but this is impossible because your hotel is in a gross, dangerous neighborhood so the club owner could save $75.

- Use the rusty hotel gym where the chlorine from the neighboring pool burns your eyes.

- Walk to a Red Robin and try to eat healthy even though they have not heard of vegetables in most of the country. So you get a grilled chicken something that comes with garlic bread and ice cream and you realize why Americans are dying.

- Go back to your room and feel utterly alone.

- Text an ex.

- Watch some movie made for TV about a woman who murdered her husband.

- Shower and get ready for your two Friday evening shows. And yes, I know you probably noticed I didn't shower right after the gym but waited 'til evening instead. You do you and I'll do me.

- Do two, sometimes three shows.

- Wake up Saturday morning and repeat a lot of Friday, including working out in the rusty-ass gym again, and hope the red itchy new thing on your knee is a rash from said gym and not from a bedbug.

- Sometimes during the day on Saturday, to pass the time, you go to whatever local attraction there is—a museum, a place where someone famous was shot, or maybe a fort.

- Eat whatever food is local to that city because it is your duty to do so. If you're in Philly, you eat a cheesesteak; if you're in Brooklyn, a cheesecake. If you're in Cincinnati, Skyline Chili; if you're in Tulsa, they don't really have a thing but someone may tell you, "You have to try our pork fried hamburger," or some weird shit. You gotta eat it. Show them some goddamn respect and then tweet them pictures of you on the toilet as a way to say thank you!

- Get ready for your Saturday night shows.

- Do two, sometimes three shows.

- Because you're a girl, you don't hook up after the show. Maybe you have a drink with the staff or maybe you go back to the hotel and get room service if they're still serving it. But usually the hotel you're at doesn't have room service at all.

- Lie awake in bed regretting that you just smoked pot because it's making you think about what you do for a living. *Am I a clown? What do I do? I tell jokes to strangers while they eat nachos.* It weirds you out and you vow not to smoke pot alone on the road anymore.

- The club owner pays you after your last show. It feels like it takes forever for them to total up your share of the money (because it does) and they act like they are doing you a favor. They tell you you didn't make your hundred-dollar bonus even though you could see every seat was filled. Sometimes they hand you a bill and you realize you thought you were eating and drinking for free but you only got 25 percent off the usual tab.

- Fly home early Monday morning and feel good about yourself because you developed fifteen new seconds of your act that weekend.

Even though the road can be brutal, it's the only way to become a stand-up. In order to get good at

it, you must get as much stage time as humanly possible. Sure, you can learn how to kill on a shorter
set. Maybe you even have a great fifteen minutes.
Or maybe you're good at local references in your
city and can do really well there. But you have to
go out on the road and do every different type of
show there is: the one for thirty drunk Harley-
Davidson guys at a VFW, the ladies' lunch at the
Carlyle, the Christmas party for firemen, the ferry
that circles Manhattan, and the comedy festival in
Staten Island. You have to do all of it or you will
plateau and go nowhere—which is fine if that is
what you want to do.

I WOULD DO anything for stage time. Actually,
let me rephrase that: I have never hooked up with
anyone to get ahead in the business. If anything,
some people I've dated have set me back. One time
my sister overheard one of the bouncers that I've
known since I started stand-up say, "Amy's gotten
so much work. Wonder how she got it . . ." Then
he mimed a dick going into his mouth. I guess I
should be angry about this kind of thing, but it
couldn't be further from the truth. I've never gotten anything from anyone I've hooked up with,
not even a Starbucks gift card—which would have
been nice.

During the week between road gigs, when I
was home in New York, I began performing at
the Comedy Cellar. That's the club you see on

I was a bundle of joy.

My ride home
from being born.

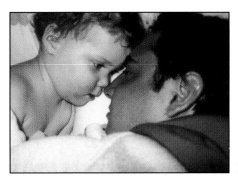

Me and my dad.

Gordon and
Sandy Schumer.

Me and Jason
looking flyyyyyyyy.

Kim, me,
Vinny (my
brother-in-
law), and
Abbott, my
love interest.

"Hey, I'm workin' over here!"

Happy campers.

At our farmhouse, two and a half.

Rocking out.

Me at age three, always
a flawless accessorizer.

At a magazine
(not-fitting) fitting.

Me as a baby model = nepotism. Also, is there anything creepier to put in a baby's crib than a stuffed sixty-year-old man smoking a pipe?

Panda, Pokey, Penny, Mouser, Bunny, and the two-headed bear.

Cincinnati, thirteen years old.

Dad at the farm.

Dad visiting me at my *Vogue* cover shoot.

Me on a horse, Chicago.

Bahamas, 2016.

Boxing in New York City. Kim puked shortly after this photo was taken.

Sisters.

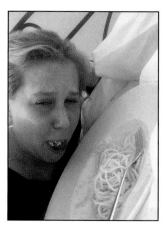

Just a gal eatin' some pasta.

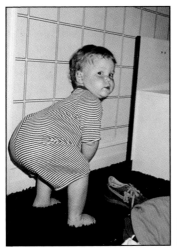

I was twerking before it was hip.

Dancing with my friend Kati in Baltimore,
sophomore year of college.

Me and my sister-in-law, Cayce, heading to *Ellen* for the first time. Cayce made this book with me.

Brother and sisters, 2016, Minneapolis.

Siblings on the set of *Trainwreck*.

Rehearsal for the dance scene in *Trainwreck*.

Me and Kev, my working partner and brother from another mother.

Writers of *Inside Amy Schumer*, season three.

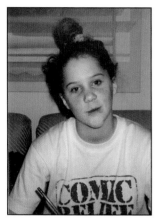

Always had comedy-
writer energy.

Bloomington,
Indiana, 2010.

Age twenty-three.

One of many pyramids with my oldest friends.

Rachel Feinstein, me, Bridget Everett, and
Poppy prepare to go onstage.

Heading home from a Boston show with Chris Rock.

A couple hours before filming my special at the Apollo.

Saying we are grateful and that we will do our best
is a preshow tradition.

Charleston, South Carolina, 2016.

Minneapolis, 2016.

the show *Louie* and in lots of documentaries about comics. I was "passed there" in 2007, which means I got to audition for the booker. I don't know the origin of this terminology, but only in the comedy world would people use such a morbid verb to signify the best thing that could happen to your career. Anyway, if the booker likes you, they then ask you to provide your availability for doing shows. If they don't like you, they say no thanks. I auditioned at the Cellar on my birthday, and Estee, who's been the booker there forever, gave me the phone number to "call in my avails," and I lost my mind I was so excited. I remember celebrating that night and getting so drunk that I got a piggyback ride from the bouncer at the bar and spent most of the night riding around back and forth, laughing and singing.

There is a restaurant upstairs from the Comedy Cellar called the Olive Tree Cafe and there is a booth in the back reserved for comedians. I was hesitant to sit there for years. Once I did, I'd stay quiet. Eventually, over time, I got more and more comfortable, and now it's the place I feel most at home in the whole world—sitting around the table with my best friends. I'm happiest when the table consists of Jimmy Norton, Keith Robinson, Colin Quinn, Rachel Feinstein, and Bobby Kelly. And sometimes we can convince Bridget Everett to stop by. We all trash each other, eat wings, and laugh. When someone dies or gets hurt we cry and laugh again. Doing stand-up and being with comics is home for me. Yes, it was completely thrilling to get my own TV show and to write and star in a movie. But getting onstage to do live comedy will always be what I chase harder than anything else.

Eventually, all my work on the road landed me some specials for TV. I had a half-hour special on Comedy Central in 2010 and then an hour special (*Mostly Sex Stuff*) in 2012. Through all of this, I stayed on the road, always touring, always writing more jokes. This is the only way to get better. I started selling more tickets in the clubs, and then small theaters, and then large theaters that seated about nine hundred people, just like in the semi-finals of *Last Comic Standing*.

The skills I developed from doing so much stand-up are the same ones I needed to write a movie and play a lead character who was based on myself. My having been onstage all these years with so many eyes on me as I degrade myself nightly is the reason my pulse doesn't change when Internet trolls try to ruin my day, every other day. One of the things I'm still most proud of is my one-hour HBO special (*Amy Schumer: Live at the Apollo*) and the fact that I got to work with Chris Rock as the director. I never would have been able to work with him if I hadn't been brave enough to ask. We'd been friendly for years, seeing each other at the Comedy Cellar, but I never wanted to bother him—because he is Chris Rock. Then one night we talked after we'd both performed on *Night of Too Many Stars*, an event to raise money for autism. My set had been strong, and Chris stopped by the greenroom and offered to help me if I ever needed it. Which sounds creepy, but it's not. He said exactly what he meant. When you have the disease of being a comic, and you see someone else with some talent and respect for comedy, you want to help. It's in his veins. It's in my veins. A little later, I called his bluff, which was anything but. He started riding around and going to clubs with me to watch my set, give me notes, and help me get better.

One day I just bit the bullet and texted him, "Will you direct my HBO special?" Again, this is the kind of confidence you can only get after years of making a clown of yourself onstage and being met with crickets. When Chris said yes, I couldn't believe it. He came on the road with me and made my set a thousand times better. Getting to work on jokes with him felt like my Make-A-Wish. I know that's not a kind comparison to make. But there is nothing else I can think of that would communicate how significant this time was to me.

One of the greatest moments of my career was hosting *Saturday Night Live*. I'm sure a lot of stand-ups dream of doing that opening *SNL* monologue. I know I have since I was a little girl. You write, rehearse, and perform the show in one week. That's all you get. One surreal, supercharged week to live your dream. One week to rush around the crowded hallways in that historic building. Nothing in my career has felt more exciting. But I won't lie, it was a grueling seven days—one that can definitely be described as athletic. You barely sleep, you constantly eat (well, I did), and you do nothing all week but write, rewrite, rehearse, try on wigs, get sewn into costumes, film promos, pose for photo shoots, rewrite, consider showering, choose sleep over showering, do table reads, rehearse, and repeat. And on the night of the show itself, you are literally running or rushing for the entire hour and a half. Stand-up comedy is live performance, sure, but *SNL* is live performance on meth.

By Saturday night, I was definitely the walking wounded, but I'd never been happier. My very favorite scene was one that Vanessa Bayer and Mikey Day wrote about two overly chipper flight attendants (played by me and Vanessa) who sing the in-flight service announcements before they are suddenly sucked out of the plane—one at a time. Live television doesn't allow for stunt doubles, so Vanessa and I had to actually hurl ourselves out of this plane door in order to make the scene work. I am a clown at heart, and my competitive-volleyball past didn't hurt, so I had no problem going for it. But Vanessa was a little more tentative. I wanted nothing more than to open the entire show with this sketch, so I grabbed her by the shoulders and I said, "Vaness! We are going to have to hurt ourselves, okay?!"

After rehearsing several times, we both felt pretty confident about the stunt. But then on Friday, the set builders moved the airplane onto a platform, which in turn lowered the clearance of the door we were jumping through by a full eight inches. *No problem*, I thought, stupidly confident. Vanessa was up first to try jumping through the new door, and she did, perfectly. But when it was my turn, I bricked my head right into the door. Everyone gasped as I lay on the mat, unmoving. My first thought was, *I will have to do this show with scabs all over my face and a bump on my forehead.* My second thought was, *Let's do this fucking thing again. We have to get it right!* By this point in my career, I had become a pro at falling face-first and getting up stronger. They iced my face and gave me some Advil, and we rehearsed it a dozen more times. I went harder every time I flew through that door and smashed into the mat. And it was worth it. My shoulder hurt for four months after, but that scene is my favorite sketch I've ever put on tape.

After being on one of the most historic stages and having the best night a comic could have in front of a live audience of millions, I woke up the next morning, ready to get back on the road. My episode of *Saturday Night Live* and my HBO special aired within seven days of each other, so getting back on the road was more important than ever. I'd burned all my jokes on those two events—meaning they'd aired on TV to massive audiences, so I couldn't use them anymore because people would know them now. Unlike musicians, comedians are expected to always bring new shit. No one wants to hear the greatest hits, so I was back to square one. This requirement of comedy is exhausting and challenging, but I wouldn't have it any other way. It's exciting and humbling to have to start over—and the payoff is even better. You feel so accomplished when you've accumulated enough material—one joke at a time—for an entire special. And when you're back to zero, it doesn't matter who you are, you're starting the fuck over. It's the scariest, emptiest feeling in the world. Even the greatest, most seasoned comics are afraid they'll never write a great joke again. But you do the work.

And that means hitting the road and getting onstage. I know I'm repeating myself, but it's my number one piece of advice to comics who are just starting out when they ask me how to become successful. Get onstage! If there isn't a comedy room in your town, produce one! Find a place with a stage and a mic and stand in front of people as much as possible. Log as many hours as you can. I still do this. I'm not bullshitting you: the money is good now, but even on my nights off, I am still onstage in shitty little rooms, rock clubs, jazz halls, wherever. Always working hard to get better. I became obsessed a long time ago, and it has never dulled.

No matter how hard you work or how sharp you keep yourself, your popularity and ticket sales will ebb and flow, but I'm very proud to say that right now, as I write this in 2016, I'm touring arenas, doing stand-up for crowds of ten to fifteen thousand people. I'm telling jokes where NBA and NHL games are played. I sold out Madison Square

Garden! (I can't believe I just typed that.) For these arena shows, I have the same opening comic, Mark Normand, with whom I've worked with the past seven years. My brother, Jason, also opens the show with his jazz trio, which means I get to hang out on the road with his wife, Cayce, who is one of my best friends and helped edit this book. Their daughter, my niece, hangs out backstage with us. Sometimes my sister, Kim, and her husband, Vinny, are there too. I get to stay in nice hotels and have a tour bus or fly first class or sometimes even travel via private jet. I feel extremely lucky, and I know better than to get too comfortable or think it will last forever. But I love every minute of it right now. It feels so great to walk out onstage after Mark says my name, to hug him and look at the crowd and give them everything I've got. I vow every night before I go on to do the best show I've ever done. I still bomb, I still kill. Either way, the crowd will let you know the truth. It's masochistic and it's noble. And I never want to stop.

TIMES IT'S OKAY
FOR A MAN TO NOT MAKE
A WOMAN COME DURING SEX

1. If she's a hooker and the next guy is waiting, but even then, check with her.

2. If she's in a rush and tells you she doesn't have time.

3. If you're on an airplane or anywhere in public. If you get away with having sex in public, get in and get out. But make sure you take care of her when you get home.

4. If you realize that your kids or parents will walk into the room. But again, take care of her later.

5. If she gets a cramp or if she gets hungry.

Note: It is okay to not make a woman come during sex if you made her come before it. I am someone who can't really come from penetration. So I hope you enjoy a nice visit with my clit before the main event!

THE WORST NIGHT OF MY LIFE

Here we go, it's time to tell you about Dan, who has already come up in this book. I thought he was the love of my life for a long time but I allowed him to hurt me in ways that I still don't understand. I met him when I was eighteen years old, and I liked him right away. He'd take his clothes off for no reason and run around without shame. We had a lot in common, especially the shameless-nudity part. I think nudity has the potential to be both beautiful and hilarious, so when given the chance, I pull a Porky Pig on my TV show, which basically means that whenever a scene allows, I'll rock out in a long "boyfriend" shirt with no pants or underwear. Anyway, Dan wasn't interested in a relationship with me, and I pretended I wasn't interested in one with him either.

Dan was fascinating to me. He grew up in Manhattan in an incredible loft and got shipped off to boarding school at thirteen. He was a bad kid—lots of detention and sex. New York City kids don't really drink underage like Long Island kids. Instead they do drugs and bang each other to feel like adults. He effed any girl who would hold still long enough for him to come. Or at least that's how he described it to me. But bad kid or not, I felt he was misunderstood and that I was the *one* person who could really love him. Which, as you know by now, was my cup of tea through most of my twenties.

The first night I slept with him was at his mom's place in NYC. The apartment was incredible— huge, with high ceilings, and decorated impeccably. There was so much about him and his home that was "cool" to me. It was "cool" that, at night, when he came downstairs to let me in the building, he was barefoot and in his underwear. Barefoot on the pavement in Manhattan. It was "cool" he had a Dexter Gordon poster in his room. And it was "cool" that he knew about art. His family friends were famous, culturally elite people. This was thrilling to me. I wanted no part of my suburban upbringing anymore, and I was smitten with him and the life he was projecting. I knew we were meant to be together, but he wasn't convinced that I was the girl for him. Maybe it was because the only poster I had in my room was of Ani DiFranco, and if you asked me who our family friends were, I would have said the Muppets. Or maybe it was just that Dan was a real don't-want-to-join-any-club-that-would-have-me-as-a-member type of guy. But I was playing the long game, and I took my time winning him over. I even drove him cross-country when he moved to the West Coast. We were twenty years old driving a U-Haul across America, and by the time we got to Vegas, he was mine. I could feel the shift in him when I'd finally worn him down. He could see the look in my eyes, which said: you. are. mine. bro.

We were together, and we were running low on money, but he still decided to buy a pair of Gucci sunglasses from an outlet store. Red flag? I chose not to notice those sorts of fun little quirks. I thought that because his parents were rich, he was rich. This was a puzzle I didn't fully solve until a year later when I was living with him and had to pedal that horrible pedicab around town so we had grocery money, which he proceeded to spend on alcohol.

And yes, when we were still in Vegas, he screamed at me at the top of his lungs and shook me so hard that I had to run and hide until he calmed down. It was the first time I saw this behavior from him. I'd never seen him even a little upset before. And how did I reward that behavior?

I moved in with him a year later. We lived together for one summer on the West Coast when I was just twenty-one. We had an apartment up on a hill and very close to the beach. Every day, I'd wake up early and teach a kickboxing class at the Y, then go play in a female beach volleyball doubles league, then meet up with him and drink and fight and fuck. It was everything you could want, if what you want is Penélope Cruz and Javier Bardem's relationship in *Vicky Cristina Barcelona*. And if you didn't see that movie, I was the Whitney to his Bobby. (Quick shout-out: I loved Whitney so much and still can't believe she's gone.)

Anyway, Dan and I would go to happy hours with friends and get drunk, and then he'd get mad at me and shove me a little. Sometimes, from the shove, I'd trip over something and fall, and get hurt. But of course it was an accident. I got hurt by accident a lot that year. He'd get jealous about something I did and would squeeze my arm too hard and I'd get a horrible bruise. But of course it was an *accident*, and he always felt terrible afterward. I'd comfort him and we'd move on until the next time it happened. But it's not like I was in an abusive relationship, right? I mean, I wasn't a passive girl. I've been easily standing up for myself for as long as I could talk. I'm the girl who would bully the bullies in middle school—defend the kids who got made fun of. I'd always prided myself on being strong, assertive, and independent. It couldn't happen to me, right?

On a regular basis, Dan would say things to me I didn't let anyone else say—passively hurtful things to let me know I wasn't as pretty as the other women he'd dated. He'd point out areas of my legs and arms and stomach he thought I needed to work on. He'd pull the shower curtain open and laugh at my naked body. Once he even pissed on my legs and feet while laughing. I'd cry and go for a walk and we'd start over. But come on, I was smart and funny and a loudmouth who spoke her mind. I definitely wasn't in an abusive relationship, right? That only happens to girls who don't believe in themselves. Right?

It proceeded to get worse and worse, and I started escaping the apartment whenever I could. I'd go to Starbucks, lock myself in the bathroom, and sit on the floor and cry. I knew I should go back to the East Coast, but I thought no one would ever love me as much as he did. I believed he was just as passionate about me as I was about him, and that if I did a better job of not making him mad, we'd be fine. I really felt he loved me. And I really loved him. I think somewhere in the course of our relationship, I started to confuse his anger and aggression for passion and love. I actually started to think that real love was supposed to look like that. The more you yelled at each other, the more you loved each other. The more physical and demeaning it got, the more you were really *getting through* to each other. And the more I was willing to stand by him, the more he'd understand I truly loved him and that we should be together forever. And he always felt so bad about what he'd done after he shouted or bruised me. Surely he wouldn't beat himself up so much if he didn't love me so much. It's not abusive if they feel really bad afterward and promise to love you the rest of your life, right? Right?

Wrong. Knowing what I know now, it's clear

as day. Of course. And being frightened and hurt
and abused isn't reserved for insecure women
who are easily intimidated, or women who come
from unstable environments, or women who have
never seen a positive male role model. I learned
from a TED talk about domestic violence by Les-
lie Morgan Steiner (these are mostly her words)
that women of all income and education levels are
affected. I also learned that I was a typical domestic
violence victim because of my age. In the United
States, women ages sixteen to twenty-four are
three times more likely to be domestic violence
victims than women of any other age. Also, every
year in the United States, five hundred women in
this age bracket are killed by their domestic abuser.
A domestic abuser doesn't just have to be someone
you live with. It means anyone you are in an intimate relationship with. I was a statistic.

What made things so confusing with Dan was
that we usually had the best time. We were manic
together. He was obsessed with me in a way that
made me feel high. We had sex several times a day.
I thought it was because I turned him on so much,
but I now believe it was because it was a way for
him to have my undivided attention. We'd laugh
until we were in tears, fuck, pledge our undying
love, and then the next moment we'd be in shouting turmoil and he'd be screaming at me and
squeezing me too hard.

One humid summer night we went out with
our friends to a new bar. We were all dressed up

and excited to get into the new hot spot. I love dancing—always have, always will. Am I good at it? Nope! But that has never stopped me. I grabbed my girlfriend and we hit the floor. Sometimes Dan would dance, but on this evening, I think because I'd talked all day about how excited I was, he wanted to sour it a little. I dance like all other white girls: in a sexually suggestive way that says, "This is what it would be like to mount me." It's completely false advertising. Also, I don't do it well, and over the years several black people have pointed this out to me—to my face. Anyway, my girlfriend and I were gyrating and body-rolling on the dance floor when out of nowhere Dan came up and grabbed my arm. He didn't like how the guys in the bar were looking at me, and he thought I was flirting with them. I left the dance floor and we drank and drank, and kissed in a booth, and then the song "Real Love" by Mary J. Blige came on, and you know I had to dance to that. It's like a law that all women turn into the Manchurian Candidate when that song comes on.

A guy came up to me on the dance floor who I would have bet my life was gay. We sang the song and danced together. We were giggling and half grinding but made no actual contact. It was totally innocent. Dan walked past me on the dance floor on his way to the bathroom and whispered in my ear, "You're disgusting." I was furious. I thought, *I'll show you disgusting*, and began to dance very sexually with another guy on the floor. When Dan came out of the bathroom he again dragged me to the booth. And that was when I did something that I'd never done before and never, ever, will do again: I spit right in his face. I don't know if I thought I was a character in *West Side Story* or if it was just the booze that gave me major balls, but I did it. And this maneuver awakened the beast in Dan and fired off my fear signal in one instant. He got a look in his eyes that scared the shit out of me, and I ran. I ran right out the door of the bar and I kept running.

I ran to our friend's house down the street, but he caught up to me. I tried to calm him down and I told him that it was probably better if we spent the night apart to cool off. That was the smart thing to do, and he was smart, so I was sure he'd agree, maybe call me a bitch, then storm away. Right? No, the smart thing did not happen. Instead, when I got out my phone to call my friend, he grabbed it out of my hand and whipped it at a nearby tree, where it shattered. He put his hands on my cheeks and squeezed my face hard. My head was throbbing, and I could tell this night was different. I wasn't safe. And I knew it.

I told him I was going to walk to my friend's house and asked him to leave me alone. He wouldn't. He followed me. My heart was pounding while I listened to his footsteps behind me on the quiet side streets. I kept walking and walking, and then for a second I didn't hear his footsteps. But it was too late when I realized he was right behind me. I tried to pick up the pace, and this pissed him off, and he pushed me onto the hood of a parked car. I banged my head and my elbow hard. This was more than he'd done before. This was an actual violent outburst. I didn't get hurt "by accident" this time. He saw the car right there and pushed me onto it intentionally. I burst into tears, kicked my shoes off, and ran down the street as fast as I could, listening to my own breath, trying to slow down my heart rate like my volleyball coach had taught me. I think Dan had surprised himself.

I heard voices coming from a nearby backyard and I ran into the open front door of this random house, sobbing, with no shoes on, makeup running down my face and a welt on my head that was already becoming a bruise. I staggered into the living room, and there sat about eight *Breaking Bad*–looking huge Hispanic gang members. They had bandanas and tattoos, they were not fucking around, and they definitely did not want me there. I begged them to let me use the phone to call my friend and promised I'd then leave. Naturally, they made me promise not to call the cops.

I heard Dan screaming for me through the screen door, and at that moment I realized that being with the gang felt infinitely more safe than being with Dan did. But I quickly understood that my presence threatened to get them caught doing whatever it was they were doing. Some of the guys went outside to try to get Dan to leave, but he was causing a real commotion and standing his ground.

I ran outside to get him to quiet down, and he got into a fistfight with one of the gang members until his eye and lip were bleeding. As the guy was pounding Dan with his fist, I instantly switched teams and began to defend Dan. When you are an abuse victim, your logic and instinct can become warped like this. It was similar to the night in high school when I realized Jeff was helping himself to my virginity, and I ended up comforting him for hurting me, even though it should have been the other way around. Here I was defending another guy who was actively betraying me. "Get off of him!" I yelled, running toward Dan, who was taking a serious beating. The gang members kicked us both off their property, fearing the cops would come.

We walked to his car in silence. Dan had seemingly calmed down. He was even laughing a little, talking about how crazy the night had been, and so I did too. I wanted to comfort him and make him feel like we were in this together. We got into the car, and I drove the fifteen minutes home. The events had sobered me right up. I tried to keep him calm. That was my only goal. He mentioned ordering food when we got home, and I let him know in a very collected, kind way that I wasn't going to stay at our apartment that night.

And there it was again. The beast reawakened right before my eyes, the same beast I'd seen earlier that night, but this time, it was much angrier. He started banging his head against the window and screaming. He took my hand and used it to punch himself in the face. He broke the side mirror with his own hand, and I was scream-crying, begging, pleading with him to stop. I agreed to sleep at home if he'd stop hurting himself. It was a bad idea to negotiate with him like that, because what came after I agreed to sleep at home was so much worse.

When we got home, I went inside and got right into bed. I was exhausted and just wanted the night to be over. I had nothing left. I begged him to leave me alone so I could sleep. But he kept tormenting me, sitting and staring at me. He shook the bed to scare me, saying, "I don't want you to go to sleep." I told him we'd talk in the morning but I really needed to rest. I told him that if he wouldn't let me sleep I was going to leave. He was quiet for a couple minutes. I closed my eyes, and then opened them again to see him standing over me, staring. I told him that was it and got up to leave. He ran to the kitchen and broke a mug—not a glass, a *mug*—over his head, and then started banging his head on a light fixture attached to the ceiling. It wouldn't break. I was screaming for him to stop, when he grabbed a huge butcher knife from a drawer. And that's when I was sure he was going to kill me. It may sound clichéd, but I saw my life flash before my eyes. I thought, *This is how I die? I can't believe it*. I thought about my sister and my mom finding out that this was how I'd checked out. This thought awoke the beast in *me*. This was my moment of clarity. I had to get away from him. Fast.

I threw a glass against the wall as a diversion and raced out the door, running through our apartment complex, banging on all the doors, begging for someone to let me in. It was just like *American Psycho*, him chasing me and gaining on me at every turn. I knocked on five different unanswered doors before one opened up, and I flung myself inside, locking the door behind me. Dan immediately started pounding on the door. I looked up at the elderly man who'd let me in and said, "Thank you so much, I need to call the police." I'd seen this guy around the complex for months, mostly shuffling to the Dumpster and back, and we'd wave once in a while. He had a bushy mustache and eyebrows that were salt-and-pepper colored, like his hair. He looked like a cartoon. It was the second stranger's house I'd entered that night. I remember thinking to myself, *How much worse can it get than the Latin Kings' headquarters?*

It was worse. I breathed the air in the apartment and it was stale and vaguely smelled like sewage. I noticed that his wife, whom I'd never seen before, was in a hospital bed near the window. Her arms and legs had been amputated and her mouth was cocked open, head to the side. I still don't know if she was alive or not, but I think so. It was a terrifying and disorienting scene. I went to the bathroom, which was full of furniture and filth, and locked myself inside with their phone. I called a cab and stayed in there until it arrived.

I walked outside, numb, when the cab pulled up.

Dan was still out there, but he'd calmed down too. I could have called the cops on him. I could have pressed charges. But I didn't want to. I felt bad for him, seeing him standing there alone. I worried about how he'd feel the next day. Even after all Dan had put me through, I couldn't dream of having him arrested. But I did finally see my situation for what it was—a case of domestic abuse. I was finally able to empathize with the millions of other women who'd been in this same situation. I was them and they were me.

I took the cab to the house of a couple that I knew. They let me sleep upstairs, and the guy of the couple slept next to their front door with a bat, which I'm still very grateful for. I flew back to New York the next day, still worried about Dan and how he might be feeling. I knew he'd feel awful and lonely and would be in a lot of pain, but I was choosing to live. I thought a lot about my sister and how I wanted to be the kind of person who made her proud. I couldn't face her if I stayed another day with a man I believed would eventually kill me.

The next awful chapter of this story—and something that it pains me to tell you—is that we got back together one more time after that, during the New York City blackout of 2003. (In that heat, I would have fucked a salamander.) It wasn't for very long, but the loneliness of New York City and my feelings for him weakened me. I think I reunited with him because I still longed to be close to him. And I wanted to punish him for hurting me so much in the past. I thought I could do more damage from the inside. I was his girlfriend, which meant I had free rein to criticize him and point out why he was the worst. I'm not proud of that. But there was a part of me that wanted to be with him again so I could hurt him back.

We finally broke up a few months later and said good-bye to each other one morning when I was fully able to see him for who he really was. I could see that he presented to the world the facade of a certain kind of man who wasn't really there. He had the poster, but he couldn't name one Dexter Gordon album. He said he loved me, but every step of the way he'd hurt and sabotage me. I realized later that he put me down so much because he was probably terrified that I'd realize he was nothing and leave him. Which is exactly what I did.

I'm telling this story because I'm a strong-ass woman, not someone most people picture when they think "abused woman." But it can happen to anyone. When you're in love with a man who hurts you, it's a special kind of hell, yet one that so many women have experienced. You're not alone if it's happening to you, and you're not exempt if it hasn't happened to you yet. I found my way out and will never be back there again. I got out. Get out.

THINGS
THAT MAKE ME
INSANELY FURIOUS

1. People who run down mountains. Have you ever been hiking and had someone run past you downhill? I secretly root for them to tumble to their—as far as I'm concerned—timely death.

2. Girls with their hair down at the gym. Unless you're covering horrible burn marks like that girl from *The Craft*, pull that shit up in a ponytail.

3. Couples working out together are vile. You can't spend one hour apart? Also, the guy showing the submissive girl how to do everything makes me retch.

4. People who act like the mayor of the fucking gym. I don't even smile at people I know at the gym because all I want to do is leave the whole time. If I make eye contact with someone I know and they look away immediately, I know they are a great person and I feel very close to them.

5. Apparently the gym and all forms of exercise, based on the first four items on this list.

6. Also, people named Jim. Because it sounds like the word "gym."

7. People who misspell the word "you're" when telling me I'm fat ("your fat").

8. People who stand too close to you while you're in line for something. Make like Onyx and bacdafucup. I wish everyone was a football field away at all times, but I understand this isn't possible, so please, just give me six inches. But twelve would be great. (No penis puns here.)

9. Clear-cut mail-order-bride situations where the guy is disgusting and the woman is beautiful and seems trapped. I pray that these women find a way to steal the man's money and run off with it.

10. Radio commercials. Every single one ever.

11. People who say "I eat to live. I don't live to eat." I wish all ten plagues upon your house.

12. Guys who don't make sure the girl comes.

13. Really drunk people. You may be thinking, *Amy, you fucking hypocrite.* But I'm not. I love drinking, but I almost never get fucking hammered anymore. Not much anyway, since college. Even when I would black out in college, no one ever knew. My speech was just a little slurred.

14. Okay, you were right; number 13 was fucked up for me to say. I do get drunk. But still, you shouldn't.

15. Watercress.

16. People who look up, like at the ceiling, when they talk. Unless a pigeon has flown onto a chandelier above my head, look down here.

17. Also, birds inside. Any bird in an airport or mall or anything makes me out of my mind, crazy furious.

18. Selective outrage.

19. Drivers who floor it when a light turns green and then brake hard at a red light. I lie to a lot of Uber drivers and tell them I'm pregnant so they will drive safer. They don't know I'm not and really neither do I. I guess I could be.

20. *The Big Bang Theory.* (The TV show, not the theory.)

21. People who judge me as a sinner. Fuck you.

22. Hotel-room deodorizers. They plug in these huge machines that make all the rooms smell the same and it's all like baby powder and funerals. It makes your eyes water and your skin itch.

23. People who talk too loud in public. I have yelled at strangers. I will say "shhhhh" and no one is exempt. I once shushed Vin Diesel.

24. People with egos that don't let them acknowledge the truth.

25. Black jelly beans. Also, black licorice makes me mad but not furious.

26. House music. It is the worst. I love going out and dancing to hip-hop but it's almost impossible to find a place that plays it anymore because they have all been replaced by this horrible excuse for music.

27. Celebrity DJs and bad-boy chefs. Questlove doesn't count. He is a drummer and an amazing DJ.

28. Grown women wearing jean shorts that are small enough to be a diaper, because I can't come close to being able to rock them. I need a denim burka at this point.

29. Talking to anyone I don't know on an elevator. (I guess this counts as small talk, which I've mentioned several times as something I detest, but it's even more unbearable in an elevator because you're trapped!)

30. People who go to Starbucks to write. Yuck.

31. People who bring a book to a bar deserve to be stoned. Don't try to look mysterious and interesting. You are reading in a bar.

32. People who eat impeccably healthy. Fuck you!!!!

33. Most kids who aren't my niece. Some kids are cute, but most need to tone it right on down.

34. Guys who try to flirt with you even though you give clear motherfucking indicators that you are not interested. JUST STOP!!!!

35. Girls who act like prudes. We've all had to clean cum off our skin while making eye contact with ourselves in the mirror.

36. Guys who don't like to have sex a lot. At least twice a week or get out of here. (I know I should be sympathetic, but I have no patience for that.)

ATHLETES AND MUSICIANS

I recently came into contact with the hugest dick you can imagine. And when I say "hugest dick," I mean largest penis. I don't mean he was a dick. But I'm getting ahead of myself. So, let me back up and properly introduce this as the chapter where I will tell you in major detail about hooking up with a few athletes and a musician. I am telling you because I think you may find it interesting. And also because even though we all know there is no holy grail of a person who will finally be the key to our everlasting confidence, because we are all just damaged little children, we still hope that someone who is killer with a guitar or puck will hold the key to eternal self-love at the tip of their tip. No? Just me? Well, read along anyway.

I will not name names. Right now, maybe you're thinking: *Fuck you, Amy!! I bought this stupid book and I want to know who these dudes are!* I hear you. I want to tell you so bad. It makes it a lot funnier having a face and name to go along with these terribly disappointing tales. But I can't do that. It's not a legal matter. It's just that I would personally like to have more sex in my life, and what guy in his right mind would get down with me if he knew he and his penis might end up in my next book?

Also, if we ever meet in person I'll probably tell you the actual names of these athletes and musicians. But in the meantime, let's start with the first athlete I hooked up with, who was a lacrosse player, of all sports. I'd been going through a particularly lonely time. As I write that, I realize every single one of the hookups mentioned in this chapter was a direct response to a breakup. I've learned the lesson that the grieving process after a breakup will not be sped up by hooking up with someone else. The way I usually advise my friends is by saying, "It's gonna take time. Let's just watch movies and go on long walks." But I don't tend to follow my own advice. I also sometimes tell a good girlfriend, "You need to have sex with someone." Are you noticing a pattern, that I am a hypocrite and a flake?

Anyway, about this lacrosse player . . . We were both newly single and he was better looking than me and from a wealthy family, but he could apparently stomach fucking me, which is literally how it felt when we had sex. I was funnier and smarter than him, but that didn't matter to me at the time. What mattered in that moment was that he was cute and he had a working penis. We went on a couple dates, which had all the excitement of watching toenail polish dry on a cadaver.

During dinner, I felt the way you always hear men supposedly feel when women are talking. I was enduring it, pretending to laugh at his jokes, letting him ask me a lot of lame questions you'd expect to hear during a job interview, such as "Where do you see yourself in five years?" He asked, if I could have lunch with anyone living or dead, who would it be? I answered, Mark Twain. To which he said, "No, it has to be someone real." And still, without even thinking twice, I went home with him. When we kissed, there was absolutely no chemistry, which confirmed our mutual lack of interest in one another. And yet from sheer muscle memory our bodies were still able to have intercourse. I think we hooked up a few times before our different levels of attractiveness and senses of humor caught up to us, and he called to tell me that he'd started seeing someone else. I was shocked that he felt our few unappealing hookups obligated him to notify me he was off the market. I said, "I understand," in as serious a tone as I could muster. We truly did a great job of wasting each other's time.

The next athlete was in the NFL. Which means he played football. This time I went to the city he lived in, and he came to my hotel. We'd been out three or four times but hadn't hooked up yet, and this was going to be *the* night. He got to my room and we had a drink and I could already feel I didn't want this. I said I was exhausted and needed to go to sleep, and when he kissed me, I just wasn't feeling it. Our chemicals didn't mesh well together.

That has happened a couple times in my life, where the kiss just doesn't taste right. It's nothing personal, just science. He grabbed my ass and kissed me and I stopped him and said good night. I made up some excuses about why I couldn't hang out with him until he stopped asking.

Another athlete I dated was the famous professional wrestler I met on Twitter. I know you're probably thinking this would be a good moment to trash wrestling, but I have no interest in doing that. This guy was a true athlete. He was healthier, stronger, and more disciplined than most people who play a sport involving a ball or uniform. When I met him, I had no interest in wrestling, though I had spent time pretending to like it for guys in the past (see chapter titled "How I Lost My Virginity"). But once I saw professional wrestling behind the scenes, I was amazed by the athleticism and theater of it. Anyway, we met when I was doing a show in Phoenix, Arizona. I was alone in my nice hotel and decided to order some crab cakes. I know what you're thinking: landlocked Arizona is world-famous for its killer seafood and surfing. But I convinced myself it was a low-carb option even though we know that outside Baltimore, Maryland, crab cakes are 99 percent bread. Turns out there was enough *actual* crab in these cakes for me to get the most violent food poisoning you can imagine. I quickly went from being completely healthy and fine to being a convulsing vessel of foul bodily fluids spouting from every orifice of my body. A couple times I had to decide between sitting on the toilet and bending over it to puke. It was a real Sophie's Choice of human waste. (Spoiler alert: there is no happy ending.)

Despite my predicament, I was still convinced I was going to perform that night. I was especially excited because the cute wrestler was going to be in the audience, and so was the comedian David Spade. I wound up lying on the floor of the bathroom in my own puke with the club owner and his kind mother standing over me. I was hallucinating from dehydration and an ambulance was called. Luckily, David Spade is a hero and he did the show for me that night. It's the only show I've ever had to cancel from illness. I once lost my voice in the middle of a set at Governor's Comedy Club on Long Island, but I still didn't leave the stage. Since my mom and I both know sign language, I signed my set to her so she could deliver it to the crowd.

So that night in Phoenix, I ended up having an overnight stay at the hospital. My very kind friend Jackie, who was working with me that weekend, spent the night sitting in a chair next to my hospital bed. When I woke up, I learned that I'd been inundated with countless messages on Twitter that mentioned the wrestler. Turns out the wrestler had led a campaign among his followers to get me to follow him. He had about a million followers, and it felt like I got a tweet from each and every one of them. He had been at the show I missed, so he knew I'd been hospitalized. As I sat there waiting to be released from the hospital, I clicked "follow" on his page and wrote him a direct message: "Okay, I'm following you. What do you want?" He wrote back, "Hi, how are you feeling?" He was really sweet and offered to pick me up from the hospital.

In addition to this very kind gesture, the wrestler was really easy on the eyes—and I figured probably hands—so we started talking and made plans to meet up. We met in Denver, had a nice weekend together, and actually began seeing each other a few weeks later. We did our best to date, despite the fact that we were both on the road all the time and I was still in love with my ex. I once even asked him if I could take a short dating hiatus from him to go to Mexico with my ex and then resume our dating when I returned. He rightfully told me no. I realize that was an insane request but I sometimes forget that a man may actually have real feelings for me.

He was so physically perfect, smart, funny, and kind. But I remember being in some hotel with him, seeing his knee pads drying on the radiator, and thinking I was in the wrong story. Naturally, I got back together with my ex. (Always a great idea.) The wrestler and I are still good friends, and I'll be very happy for whatever lucky lady ends up with him, even though he's a recent ex and I usually wish rare Amazonian skin diseases on their new girlfriends. Which brings me to the musician.

The musician was probably the saddest experience of all. He's famous and I'm a fan. I would never have ever ever ever thought he'd be interested in me. Any of these guys actually—these are dudes who have access to tiny models. But what I've learned is that guys are guys, no matter how famous or hot, and they all basically want to hook up with anyone they're even moderately attracted to who will hold still long enough for them to rub against them. Does that sound like an insult? Because it's actually something that I love about men so much. I love the simplicity of the drive they have to fuck. Their biology is beautiful to me. We ladies work so hard to be attractive for them and we really don't need to. Their driving force is to put their penises in our buttholes. Meanwhile I'm worried if he can see the roots of my highlights. I have thoughts like, *Should I get a French manicure?* HE DOESN'T CARE. HE WANTS TO JAM HIS WIENER IN YOUR POOPER!

Anyway, I met this musician for lunch. I thought we were just friends but he hugged me in a masterful way I will never forget. He slid his hand along my lower back, starting at my hip inside my leather jacket. When he hugged me I realized, *Oh, this is a date*. We were both going through breakups, so we complained about our exes and ate ramen. We were having such a good time that we made plans to meet up later that same evening. I was very much not out of the woods with my feelings for my ex, but revenge-dating a rock star seemed like a pretty good plan.

We met up at the Bowery Hotel and had some

drinks. Showing up to this second location for the second date in one day with this guy totally freaked me out. He was now going to be evaluating me as a woman he might want to hook up with, or date, so I of course lost all my self-esteem while I was getting dressed to meet him. I got nervous and I put too much into it. The early hangout was lunch with a friend, but this was a fucking date with a fucking rock star! He commented, "You're like a different person than you were earlier today," immediately detecting my plummeting confidence. We walked around and watched some stand-up comedy at a nearby club. I told him I'd had a great time and tried to say good night, but he talked me into one more drink at the hotel. The bar was closed by then so he suggested we order drinks from room service and went up to his hotel room.

By this point, I'd accepted as fact that there was no way he was attracted to me, and I figured he must have just liked hanging out with me. This is how it's been my whole life. I've always assumed that men see me as just one of the guys, so when someone is interested in me as a girl I am floored. This hang-up has gotten better over time, but it's not completely gone. Anyway, we had a drink in his room and when I got up to hug him good-bye, he kissed me. We didn't have good chemistry but I was flattered, and this was the first person I'd kissed who wasn't my boyfriend in the last four years, so I went with it. We got in bed, we got naked, and I couldn't have been less present. It was like what I would imagine Pat Sajak feels like at this point on *Wheel of Fortune*. If you look deep into his eyes, he is a full-blown zombie.

I could see the two of us like I was out of my body and I felt so sad for us: a rock star and a whatever I am. But no matter who you are, you still feel all the same shit as everyone else. We both missed our exes. We didn't do much of anything. We touched each other and tears started rolling down my cheeks. I wasn't crying but they were just coming out. He noticed and held me. We lay there in the dark, eyes open, listening to each other breathe. I was in so much pain at the time and I could feel his pain too. We didn't judge or want anything from each other. After he fell asleep, I slipped out of the room. I'm grateful he was so sweet and as sad as I was too. I felt less alone for a couple moments, and I'm sure I was the most disappointing hookup of his life. Which I am actually a little proud to say. It's good to stand out, even in that way. He will never forget me!

I'm now seeing a real pattern in these stories: I have been a huge disappointment to hook up with. I've always thought of myself in these hookups as the one who was shortchanged by a bummer guy, but upon further reflection, it seems like it really was me who was the bummer. Interesting. Oh well. No time to unpack that. On to the huge cock.

I want to preface this story by saying I have no interest in hockey. I have gone to a couple games and had fun—but that's mostly because I went with my sister, and we gave ourselves fake bruises.

We only went to Rangers games at Madison Square Garden, and I'd wear a neck brace and two black eyes, and put Band-Aids all over Kim. I don't know why we used to do that, but we liked to look like we had gotten all bloodied. Most people would ignore us and look away as quickly as possible, but some people would ask what happened and we would say we got into a thing with each other.

Kim and her husband love hockey, and they always talk about one of their favorite players. They love how he plays and are always mentioning that he's funny and cool off the ice, too. They bring up this dude all the time with me. He followed me on Twitter, so I followed him back, and when I told my sister he was following me, she flipped out. She was like, "You have to message him! You would love each other!" So I did. I told him he was my favorite player, and I think I said if he ever wanted to come see a stand-up show to let me know. He showed me enough respect not to pretend to be interested in seeing a comedy show and instead asked me if I wanted to get a drink. I said yes and was very excited that Kim would think I was the shit. She never does.

On the day of our date, I went to the location we'd agreed on and waited for nearly forty minutes. He was texting me saying, "Sorry, leaving soon!" I left the place angry but got a text shortly after telling me that he was very sorry and that he would meet me anywhere I wanted. I made him go to Fat Cat, a basement bar in the village that has jazz music and Ping-Pong. When I arrived and saw him from across the room, I realized he was with all of his friends.

So I was now on a group date with a bunch of rowdy guys. I was yelling over the music and trying to communicate with him, but we had all the rapport of the Pope and Rick Ross. We didn't know what to talk about, couldn't hear each other, and didn't understand each other's sarcasm. I finally gave up and started talking to his friends. They were treating me like some whore that their famous athlete friend was gonna bang—which, in their defense, was what I was. Except I didn't have the patience to stick it out. So when he told me that they were going to another bar, I said I wasn't and started to say farewell to my sister's favorite athlete. He said, "Well, no, I'll just go with you then." I was shocked. He didn't even say good-bye to his friends. We went to one more bar on the way home, and I watched him play a dumb golf arcade game and listened to him discuss his dreams and his family. I couldn't believe I was going to hook up with this beautiful, tall, talented guy whom I could barely understand or connect with. He was using hockey terms, thinking I was a huge fan, but I'd only been to a few games in my life and understood nothing. He asked me exactly zero questions about myself, and that was the perfect amount. I wasn't interested in building a future with this guy, I was just sticking around to see if he'd be willing to hook up with *me*. Even though in my eyes we were a physical mismatch on the level of Miss Piggy and Charles Grodin in *The Great Muppet Caper*. Or Kate Hudson and anyone I've ever seen her paired up with. I often feel this way with men who have been willing to be physical with me. Fortunately, most men are driven toward a wet hole more than a perfect face—especially late at night.

We went to his apartment, and he put on the TV show *Workaholics* and went down on me right away. I thought he was such a sweetheart for doing that. I came, thinking he was a prince. But then I saw the reason for his chivalry. He took his dick out and I became a cartoon. My jaw hit the floor. Which, coincidentally, was the only way his dick was going to fit in there. I have a small mouth, and the size of this hog was like nothing I'd ever seen. No way was that going near my vagina. I felt like a musician performing on the deck of the *Titanic*, knowing there was nothing I could do but go down. I felt like I was trying to fit an entire Thanksgiving turkey in a toilet paper roll: not happening. He tried to act like his dick wasn't that big, as if it were a normal size and I was just being skittish and weird, but after several attempts, I determined I could not fellate this fellow. Feeling badly, I tried to be a team player and said we could give sex a go. I lay back and tried to think of a more relaxing environment, like Guantánamo Bay or the shoe display at the Holocaust museum, but it wasn't going to happen. He encouraged me to try to make it fit, to which I said, "I'm not going to try to force it in and deform my pussy just so I can have sex with you once. Sorry, bro. I'd rather not have to pick up my NuvaRing off the subway platform because it keeps falling out of my new gaping vag, courtesy of your endless BFG of a cock." I was making him laugh and this was clearly not his first rodeo with a girl chanting, "Hell no, water buffalo!"

So we did the only classy thing we could do. We made out while I jerked him off in my general direction. When he came, it landed mostly on my stomach. I got up to clean myself off and he said, "Where are you going? You got a mess on you!" and he went to get me a warm washcloth and a dry one. I then watched this member of the NHL clean me very carefully. Maybe he was afraid I'd try to steal his DNA like a hip-hop wife, but it was the sweetest thing to witness. He looked like a little boy working on a science project. I got dressed, and he seemed legitimately confused and sad that I was leaving. He asked if I would stay and watch a movie and when we would see each other again. I felt like we were starring in two different movies. I explained that I had had a great time with him and that we would never see each other again. I did the walk of shame at four thirty a.m. You may be recalling an earlier chapter where I told you I'd only had one one-night stand in my life and thinking this counts as number two. But I don't consider it a one-night stand unless sex occurred. Sex where a penis enters your vagina or butthole. (Why don't I write romance novels? My prose is so arousing!)

I called my sister in the morning from a Starbucks and told her what had happened and we both laughed so hard we were crying. I'd only gone out with him so she'd think I was cool, and that is definitely not what happened. She thought it was the saddest thing she'd ever heard. We still laugh to tears whenever he takes the ice. Does that sound mean? Did you have a moment reading this story when you felt bad for him? Please don't. Please don't shed any tears for this rich, famous, and perfect-looking athlete with a huge cock. He's just fine. He has no doubt had many wonderful sexual experiences aside from with me. He's now married to a gorgeous, tiny woman, and whenever I see pictures of them I think, *Good luck with that, sweetheart!*

I've always been a sucker for magazines—even the ones that tell me I am doing everything wrong as a woman. I grew up covering my bedroom walls with magazine photos of Jason Priestley and Luke Perry. I'd steal *Redbook* from my mom and *Mademoiselle* from my dad. Hahaha, just kidding; my dad didn't read *Mademoiselle* but I thought writing that would create a good funny rhythm. *Amy, stop explaining your jokes and get on with it.* I buy and flip through tabloids, which I believe causes cancer. I'll also buy a *Time* magazine if I feel like looking like a genius, and I put it on top of the stack so if anyone sees me, they think, *Hmmm, what a smart, important girl. I wonder what's under that—* Newsweek? The Economist? I can't think of any other smart magazines, which lets you know I'm Long Island trash who came close to not graduating high school.

Anyway, I like magazines on a flight or when I'm laying out on the beach hungover. I've never thought too hard about them, and I definitely never, ever imagined that I'd actually be in them, much less see my face slapped on the cover. My first few appearances in magazines were as a writer. After I'd been doing stand-up for a few years, I started receiving offers to write funny articles for women's magazines. I wrote for *Cosmo* a couple times, and it was really fun. I wrote about things similar to what I'm covering in this book. So when I was asked to write an article for *Men's Health* magazine, I was fired up. I pride myself on being a comic who appeals to both men and women, so I was excited to get exposure in a dudes' periodical as well.

I met with Ryan, an editor of sorts for the magazine. He was forty-five minutes late to our meeting—never a good sign—but he was really apologetic and complimentary of my stand-up, so of course, all was forgiven. We got down to business and brainstormed what I'd write about: sex! My cup of tea. All good in the hood.

Ryan and I started discussing the photo to go along with my article. I had some concepts I thought were pretty funny: me holding a copy of the magazine with a front cover that read "The Daddy Issue," or me dressed as a sad stripper next to a "No Jokes in the Champagne Room" sign. Ryan laughed at my sick ideas and said he'd pass them along to the art department.

Over the next month and a half we settled on the finished piece. A few weeks later I was backstage getting ready to film the stand-up portion of my pilot for Comedy Central when I got an email from Ryan putting me in touch with the fact-checker about one last sidebar. And that's when I saw the layout of the article. It was accompanied by three huge pictures— and I couldn't help but notice that *not one of them was me*. Each one featured a very slender, heavy-titted model, whose ages ranged from old enough for military service to too young to rent a car.

Minutes later I had to go onstage in front of cameras under bright-ass lights and tell jokes that were supposed to be funny and empowering, but all I wanted to do was throw in the towel and switch to the path that *Men's Health* obviously saw for me. This path probably involved writing in a broom closet for the rest of my life or standing at the bottom of a hole putting lotion on my skin that they dropped down in a bucket for me. Or at least that's how they made me feel. I could just hear them saying, "Schumer's a very fun girl. Bright, with a face for podcasting."

I emailed Ryan and asked about the pictures, and his reply was something along the lines of, "Sorry, it wasn't my call! Now's the time we really need you to sign off on that sidebar."

I was brushed off. And even though I can imagine everyone at *Men's Health* shaking their heads and saying, "Ugghh, just another crazy homely woman creating problems because she's not hot enough," I told him I wouldn't do any more work until I got some answers. So Ryan—who was really a nice guy, just doing his job, probably—put me in touch with the editor, a man I'll call Jake. And here is the reply I got.

> Hey Amy—
>
> Just read your note to Ryan, and I apologize if there's been any confusion over the art treatment for your story. In fact, we very rarely run author images with any story, and that applies equally to Amy Schumer and Jonathan Safran Foer and Jesse Eisenberg and Augusten Burroughs and Garrison Keillor. All well-known names, all people we turned to for wit, intelligence, and nicely turned phrases, but not for photo shoots. So you're in very good company among the non-photographed.
>
> When I heard your complaint, though, I winced a little. I hate for any of our contributors to be smarting over a detail of their piece. So we've hunted down a good photo of you—you're right, there are plenty—and have incorporated it into the spread, so everybody knows who wrote this, and can congratulate you when they see you on the street (or marquee).
>
> Please, accept my apologies.
>
> Now, you want to write a funny essay about double standards in male beauty and female beauty? Game on.
>
> Many thanks for the sweet piece, in any case. Our guys are going to love it.
>
> Best,
>
> Jake

• • •

Jake,

I appreciate your response. That's certainly an impressive list of authors. But I feel the need to point out that not one person on that list is a woman. I know you are aware that there is a difference. Were the nature of their essays sexual and did you run a picture of younger thinner dudes above their words? I'm having trouble finding the humor in the double standard at the moment.

Thank you for including a photo of me. [*The photo they ran was pinky-nail-sized, smaller than one of the models' nipples.*] I would like some more details about that. Is it very small next to the giant model shots? I think that may just highlight the situation. What is the picture? I would like to see it. I know it's too late to pull the whole story, but I would prefer that to feeling swept under the rug.

I do not accept your challenge for a follow-up story. Pardon me if my trust and faith in your publication has been shaken. I'm sure you are a great guy who is fun to get a beer with and has a good relationship with his exes, so know that this is not personal to you or your team. But I will not take this lying down. (You can have your comedic experts on staff add a joke after this line.)

Amy

. . .

Amy,

Damn. I was doing much better after your first note.

Truly, I'm sorry you're angry. We simply sought the best person to write the piece. And you were that, which you showed on the page.

Design/photo/artwork is an entirely separate realm, in my mind, so it never occurred to me that you'd be the photo subject for your own piece. You already did your part with the writing.

Think of a financial story: the writer expresses her expertise on money, and the artwork depicts cash. Writer does one part, photographer does the other, supporting the same idea. Then magazine people mesh words and images together on the page.

That's what we do all the time, and in this case, too.

Not sure I can ever convince you, so I'll stop trying. But it's exactly what happened with this story.

Jake

. . .

Jake,

Thank you for your financial advisor comparison. We are totally on the same page now. Want to get a drink sometime? I'm on a diet. I'll give you a heads up when I'm under 110.

Amy

Amy,

Ha. Phew!

Yes, let's grab a drink. I'll have beer, you can have water, and all will be good.

Happy to send you a copy of *The Women's Health Diet* to speed you on your way to 110.

Cheers,

Jake

• • •

Jake,

I hope you are blessed with daughters. All joking aside, is it too late to pull the article? I honestly don't want it to run.

I think the picture is distracting and has nothing to do with the piece. You look at the design, image, and photo as 3 separate things, but I believe the reader experiences it all together.

Amy

• • •

Amy,

Presses rolling. I hope you win an award for it.

I have two sons. Maybe they'll marry somebody's daughters.

Jake

And that was that. I don't know if Jake could tell I was being the biggest wiseass on earth, but interestingly enough, some time later, after that issue of the magazine was published, he added a large photo of me to the online version of the article, along with his defense for having initially chosen the model pics over a picture of me. Needless to say, my opinion of magazines shifted a lot after this experience. What was once just a glossy, mindless form of entertainment became something that seemed a little darker.

I know I don't look like the models they use in *Men's Health*. Their aesthetic is pretty consistent: a Svedka vodka–style fembot chick who just got out of the shower, with huge breasts on an otherwise young-boy body and an expression that says, "I'm sexy and powerful unless that's not what you want, master." Bless those gals; they work hard. So do the Photoshop editors, but I'm not going to buy into what the editors and their advertisers want. I'm not going to accept that that's the way it should be just because that's the way it is. People like women with more to their bodies too. Some people like a thick ass they can grab on to and a back they can touch without being met with a row of ribs. Nothing wrong if you enjoy the ribs. Just saying. I'm beautiful too. I am worthy of being in front of the camera. I can hear them around a conference table in their soulless office now: "She's just mad that she's busted; she should get over it!" But it's not that simple.

I'm mad because girls as young as eight years old are being shamed about their bodies. Fifth graders go on diets and admire Instagram pics of celebs in waist trainers. Some of the people I'm closest to have struggled with eating disorders. I'm mad at an industry that suggests that painfully thin is the only acceptable way to be. Please don't get on me for skinny shaming. If that's how you are shaped, God bless, but we gotta mix it up, because it's upsetting and confusing to women with other body types. When I'm onstage performing for over ten thousand people, I look out at the crowd and about half of the women in the audience have their arms folded to cover their stomachs. We're endlessly shown that being dangerously thin is the only way to be valuable—or even acceptable.

Why can't girls above a size 4 walk a runway? What are they afraid of? Will the whole runway tip over? Do they think models size 6 and above can't make it to the end of the runway without stopping midway for a burrito? Enough, enough with these waifish elves walking your impossible clothing down an ugly runway with ugly lighting and noisy music. Life doesn't look like that runway. Let's see some ass up there. And not just during the specially themed "plus-size show." We girls over size 6, 8, 10, 12, 14, 16 . . . we don't want a special day, we want every day, and we want you to get out of our fucking way because we are already here! You are living in the past, all you dated, strange magazines representing the weird fashion world that presents bizarre clothing that no one I have ever met wears.

Now that I've been on some of these magazine covers, I can tell you that even the chick on the cover doesn't love this situation. When you pose for a cover, a lot of magazines don't allow you to choose how you look or what you wear, and they generally Photoshop you until you look like everyone else. Google "magazine covers women," then click "Images," and you will get a screen full of dozens of magazine covers. Now squint just a little bit, and you'll see: everyone looks like the same person. It's sick. Why are we taught that we all need to look like one girl? Some of us want to look like ourselves. How we were born, a little goofy with some rough angles and some beautiful ones. I have been lucky to be part of some photo shoots that gave me license to look and feel like myself, thanks to photographers like Annie Leibovitz and Mark Seliger. Underappreciated fact: photographers are *artists* who enjoy mixing it up and presenting creative and varied images to delight and surprise people. Can you imagine photographing women in the same cover-shot pose all the time? There is nothing wrong with celebrating beauty, but beauty comes in many forms!

And how about we all agree that we don't need to slap a warning label on the page any time we show some form of "alternative" beauty? The "plus-size" label sends an us-vs.-them message: *These are the special magical plus-size ladies who are still lovable and beautiful—despite their size.* Why create categories for women's bodies? "Plus-size" is a pointless term that implies anything above a certain size is different and wrong. When *Glamour* put my name on the cover of their "Chic at Any Size" issue without asking me, I was frustrated, because I don't want to be a part of that message.

A few days after I got Jake's last email in that fun pen-pal exchange, I got out of the shower and stopped to look at myself in the mirror. I looked blotchy and messy and not at all like the girls in those magazines. But I was still fucking beautiful. I'm a real woman who digests her meals and breaks out and has sweet little pockets of cellulite on her upper thighs that she's not apologizing for. Because guess what? We all have that shit. We're all human beings.

I'm mad at myself for wasting any time caring about a magazine that runs articles with titles like "How to Tell If She's Good in Bed" and "Nine Ways to a Stronger Erection." What the fuck do I care? I want no part of that noise. I want something else. Women's magazines, I'm looking at you! Maybe run some fun photos, make some waves, and add more than one article per issue about women who are smart, creative, or interesting. I know there are bigger problems in the world. But this is something I care about deeply. This is my thing. I want to shout it from the fucking rooftops: You can't shame us or label us anymore. Join us instead—and EVOLVE FASTER so we can all work together!

I don't think magazines are the enemy. But I think they can do better. I want to be a part of that. If more magazines will have me, I will continue to scrunch up my nose and laugh on their covers; I will continue to pose pantsless with fire Photoshopped on my crotch; I will keep running fearlessly through Chinatown in shapeless silk pajamas and a blizzard of confetti. Beauty doesn't have to be so strict, stringent, and serious. Some of these magazines have sold us short. They have asked us to believe in their labels and their sameness. For a minute, I subscribed. But that minute is up. And I hope it's up for all of you.

Photo taken in an amusement park photo booth.

SECRET BAD HABITS

Kim and I got really fat one summer. I'm not fat-shaming us. It was worth it. We both like to expand and contract like accordions depending on the season. If it's hot, we drink white wine and tequila; if it's cold, we drink red wine and scotch and tequila. So, basically, we always weigh around the same. I usually weigh anywhere between one hundred forty-five pounds and six million pounds. That summer we were not wanting for anything.

I was told by someone somewhere at some point that I should listen to my body. If my body wanted ice cream, it got ice cream. Cinnabon? Okay! Cinnabon ice cream is a thing? Pick it up and put some pretzels in it—and oh, they must have forgotten to add peanut butter. Not a problem. I'm on top of it. Amy, you had a bottle and a half of wine tonight on your own because you felt your "body needed to relax." What is a good way to go to sleep? Good question, Amy. How about ordering a gluten-free pizza and also pasta from Seamless and putting the pasta on top of the pizza and eating it? Good call. But a word of advice: if you're gonna get pastitzza (which is not a thing, except for with me), only order it if you're already falling asleep and you'll be woken up by the buzzer when the delivery guy gets there. Cool idea!

I was blessed with a mother who made junk food completely contraband in our house. This means it was bad and is not another word for "condom," as I suspected before my editor explained it to me. If you're thinking my mom did me a favor, *ehhhhnnn* (buzzer sound). Her restrictions did not have the desired effect. Instead of giving me a healthy in-moderation-only attitude toward shitty-for-you food, I acted like an Amish kid on Rumspringa any time I was near it. I'm talking any time I was around soda or pizza at a birthday party, I would wile out. I went full-metal-jacket crazy eating it all. Especially as a little kid.

Once when I was nine years old, I went to the circus with my friend Lauren. Her mom innocently offered to grab me something from the concession stand, and I was like, "What do you mean? I can have whatever I want?" She said—get this— "Yes." In that moment, the whole world stopped around me. My vision blurred, and I blinked maniacally, unable to respond. She must have thought I was waiting for her to read me the menu of options—which is what she did.

"Well, honey, they have peanuts, popcorn, cotton candy, pretzels, giant chocolate chip cookies, lollipops, soda, and hot chocolate."

To which I answered, "Yes." Then, I ate so much, it's a miracle my little stomach—which had now become a piñata containing everything in Willy Wonka's factory—didn't explode all over a dancing elephant.

Every time I went to a birthday party where junk food was made available to me, I'd return home to my mom at the end of the day very, very ill—my chin sticky with dried soda and Cheetos dust under my fingernails. All my friends who were allowed to eat that stuff in moderation were so confused as to why I would eat myself sick. Just like Italian kids who are allowed to sip a little wine with their dinners and never end up binge-drinking as teens, most kids can handle moderate exposure to this food. But I had to be secretive about it so my mom wouldn't find out. I had friendships based on who lived near bodegas and candy shops. There was one girl I didn't care for even the slightest bit, but I knew if I went to her house, I could get enough Sour Patch Kids to kill a large giraffe, which I did. RIP, Smokey.

In college, my roommate Denise couldn't leave her food lying around because I'd come home from class or the bar and find a box of Twinkies and eat the whole thing. She'd make a tray of lasagna, and I'd slowly, square by square, eat the entire dish. I'd wake up like Garfield to her screaming my name. I had to tell her to start hiding it from me. I couldn't even know it was in the house. She started running out of places to hide her snacks because I would always find them. I would ransack my own apartment like the Gestapo. One night she brought a guy home, and he found a box of Devil Dogs under her pillow. He was really weirded out. She was totally embarrassed and blamed me, but I of course acted like I didn't know what she was talking about.

Even as a full-grown adult woman, I still have this habit. I curb it within reason. But there is no other way to describe that particular summer: Kim and I got fat. I was just about to start filming the second season of my TV show, so I panicked and asked her to lose some weight with me. There is no reason she should have said yes. She's very married and is not on camera very much. Kim is one of those girls with a natural *Playboy*-model type of body—the kind that, if it were mine, I would have had so much fun with by now. I'd be carrying every disease known to man and monkey. Instead, I'm shaped like a cactus, and when I don't shave for four hours I feel like one, too.

But Kim agreed to work out and eat well with me because she is kind and knows my favorite thing to do is eat and drink with her. She was all too aware that I'd throw away our health plan the second she agreed to booze or a cookie, so she had to join me in the diet if she wanted to ensure I stuck with it. She keeps me from eating and drinking myself to death most of the time, but when she is having a moment of weakness I can sniff it out, and I strike like an MMA fighter avenging his closetedness.

So we signed up for this CrossFit-type insane workout and actually went most days. It's one of those programs that puts you through Navy SEAL–style guerrilla warfare training that is completely over-the-top and unnecessary unless you're a runway model or about to compete in the Hunger Games. But we went. Every day we were on the verge of death. Sweating and wheezing. Walking out shaking and dizzy. It was horrible doing these workouts that were originally developed for people who needed them TO SURVIVE. Pilates was developed by Joseph Pilates, who worked with soldiers during World War II. He created his method to help very wounded soldiers get back into shape. Now it's mostly used by housewives who want child-soldier abs and who refuse to let their asses go where gravity is inevitably dragging them. All these boot camps and diets where they teach you to survive on minimal amounts of food like a prisoner of war are just not right. But Kim and I were committed to getting healthier, so we went.

The instructors were all gorgeous—girls in tiny spandex shorts and sports bras, with perfect hair and flawless faces without makeup. I think it has now been established that without makeup I look like Charlize Theron in *Monster*. The guys were also in ridiculous shape and were super hot. But there was one who was so beautiful and charismatic that it was confusing. I don't know if it's because we were so light-headed or because he was actually funny, but he kept us laughing and having fun while we sweated and sucked wind like George Burns on an elliptical.

This particular instructor, whom I'll call Neal, looked like a fake Greek sculpture of a man; he was so handsome you couldn't look at him for very long. He was toned and tanned to perfection—beyond what you are imagining now. He spread his attention evenly in the class, walking around and winking and squatting next to us as we did wall-sits and crunches. He'd literally take a knee and encourage you with a hand on your lower back. I think every girl left the class with a stupid grin, giggling, "Bye, Neal!" Kim and I are smarter than those girls, right? We're annoyed by physically perfect people, because *fuck you*. They can't also be funny. YOU AREN'T ALLOWED TO HAVE IT ALL! But even we were not immune to his charm. We would roll our eyes and look at each other like *What the fuck?!* because we couldn't believe how hot he was and how he could reduce us to smirking schoolgirls. He always made it very clear in class that he was available via the Internet to provide extra personal training outside of the usual class sessions. He'd say it over and over during workouts, and while I felt stupid even mentioning it to my sister, one day I said, "I kind of feel like he was saying that specifically to me . . . not just because he thinks I need help, but because he kind of likes me."

I was fully ready for her to tell me I was an idiot and needed to slow my roll and remember that my current Mrs. Potato Head shape was what got us into this mess in the first place. Kim has often messed with me when I have a crush on a guy and he has zero feelings for me. There was a guy who worked on season one of my TV show whom I was crazy about. So cute—this little bike-riding hipster who wouldn't give me the time of day, even though I was literally paying for his time of day. One afternoon while shooting, Kim said, "Oh my God, Aim, don't turn around, he is looking at you!" "Really?!!!" I shrieked. I slowly turned around and he was sleeping on a pile of equipment. What I'm saying is that not only does Kim *not* lie to me about guys having no interest in me, she enjoys it. But after I asked her about Neal, she said, "Dude, me too, I felt like he was saying it to you!" This was all I needed.

I've talked onstage and in these pages about how I can have low self-esteem at times. But I'm also always completely ready to accept and believe the fact that I am prettier than I ever realized. On the evolution chart, this guy and I were at opposite ends. I was dragging my knuckles, sniffing around for bananas, throwing my own feces at tourists, and he was a Disney prince but with more sex appeal. I reached out and was all, "Can you help me with my diet?" and he was all, "Sure, let's meet up at this healthy-eating place," and I was all, "*Here comes the bride*." So we met up and we hung out a couple fitness-based times before I texted him while a little buzzed one night saying I wanted to make out.

On our next few dates, he'd let me know he was interested but also stomp on my ego, saying things like "Looks aren't the most important thing to me." *Wow, thank you,* I thought. *I really lucked out—I am so busted looking, but I still have some qualities for which you can muster an erection.* We wound up hooking up a couple times, and I could tell that he hoped I was going to just blow him. But he didn't realize how lazy homegirl is. I've given maybe eight blow jobs to completion in my life. I have to really love the person and feel they deserve it, or just be in a dirty mood. But they still need to deserve it. So, yeah, eight total. No joke. We had sex a couple times, always at my place.

To be honest, I never really enjoyed making out with him because the whole time I was thinking, *Why would he do this with me? It makes no sense. What does he have to gain from this?* It's not that I was down on myself, but it just didn't add up. I saw all the girls who were actual real-life, young-as-fuck supermodels in class swooning over him. But there he was with me, eating my dumb-ass pussy. Not ass pussy, but my vagina. Anywho, the point is he was hot and I am me, and we never went to his apartment. Always mine. Until one night. And that's when I found out about his secret bad habit.

We all have habits we don't want people to know about. Most are fairly harmless, but we still keep them a secret because we feel like we should.

Some people only eat fast food in secret, and some people, like my sister-in-law, watch reality TV that is so trashy it should be illegal. How do I know that? Because I watch it right there with her and make her watch even worse TV. Some people like to eat the inside stuffing of their couch. Only God can judge you, brotha!

Anyway, the night I found out about Neal's secret, I had taken him to an event with me. We were progressing—he was hot enough and had enough confidence to actually confuse me into thinking he was cool and that we might even start dating for real. (Typing that just made me short of breath.) So we went to a fund-raiser for a disease, Lyme or alcoholism or something, and it was embarrassing to be there with him, because everyone was looking at me like, *Give me a break, bitch*. And they were right. Not that I don't deserve someone hot like that, or whatever I'm supposed to tell myself, but there *is* a line. You can be with someone kinda a li'l bit hotter or less hot than you, but if the levels are too off, people are furious. It's sick and sad. But I wasn't surprised. His hotness was just in the ridiculous range. I felt like we were in that scene from *The Little Mermaid* where Ursula sings the song about stealing Ariel's voice and I was one of the weeds on the floor and Neal was Ariel. (Hmm? Don't worry about it. All my metaphors aren't gonna hit.)

I got myself nice and drunk to deal with the humiliation—I don't care what anyone says, it's a great technique. We left hand in hand, excited about continuing the evening together. Walking to the car, I thought, *Maybe we will have something more. Is this my next boyfriend?* In the car, I was feeling good about "us" and I said, "Let's go to your place." "Okay," he said, "but it's kind of a mess." I let him know I wasn't the type of girl who would ever care, and off we went.

That night, we walked past his nice doorman to the nice elevator and walked down his nice hall and he opened his nice door—and there it was. What had probably once been a beautiful studio apartment had become an overstuffed locker. It looked like a garage door had opened on *Storage Wars*. The mess was bad—the kitchen and bathroom were black with mold, all porcelain surfaces coated in hair and grime, and there were unwashed dishes and towels covering every inch of the counters. I'd seen messes in men's apartments. It's not that uncommon for a guy to have a disgusting apartment, especially if he's single. I actually think it's endearing. I love a guy with a shitty apartment with nothing hanging on the walls. I like for guys to dress basic and be hanging on by a thread with their style. I don't trust a guy with taste. It seems unnatural to me.

But Neal's apartment went far beyond endearingly dirty. It was more than dirty. It was like *Jumanji*. Filled to the brim with unnatural things that didn't belong in an apartment. I mean, there were piles upon piles of just stuff. Piles everywhere. Piles of books and clothes and sneakers and furniture sitting on top of other furniture. There were magazines and papers stacked in tall symmetrical towers, but there were also messy mountains of stuff. Like big, haphazard pyramids made of boxes of merchandise and exercise contraptions and unopened packages. There were bottles of things, protein powders and health-food products. Junk mail and paperwork, CDs, rolled-up posters, jump ropes, empty grocery bags, knee pads (knee pads? WTF) . . . It was a nightmare to look at. A filthy, stacked-to-the-ceiling nightmare. There was barely room to walk around. You had to walk sideways through the narrow pathways he'd cleared. This boy was not a collector. He was a hoarder.

I instantly sobered up. Now I had to act. *I'm an actor*, I told myself. *I can do this.*

"I told you it was messy," he said. "Is it bad?"

"No!" I shrieked too loud and fast. "It's a really nice apartment."

I shut myself in the bathroom and noticed a bra and girls' things hanging on the door. I'd previously been suspicious he had a girlfriend—some little model walking in Paris at Fashion Week, I had guessed. Even though I've never been to Paris and I don't know when Fashion Week is. (It seems like it's every fucking week though. Does anyone else feel that way?) Anyway, I don't think this bra could have belonged to a recent girlfriend. Based on the expired time stamp of everything else in that apartment, that bra could have been hanging there for years. It could have been Amelia Earhart's bra. I stalled in the bathroom, marveling for a moment at the fact that a man so perfectly waxed, so expertly coiffed and immaculately molded, could emerge from this bottom-of-an-orangutan-cage bathroom every morning.

After I pulled myself away from deep breathing in the bathroom, he continued leading me around the apartment through the pathways he'd cleared. It felt like being led through a maze. It smelled dusty and like his dog, a sweet pit bull who followed us single file through the pathways. He offered me a drink and I said no. That's how bad it was. I never turn down a drink when I'm with a new guy. I typically use dating a new guy as an excuse to go on a Keith Richards–type bender. But I just couldn't see myself touching my mouth to a wineglass that lived in his apartment. He led me to the only clear area—the love seat in front of the TV, which he obviously sat in frequently since it wasn't covered with stuff. He made room for me on the love seat and we watched TV. Rather, I *pretended* to watch TV, unsure of how to leave. *Does he know how bad it is? If he does, he could be planning on killing me.* I looked at him to see if he was on edge. Nope, he was laughing hard at whatever MTV nightmare we were watching.

So what did I do? *Well, Amy, you obviously left. You thanked him for a lovely evening.* No, no, good friend, that is what a normal person would do. What I did was let him lead me to his mattress that had no sheets on it, and he went down on me. It was an out-of-body experience. I was looking around the room at the stacks of things he had accumulated over the years. Gifts from Nike and Adidas. Dog toys and a broken lamp stacked on top of a broken desk, covered in even more magazines and CDs. The dog and I made eye contact. I felt like we were sending each other the same message: "HELP!" I got dressed. I specifically remember putting my boots on and making myself pause to feel what it felt like to be in my thirties and having a sexual encounter like this. *Never again*, I thought. I said good night and walked back out to the city street full of steaming trash where things were nice.

It was three a.m. and the garbagemen were pulling up right as I entered the clean night air. I was clearly beginning my walk of deep shame and they knew it. They howled at me and I laughed at myself. There was no denying the state I was in. I went home and showered for eight years. The next day Neal said to me, "You inspired me to get my place together." I didn't know what I had said to make him do that but I thought this sounded like pretty good news.

"Oh, cool, you're gonna get rid of some stuff?" I asked.

"No, I'm going to get some new furniture."

I couldn't think of anything to say. I don't know what caused his condition. My only guess is that maybe he grew up without a lot and struggled— and maybe material things and name brands and just having stuff makes him feel successful. He could measure his place in the world by how much he had accumulated. This analysis is based on watching about three episodes of *Hoarders* and asking no one. I have no information is what I'm saying. But like every other girl I'm friends with, I like to diagnose people without any research.

He called me a few days later and I hung out with him one more time, just as friends, at my place with my sister. I didn't want to suspiciously disappear after seeing his apartment, but I couldn't go back there. And since Kim and I had already declared victory in our weight-loss journey, given our impressive combined loss of six pounds, I had no reason to attend his fitness class anymore either.

He wasn't a bad guy at all—he was quite the opposite. I've seen him in passing since then, and he's doing very well for himself. I wonder if he knows he has this affliction. I mean, this guy very clearly grooms himself within an inch of his life. His body is an absolutely immaculate temple. But his actual temple, on the other hand, is maculate. I don't know what that means. But it is.

Sometimes I think I have the opposite problem. Most of the time I throw away shit I need. I can never find anything I need. I even lose my Nuva-Ring a few times a year, and that is supposed to be inside me. All human beings have secret compulsions and habits. Including me. But now any time I see someone who is so physically beautiful they almost don't look human, I remember there's definitely something totally fucked about them that will bring them right back down to earth. I'm kind of grateful to the guy because he made my pastitzza-as-I'm-falling-asleep habit seem a lot more forgivable.

MOM

———

I have trouble with people who maintain that their mothers are perfect. Are you dating a guy who can't make a decision without running it by his mom first? Break up with him. (Unless his mother is Caroline Manzo from *The Real Housewives of New Jersey*, but she is the only exception.) Definitely end it with this guy if he and his mother have one of those dynamics where you can tell the mom always kind of thought she would end up with her own son. Trust me—leave. Do you think your mother always has the answer to everything, including great suggestions about your hair, clothing, and relationships? I recommend you examine your view of her. I want to be patient and let you discover it in your own time. That's a lie. Actually, I just want to pull the entire rug out from under you and rush you to see the light.

Everyone's parents have fucked them up in one way or another. This is part of the natural order. It's the circle of life. Mothers are people—not

angels from heaven or *Ex Machina* error-free service bots. Just because they pushed you out of their
vaginal canals does not mean they have all (or any)
of the answers. Before they had you, they were
flailing around like idiots, just like you are right
now. My point is, they are just people. Most likely
extraordinarily flawed people.

Which brings me to my mother. Yes, yes, just
like your mother, she did her best. But I was one
of those kids who grew up thinking my mom was a
saint. An actual goddess walking the earth. I worshipped her. But one day, I learned my mom wasn't
perfect. The day I learned this also happened to be
the day my childhood best friend, Mia, and I fell
out forever. It wasn't a wacky coincidence. My
mother was having an affair with Mia's father.

I met Mia on the first day of fourth grade when I
was nine years old. I was the new kid at school and
no one would talk to me, except her. She was the
only one who didn't mind my bossiness and inces-
sant lying. I'd just finished telling everyone at my
new school that I was a bikini model from California, along with several other fabrications that
didn't exactly win them over. I remember thinking
she looked like Tinker Bell, so lovely and scrappy,
when she approached me at the lunch table to say
hi. She had dirty-blond unbrushed hair and was
beautiful, tiny, and fragile. We became instantly
inseparable. We had a few other friends who came
in and out of our world, but I only saw them as

a hindrance. I thought she was fascinating, brave, and confident.

I became a part of Mia's family and she became a part of mine. She had an older brother my brother's age and a younger sister my sister's age, so our families were perfect matches. We had sleepovers as often as our parents would allow us, and we spent our time choreographing captivating dances that we showcased for anyone we could get to hold still for five minutes. Our choreography secret was to match up the dance moves to the words in the song. For example, for Paula Abdul's song "Cold Hearted," we would shiver and act cold when Paula sang the word "cold." We'd point to our hearts for the word "hearted," and when that future *American Idol* judge sang the word "snake," we would—guess what?—each make a snake motion with one of our arms, slithering it up our fingers, wrist, and elbow. Calling all *America's Best Dance Crew* choreographers, we got you if you need help!

I had no doubt in my mind that we'd one day marry twin brothers and all live in a house together. It seemed like nothing could ever possibly come between us.

Our parents met at temple and became close friends. For those of you who aren't Chosen Ones, temple is a very regular part of life for Jews. We'd go to Shabbat service Friday night and the kids would go to Hebrew school Sunday mornings. Every summer my family would join Mia's at their

lake house in upstate New York. It was five hours
away by car, and her parents would drive in their
station wagon that always smelled like cats and
stale Fritos, but I didn't mind as long as I could sit
in the seat in the back that faced the cars behind us.
We'd wave to the drivers of those cars, then give
them the finger and disappear—greatest gag in the
book. My deathly carsickness, which I've always
been prone to, was worth having just to see the
change in the faces of the people who were just trying to get from point A to point B and really didn't
need to deal with some stupid-ass kids telling them
with their small fingers to fuck off. But we'd laugh
our heads off for the whole ride.

Mia's mom, Ruth, was similar in stature to my
mom—kind of short, blond, with a killer bod.
Given my blind spot for seeing my mother as
nothing but perfection, I remember thinking that
Ruth wasn't as funny or bright as my mom. But
she was kind and didn't take any shit from Mia or
me. When we were thirteen, she caught us smoking Virginia Slims and drinking Boone's Farm on
her roof (like a couple bosses) and she was not having it. She was a good mother and always took care
of me like I was her own, like when she yelled at
me when I snuck a *Redbook* magazine over to her
house to share the sex articles with the other kids. I
remember reading aloud that it entices a man if you
dress up in his tie and nothing else. We were probably nine at the time, and she chewed me out, like
a real parent. I recall feeling sorry for her, merely

because she wasn't my mother. In fact, I always felt bad for any woman who had to be near my mom because they weren't her. She was, in my eyes, a queen.

This is a lot, right? I know.

As for Mia's dad, Lou, he was a smart, over-weight businessman who wore huge, thick-framed glasses. There was nothing flashy about him. He adored his family and they adored him back. He worked long hours so he could provide them with the best life possible. They were the standard nice, Catskills-going Jewish family on Long Island.

The summer I turned thirteen was a great time for Mia and me. We were becoming teenagers and we got to hang out constantly up at the lake house. After our parents would go to bed, we'd come alive, sneaking out and meeting up with local boys on the beach to drink and get felt up. When school started in the fall, we were never apart. She was so unself-conscious and strong. Not physically—she was basically a string bean—but she knew what she stood for, and I wanted to stand for it right next to her. She was whip smart but could be totally silly and without any ego, and she always made me feel like she wanted me around. I felt I'd met my soul mate. I had.

And then one day after school I came home and saw my mother slumped on the couch. She'd clearly been crying hard. Her eyes were almost sealed shut and her nose was really red. She was usually composed, deliberate, and happy, and I'd never seen her cry like this. It felt like the ground was shifting beneath my feet when she reached out for me with both arms.

"What is it? What happened?" I asked her. She opened her mouth to explain the tragedy to me but the tears started again and she couldn't catch her breath long enough to tell me. Because she couldn't communicate vocally, she had to sign it to me. Since she is a teacher of the deaf, we all know a good amount of sign language in my family. Slowly, her hands trembling, she rose and signed to me, "I am leaving your father. Lou and I have fallen in love with each other." I signed the word "again" because I needed her to repeat herself. Again she signed, "I am leaving your father. Lou and I have fallen in love with each other."

I was not shocked that she was leaving my dad. I wasn't ever under the impression that she was too fond of him. I'd never seen them hold hands or kiss, and she'd always expressed an air of vague annoyance toward him. Even though my dad was funny and handsome, it was hard for me to believe my perfect mother had stayed with my imperfect father for so long. I thought of her as Mother Teresa for staying with a man who never deserved her. Looking back now, I of course realize how unhealthy it was that as a teen, I had such a strong sense of alignment with one parent against the other. My father was no angel. He drank in secret and I know he did dirtbag things behind my mom's back (in their earlier days, I'm pretty sure she once walked in on him getting head from a hooker), but he never pretended to be perfect.

When she told me that she and Lou were in love, it didn't register who she was talking about because it seemed so unlikely. My first thought was, *That's funny, Mia's dad's name is Lou too*. But then I put two and two together. Flashes of dinners and trips and moments at the temple with our families shot through my brain. Even though I'd always found him to be plain, he must have been special somehow, because my mother was in love with him—and I never questioned anything my mother said or did.

She sat there on the couch looking so helpless and sad, seeming so alone and without hope. I decided in that moment that I'd be her savior. I threw my arms around her and said, "Well it's about time. I always knew you were too good for Dad. I'm happy you're in love." When my mom heard these words, the wave of hugs and kisses and praise that came my way was overwhelming. I believe no one has ever been as grateful as my mom was in that moment. Looking back now, I'm horrified that she let me play that role. To allow your thirteen-year-old to be your support system while you are simultaneously ripping her world apart is not a kind thing to do. I was a child, new to my teens, and she was treating me like a seasoned psychiatrist. And because I was the kid who always followed her lead, who outright *worshipped* her, I thought this must have been completely appropriate. I actually felt *honored*.

After she stopped crying, I bravely sat next to her in silence. And then, as I had always been trained to do, I felt fine. I believed everything was going to be OKAY. When we were kids and would fall or get upset, she'd never ask if we were all right. Instead, she'd say, "You're okay," in an upbeat tone and trick us into believing it. This is how we were raised: we were always oppressively OKAY.

I went to bed that night feeling OKAY, if a bit uneasy. I woke up in the middle of the night and couldn't fall back asleep. I had a headache. I lay there, staring at the ceiling, hoping it had all been a nightmare. I was thinking about Mia and her family when I heard the back door being unlocked. I moved my curtains aside to look down at the driveway and saw that my dad was home. I took a step toward my bedroom door and paused. What would I say to him? Did he know? A sudden, sharp pain in my temple stopped me in my tracks. I winced and lay back down. I'd never experienced a headache like this before. A faint, almost inaudible knock on my door was followed by a whisper: "*Aim?*"

The door opened and my father was standing there. "Hey, Dad."

He sat down next to me. "Hey, baby, I heard you moving around in here. Why are you awake?" I told him about my headache, and I looked in his eyes and could see that he had been briefed on his new shattered life. He seemed calm though—collected on the outside, but still broken behind his eyes. He used his thumb to rub my temple. I breathed in his smell deeply as he softly sang a sleepy rendition of "It Was a Very Good Year" by Sinatra. My dad sang this song often. His nightly standards also included "You've Got to Hide Your Love Away" and "They Call the Wind Maria." To review, these are songs about lost youth, stuffing down your feelings, and a hurricane. Not really a ray of sunshine for a kid. It hit me that this was probably the last time he would sing them to me. I felt a heaviness in my chest that stung and pulled me back into a deep sleep.

I woke up to pancakes, eggs, and orange juice on the table. My mom was bright-eyed and cheery and had an "It's gonna be a great day" way about her. She talked to me as if everything were normal. She made no mention of the previous day's events and neither did I. Then she asked if I wanted Mia to come over after school.

I thought, *Is this a joke?*

But I said, "Okay." And my mom explained, "I don't want all of this to harm your friendship." Hearing her say this made me believe it was actually possible. I thought, *I learned everything I know from this adult, and I trust her completely. If she's acting like this is all OKAY, then sure, there's nothing complicated about remaining best friends with Mia when our parents are having an affair. Nope. Nothing at all.*

In retrospect, I wish my mother had been visibly affected by what was going on. How could she get up so early and smile so brightly? But that was always her MO—to decide on a new reality that made sense to her in the moment and force us to live in it with her. I know there is a lot that she hid from me and plenty I don't know about what happened with her and Lou. But I wish she'd considered the ripple effects of her actions and then fought her desire to have this affair. At the very least, I wish she could have just been honest that she was weak and lost—that she pursued Lou because of the bad place she was in. I can't speak for her, but I don't believe she tried hard enough to think about everyone who would be affected by the relationship. Even worse, she got me on board. She made me my favorite breakfast and recruited me to be the cheerleader of her mistake. There was no "*How are you feeling today, Aim? This must be a lot for you to deal with.*" So I acted like there wasn't. In the meantime, the stress and agony that was suddenly bubbling to the surface had nowhere to go, so it was promptly internalized.

I had a blinding pressure cooker of a headache for years to come.

As Mom cleared the dishes, I asked her where Dad was. "He's moving his things into the office," she answered with a frightening Stepford quality. *Bam*, pain—right at the front of my head. I went off to school anyway, feeling that I needed to be as sunshiney and strong as my mother. Nothing was a big deal as long as we didn't act like it was. When I sat down in my chair for math class, I immediately saw that Mia's desk was empty. I stared at it. Headache. Shooting, searing pain. Then just as the second bell rang, the classroom door flung open and Mia ran to her seat without looking at me. My eyes were fixed on her all forty-two minutes of class. She didn't even glance in my direction. She looked cool and relaxed like always. *She must not know*, I thought. *What am I going to say to her? "Hey, Mia, your family is ruined because our parents are two sad and lonely people who chose some fleeting moments of joy over keeping their families happy and safe. Do you want to go get some Sour Patch Kids after school?"*

The bell rang and class was over. I packed up my books, breathed through my headache, and approached her. "Hi," I said.

"Hey," she said, and handed me a folded letter, while smiling like everything was fine. "Please give this to your mom, and promise me you won't read it." I nodded my head and I meant it. She skipped away and I immediately stepped into the bathroom and furiously opened the envelope. I was too curious. You definitely would have, too.

It was an utterly hateful letter to my mother—written by Mia. Each word more hurtful than the last. It was filled with angry questions and accusations, like *"I thought you were an angel but you are the most evil thing I've ever seen. I hope you go to hell . . . You've ruined my family. How could you do this?"*

Three spite-filled pages. I couldn't believe that someone—Mia especially—could write something like this to my mom. In my mind, my mom was innocent. She'd painted herself as a precious victim, and she had successfully brainwashed me into believing in the romantic forbidden-love story she was living out with my best friend's father. As far as I was concerned, my mother was Hester Prynne in this situation, and I wasn't going to let these people burn an innocent woman at the stake for following her heart.

I marched down the empty hallway and stopped in front of the door to the biology class I knew Mia was in. Without thinking I barged in. "I need to talk to Mia," I told the teacher. He must have heard the "don't fuck with me" tone in my voice because he let her walk right out. She came into the hallway and shut the door behind her, at which point *we were off*. "I told you not to read it!" "Fuck you!" "How could you?" "I hate you!" Back and forth—both of us screaming and crying until two teachers had to break it up. While being guided away from each other we locked eyes. We both looked surprised. I was taken to the nurse's office to calm down, where I lay on a cot and breathed heavily. By the time my mom came to drive me home, my head was throbbing, my temples beating like a heart.

In the weeks that followed, I got used to the headaches. I had to witness Mia's mother sitting on our doorstep, begging my mom not to do this to her family. My mom did it anyway. I had to see Mia in the hallways at school while I was aching to talk to her. Hold her. Be with her as I had been every day for the last five years. It was devastating to go through such a confusing and stressful experience without my best friend. We stopped going to the temple where I'd just had my bat mitzvah. It was too uncomfortable to show our faces there after my mom had wrecked a home in the community. Thus ended an important chapter in my relationship with Judaism, the religion in which I had been raised, spending every weekend of my whole life studying and celebrating. My friends and my religion were gone. The whole town knew, and instead of being angry with my mother, I stood by her with a vengeance. I looked them all dead in the eye, daring them to just try to fuck with either of us.

I had to watch my father move from the office into a sad, sterile bachelor's apartment on Long Island with a roommate. My mother rewarded my loyalty—or perhaps paid for her guilt—by giving me the master bedroom she used to share with him. Mia and I avoided each other for the rest of middle school and high school. I felt the familiar shooting pain in my head any time I would pass her in the hall or on the street. I missed her all the time. I still do. She reached out on Facebook a couple of years ago to congratulate me on my success, and I immediately gushed about how I missed her, how sorry I was, and how wrong my mom was. She never responded.

As for my mom and Lou, their relationship

lasted all of a couple months. It was a very strange experience for me and my siblings. One year earlier we'd been on family vacations with Lou's family, and now he was coming along on *our* family vacation to San Diego—as my mom's boyfriend. He'd moved out of his family's house and gotten a place of his own. It turned my stomach to watch them hold hands. I remember ordering clams and sucking them out of the shell the way we always did with my dad. But Lou insisted we use our forks. Watching him with my mom at the hotel pool, I could tell she was already over him. My brother, sister, and I all felt the same heaviness in the salty San Diego air, but she did her usual act of pretending everything was fine. She expected us to do the same, but this time we did not oblige. Something about that trip finally lifted the veil for me. I was beginning to see her for the flawed, confused, lonely human being that she was. No worse than the rest of us. But my imaginary image of her shattered and has never returned.

She broke up with Lou on the flight home.

In the years that followed, she dated several other men, swearing that each was "the one." And through it all, I remained intensely close to her—all the way up through my twenties. I used to bring her to comedy clubs with me and we were very much a part of each other's daily lives. We were enmeshed, with not a single healthy boundary between us. And I was always defending the questionable choices she made in relationships.

We have had a different journey than most mothers and daughters. Maybe it helped my mom cope with life to manage and guard our relationship so closely. She couldn't control or deal with reality, but she could control me.

Now, in our thirties, my siblings and I have begun to become more vocal with each other about the hardships of growing up with our mom. We've each had our own specific struggles, but they're rooted in the experiences we shared of being emotionally suppressed or manipulated by her. As it turns out, being OKAY ALL THE TIME as a child makes for a difficult entry into adulthood.

When I was about to turn thirty, I was beginning to think about writing a book about my life (which eventually became *this* book). I went back through the journals I've kept from the age of thirteen and started reading what I'd written about Mia and Lou. As an adult reading the words of a child who was telling this awful story, I was able for the first time to separate my mother's actions from my adoration of her. It became very clear that she manipulated me in unhealthy ways, and that the remnants of that manipulation were still a part of our present-day relationship.

With all this pain refreshed in my memory from reading my old journals, my mother happened to call to discuss my upcoming birthday. I remember her cheerful tone—the same one she'd had that morning so long ago when she made me pancakes right after turning my world upside down. "I know what we are doing for your thirtieth," she said. "We are going on a helicopter ride around Manhattan and then we'll get hibachi and massages!" I was suddenly flooded with anger. I told her, "I don't want to go on a *Millionaire Matchmaker* date with you for my birthday!" *This is not OKAY. Those are all things SHE would want to do on HER birthday*, I thought. And then I was fully furious. I wasn't just mad at her for having a short, destructive affair with my best friend's father when I was thirteen. I wasn't just mad at her for the string of other men who came into our lives after Lou. I was mad at her for manipulating me into supporting her through all this. And for making me believe the lie she was selling—the lie of her projected flawlessness and innocence.

So at the age of twenty-nine, I began to forge a new relationship with her—one with Fort Knox–level boundaries. Redirecting a relationship between two people who've been abnormally close for thirty years is not an easy thing to do. We had a period of my expressing my feelings about the past, followed by a period of our not speaking. I tried again and again to lay it all out for her, to explain my grievances and pain. And sometimes she did try to listen to where I was coming from. She stopped just defending herself and started to hear me, but ultimately I think it was too much for her to accept the gravity of what she had done—and the effect it had had on me and my siblings. We finally landed in a place where we have remained for several years. We are kind to one another but I keep my boundaries clear. We speak regularly and keep each other up to date, but far less frequently.

Now, after some years of reflection, I understand her a little better. Like all of us, she's a product of her own fucked-up childhood. She was damaged by her own mother, who was an emotionally neglectful narcissist. I have no idea what it must have been like to be in her situation when she started the affair with Lou—to have three kids and a husband who didn't make her feel loved. But I still wish she could have just been honest with us. And with herself. We're all trying our best, making mistakes, and hanging on by a thread. I wish she could have showed us an authentic emotion or two, allowed us to accept weakness and vulnerability as a part of life. Life is full of pain and disappointment. I've made a whole career out of pointing this out and reliving it in ridiculous ways so everyone can laugh and cry along with me. I wish my mother understood this too.

It's relaxing sometimes, just being human.

I still have to work hard not to internalize my feelings so they don't manifest themselves in the form of headaches and other physical problems. And I'm still at my core a girl who longs for her mother. We all are. When I think of the moments in my life that I've felt the most comforted and loved, I think of her. Being tucked in at night, or walking into the house starving from volleyball practice to find dinner already waiting on the table for me. Feeling her arms around me as she carried me through the swimming pool. The safety of wrapping my arms around her as she slowly moved through the water, guiding me, loving me. She is still the person I want to talk to when I wake up from a nightmare. When I call her in the middle of the night after a bad dream, which happens a couple times a year, she always picks up the phone. *Always.* When she tells me, "It will be okay," I believe her and go back to sleep. I love her.

But make no mistake, if I knew I was going to eventually *become* her . . . ? If it were like *World War Z* and I had five seconds until I transitioned into fully *being* my mother? I would hara-kiri myself without a second thought. If you're a parent reading this, chances are you're not as tricky as my mom. I know she is a rare flower. But don't go patting yourself on the back too quickly. No matter what, you're still going to mess up your kids too. And they're going to hate you for a minute (or two or three) while they pick up the pieces of their childhood. Anyone who claims to skirt this system is just lying. And that's a far worse offense in my book.

No matter what my mother put me through, I'm still grateful to her for raising me to believe I'm talented, smart, and beautiful. She made me who I am—someone who, ironically, places the highest value on being vulnerable, honest, and real. I wish

we could have a normal mother-daughter relationship. If such a thing exists. I don't know if that's
possible for us, but I believe family is a constant
negotiation. I have never given up on her. I can't,
and I never will.

NYC APARTMENTS

Last year, I bought my first apartment in New York City—an absolute dream come true. I've lived here pretty much all of my adult life, but always as a renter, and I've always wanted to *own* a place here. I was born in Manhattan, and after spending the first several years of my life here, I had to admire it from the far reaches of suburban Long Island for the rest of my childhood and teen years. As soon as I could make my way back after college, I did, and I've lived here ever since—in almost every corner of this island, I might add. Even after my career picked up, I stayed in New York instead of moving to Los Angeles, like most people in this business end up doing. I will never leave. It's home, the place where I can absolutely be myself—even if being myself means I have to nest with cockroach carcasses, rat droppings, and even worse, boyfriends.

I fucking love New York. It just makes sense to me in a way no other place does. Growing up in the suburbs wasn't for me: big houses separated by big yards and fences on wide streets. Big parking lots outside of huge stores. When you're in the city, everyone is so unquestionably close to everyone else, physically, that there's no choice but to bump into other humans at all times. It always seemed so *cozy* in comparison to Long Island. Like in the movie *Beaches* when they share a shitty apartment in New York and sing Christmas carols. That's what I longed for when I was a kid, imagining myself as a grown-up with my own place.

There's more than one benefit to being on top of each other all the time. Everyone has to walk the same streets, smell the same gross hot-garbage stink, and no one gets to be better than or different from anyone else. The painful humanity is everywhere. The fucking queen of England could knock into you on the subway and you'd be like, WATCH IT, CUNT. Hahahahaha. I've never called anyone a cunt on the subway. But that image really made me laugh. Someone please make a cartoon of that.

I've lived in nearly every neighborhood in all the boroughs of New York City, with the exception of the Bronx and—*of course*—Staten Island. No offense to the Wu-Tang Clan—I'm on a strict no-Shaolin (Staten Island) policy. So many of the important life lessons I've learned are written all over this city—the streets, subways, bars, restaurants, theaters, parks, and comedy clubs. Fortunately, those lessons have all been completely obscured by a fine mist of urine and spray paint, with a confetti of bedbugs and survival sprinkled into the mix. This is the magic of NYC: you're always starting over and moving fast. That could actually describe a lot of things in life: my relationship with my mom, my career, my digestive tract. I have, in essence, learned nothing, other than to *keep moving*.

I'm used to moving. I've been a comic on the road for over a decade. And before I went away to college, our family changed residences just under ten times. But it's nice to be in one place now. I love my apartment. It's full of all the things that make a home homey. In the bedroom, a great bed with soft jersey T-shirt sheets, and of course, my disgusting stuffed animals. In the kitchen, a good frying pan for eggs every morning, and a bunch of fancy teas that I never drink. Also a bunch of wine that I *do* drink (enough to outlast the apocalypse). And in the living room, there must be a good-size TV. It can't be humiliatingly small, but can't be too large either—I don't need to watch *The Bachelor* on IMAX. I just need to DVR *SNL* every week and be able to see the whites of the Bachelor's eyes. It's a one-bedroom on the top of a four-story walk-up, and the lobby and hallway are kind of gross and no one wants to visit me because there are a lot of stairs to climb to get here, but I don't care. It is MINE and it took me thirty-four years to get! For the last ten, I was always renting something, living with a new roommate, constantly moving around and storing stuff at my mom's place. It's exhausting to think about how many times I moved and how many landlords I paid more than 50 percent of my monthly income.

I never wanted to compromise and put down stakes in any other city. It always had to be New York for me. I know I can be a flake, but this is one goal from which I never deviated. Even if it meant I had to live in a shoe box, I never cared, as long as it was a New York shoe box. My first New York apartment was on Orchard and Hester on the Lower East Side of Manhattan. It was a studio that cost $800 a month—and it was *tiny*. A tiny apartment in New York is unlike any other in the country. I've gone and stayed with friends who worked as production assistants in Portland, Oregon, who'd describe their apartments as small, and then I would walk into a large one-bedroom with a balcony and think, *Fuck you. You have no idea*. Small in New York is small for real. Like you can reach over and flush your toilet while standing at your front door, which thankfully has nine locks. And you don't even have the spare real estate in the corner that is your kitchen to stock some box wine, because the container is literally too big for your fridge. I was twenty-two years old at the time and couldn't afford the rent on my own, so I put an ad on Craigslist for a roommate. Yes, a roommate—in a studio apartment. Hey, I said I wanted cozy, right? This was it. This is a reality that many New Yorkers have lived. The apartment was maybe about thirty feet by twenty feet, and it was filthy when I moved in. My mom and I scrubbed it clean and decorated it cute. I made the bed with my favorite sheets, and I was in heaven that it was mine.

I got a response to my Craigslist ad from a girl named Brittney who was from the South and coming to the city for art school. We spoke on the phone once and she moved in. I know this sounds like the setup to a shitty horror movie, but she was sweet and clean and we got along great. We never fought. We couldn't afford cable but we had a little TV, so we watched DVDs of *Sex and the City* and *Will & Grace*. Now that I think of it, it may have been the best time of my life.

After paying rent, I could barely afford to eat. Fortunately, we lived in Chinatown, where food can be very cheap. There was a dumpling factory right around the corner from us, and for five dollars you could get a huge bag of them—enough to eat for a week. I ate a record-breaking number of dumplings that year. No nutrition, but delicious. My face would swell and lips would blister from the salt. Because the only way to consume them is by drowning them in high-sodium soy sauce.

The price of real estate—or just the price of rent—in this city can really warp your judgment. Rent is so high and good places are so scarce that sometimes you talk yourself into very bad ideas. Case in point: When I moved back in with Dan after the blackout of 2003, I told myself that my instinct to make it work with an abusive ex had nothing to do with his nice two-bedroom apartment. But of course it did. Not that I wasn't enjoying folding my Murphy bed into the wall every night. It was a great way to kill the bugs in there and have space to lie on the floor and cry.

Dan was living with his friend Rob at the time, in Murray Hill. Both he and his roommate were children of privilege who could always rely on some rich relative to give them dough when the going got tough, but they had no jobs and no money of their own. The neighborhood was vile, home to young corporate America, shitty bars playing shitty classic rock, and shitty white kids drinking their parents' money away. I'd take the subway to work and sling rib eyes all day at the steakhouse in Grand Central Terminal while Dan would do God-knows-what. He tried his best to be reliably sane for a while, but he eventually started acting nuts again and was scaring me. Remember: this was the same boyfriend who pulled a knife on me. I knew it was dangerously stupid to continue living with him, but instead of moving out myself, I convinced him to move home with his mom. Which wasn't a tough sell because she happened to be a kind person with a dope-ass apartment. Right at the same time, Rob had been invited to travel around Europe with a cousin, but he didn't want to go and leave his girlfriend, Mary, behind. But Mary was sick of him and was eyeing the apartment, so she convinced him to go. After both boys left, Mary and I lived there alone. I remember the day Dan and Rob were both officially out of the house. Mary and I jumped on our beds like little girls to celebrate our healthy relationship decisions and getting them out of our lives. But mostly I think we were delighted at how funny it was that we'd evicted our boyfriends from their own apartment. The bottom line to this sad story is that I would have done anything to be able to live in the city I loved. And even though "anything" included making a regrettable choice with a dude, I still take it as a good sign that I was persistent enough to fight my way from one gross overpriced domicile to the next.

I was always pushing and struggling for the easiest setup and the cheapest rent. I once shared an apartment with a married couple in Brooklyn who needed a roommate to make rent. Or so they said. They'd give me lots of attention and make me feel really wanted, but I soon figured out it was because they didn't want to be alone together anymore. I see now that my presence was meant to distract them from their impending divorce. Some couples have a kid to try to save their marriage—these two had a twentysomething waiter/stand-up/actress who ate more than her fair share of pantry items she didn't purchase. Their tactic didn't work and they eventually split up, but they helped me get by for a while—so shout-out to that couple who prevented me from having to move back in with my mom or eject myself to the suburbs.

I'd also like to give a shout-out to the single-lady roommate who'd descend the stairs completely naked from the waist down, sometimes to get attention from my boyfriend. Here's to the old guy who was still living in my new apartment on the day I moved in. My roommate and I had to pack all of his clothing and box up his huge collection of vintage nudie magazines. One of them featured a girl wearing a varsity sweater, and she looked so much like me. The magazine was called *Babyface*. I was flattered there was a market for girls like me, who resemble that eighties doll Kid Sister or one of the Garbage Pail Kids. Oh, and one more very special shout-out goes to the roommate who invited exactly one-third of Manhattan to our place for a Halloween party, which ended when I found an aggressive dude ass-fucking a woman in a cowgirl costume in my unlocked bathroom.

All in all, the common thread in my sad string of NYC apartments is that I put up with a lot of vermin and weirdness and "coziness" so I could be where I wanted to be. I believe you should fight for what you want. I'm proud of almost every housing decision I made in the sense that they kept me in the city where I needed to be. I wouldn't have made it this far as a comedian or human if I hadn't stayed here.

I guess I only strayed from this pattern when I

would get distracted by a guy and moving became a dating tactic—a not very sly but surprisingly effective dating tactic. Besides the aforementioned time I moved back in with Dan, I set up a real nice home life with my boyfriend Rick when I was twenty-five. He wasn't at all ready for us to live together but that didn't stop me from pressuring him to let me move in with him. I've lived with four boyfriends in my life and I've tricked each of them into it. It always ended poorly. I don't think I even wanted to live with Rick, but I wanted him to want to live with me. Being a woman is so fun!

Anyway, Rick and I lived together in Brooklyn in a small but not completely horrible one-bedroom apartment. We'd work hard all day at our respective restaurant and office temp jobs, and then I'd do a stand-up show at night, which I was just starting at the time. Around ten p.m. one of us would make dinner, then we'd watch a movie we'd gotten in the mail from Netflix. We'd drink wine, smoke pot, and eat ice cream. The fridge was big enough to house all of these things! It was heaven. What more is there to life than being stoned and full and having sex, unless of course you're too full? Anyway, after living together for a while, Rick and I were in love and really excited about each other. We would make each other laugh and gaze into each other's eyes—and it felt like life was going to be all right. But I was with him during a big turning point in my life—when I got the full-blown comedy disease (which I told you about in

"How to Become a Stand-up Comedian"). I had it bad, and the only cure was to get on the road and do more comedy. I couldn't imagine putting anything else first in my life. Not even a guy I loved. I was also learning that I was an introvert (one of the first things I told you about myself in this book) who worked best when she had large spans of time to herself. So even though the fake-married life was nice for a while, I realized it wasn't for me. At least not in that moment in time. After we broke up (when I was on *Last Comic Standing*), I basically lived on the road for a while.

You'd think I would have learned my lesson about living with a guy, but not too long after, I became infatuated with this hot dude from my acting class, Devin, and eventually ended up moving to Astoria just to trap him into dating me. Which worked. But the joke was on me. Not only did I move into the worst part of Queens, but I also got bedbugs, the 9/11 of bugs, which provide both a logistical and existential nightmare when they come into your life. They are nearly impossible to get rid of—so I had to subject my poor elderly stuffed animals to a scary ride in a high-heat dryer. And everyone I knew was quietly reevaluating their friendship with me. This is not an exaggeration and it's another classic New York story—some people will straight-up take you out of their phone when they learn you have been hit with this plague. But bedbugs aside, there are many beautiful places in Astoria—just not where I lived!

I went to the grossest carpeted gym of all time there. It was billed as being "just for women"— which almost always is code for "subpar." The whole thing was built on a slant, so when you'd run on the treadmill, one leg would take all the weight. There were a lot of Muslim women in the neighborhood, and they would be on the ellipticals in their burkas while their husbands sat in the lobby area, waiting for them to finish their workouts, staring at the rest of us while they waited. I've been more comfortable getting a pelvic exam from a gynecologist with Parkinson's. *Amy, that is unsympathetic to people with that horrible disease and now we are mad and writing about it on message boards.* Okay, you're right, I'm sorry. But relax: my first-ever gyno actually had Parkinson's and it was awful. He was a million years old, and I found out that he'd died when I went in for one of my annual checkups. The new guy told me the news while his fingers were inside me and my ovaries were being squished. The previous sentence is also the title of my next book.

In defense of the Rick and Devin situations, I think there is a lot to be said for just picking up your things and moving to the neighborhood of the guy you like. When you're a child, you're friends with people based on proximity—and I've found it's the same for men. That's why so many of them sleep with their nannies, because THEY'RE THERE! And besides, I'm still great friends with both of these guys. They're both amazing actors, and Devin Dane (hahaha, his real name is Kevin Kane) has become my working partner in everything I do.

I feel like I could write a whole book on all the gross, weird places I've lived and all the bizarre or wonderful roommates I've had. Each place was just a temporary stop on the road to getting me where I wanted to be. I never quit moving and I didn't bother getting too comfortable because I wanted to be ready for whatever came next.

Now that I finally own a place, maybe I will stay for a while. I have everything I need. I even live near a small body of water, where I like to do my preferred form of exercise—a long geriatric walk while nibbling on a scone. And, guys, I got a wine refrigerator for my kitchen! (Is that not relatable? Have I sold out from my days of drinking single-serving box wine with a straw? No, because I still drink those too. It's just that I recently learned that I drink my chardonnay too cold, and I didn't even know that was possible, but now I am dedicating my life to correcting that error!) Anyway, as long as I'm in this city, not too far from my second home (the Comedy Cellar), I'm happy.

I suspect I will never stop moving. Literally. I might live in a few (hundred) more apartments, but they will always be on the same island of Manhattan and I will continue to circle this same pond over and over again, until I am an elderly woman. I know there are probably bigger, better bodies of water in LA, but I'm pretty sure it's illegal to transport a baked good from one location to another there. Can you imagine walking into a Beverly Hills SoulCycle with a fistful of quiche? I have to do that sometime. But even if they were cool with it, LA would never feel like home to me.

BLACKOUTS AND STEM CELLS

I pay my taxes. I vote—for my favorite reality show contestants, but also in elections. I call my friends on their birthdays. I use a bath towel no longer than a week before washing it. I drink the recommended amount of water daily. And I can hold my liquor. All of this makes me a grown-up. Actually, as I write this, my twenty-four-year-old assistant just brought me a snack of crackers and hummus, so maybe I still have some work to do.

But when I was in college, I was a far cry from adulthood. I did none of the things listed above. By junior year of college this is how I drank: I'd have two beers in my dorm room, then go to the bar, where I'd enjoy about four martinis. Four *real* martinis—I'm talking Ketel One up and dirty, and I would always go back to the bartender and complain that they'd made it too dirty so I could get more vodka added for free. Everyone else ordered normal college stuff, like vodka cranberries or Jack and Cokes, but it was always beer and martinis for me. And then sometimes I'd end the night with some wine or champagne, even though I had nothing to celebrate.

As it turns out, I also won the genetic lottery and am one of those chicks who is prone to blackouts. For those of you who haven't been to high school or college parties, blacking out is when your mind goes to sleep but your body keeps right on doing whatever your drunk-ass self thinks is a good idea. Blacking out is NOT passing out asleep in a drunken stupor. It's quite the opposite. Your brain is sleeping like an innocent little baby, but your body is at a rave and it keeps making decisions. Decisions such as, *Let's eat something called a "walking taco" from a place in Chicago where you eat a taco mixed in a Fritos bag and jam handfuls of it in your mouth.* This is why blacking out is incredibly dangerous. You might look like a regular drunk girl, but you're actually a zombie who won't remember shit later. A really thrilling part of blacking out is the fact that sometimes you wake up while you're *still doing* whatever horrible thing you chose to do when you fell into it. You suddenly reemerge in your body like a time traveler and have no idea how long you've been out.

My most memorable (technically my *least* memorable) college blackout happened this way: My brain was completely checked out and then all of a sudden I was back in my body and aware of everything. I looked southward and there was a stranger

going down on me in my bed. Huh? What? Hello?!!
I'll say that again. Someone I had never in my life
met or seen before was tonguing my vagina like he
was digging for gold. I had a boyfriend at the time
and this was not him. I didn't know this dude, but
he was obviously getting to know me. I lightly
tapped him on the shoulder because I didn't want
to startle him, and also because what do I know
about this guy at this point? Obviously, I know
he's a true gentleman—he's going down on me,
and that is a move worthy of knighthood. On my
vagina's very best day—when I know I may have a
visitor soon so I've just showered and really tended
to it with care—it still smells like a small barnyard
animal. A freshly washed goat or something of that
size and potency. A cute one that you'd want to buy
little pellets for and feed at a zoo. That's on its best
day. On its worst day? After a night of drinking?
It's probably like an unwashed shark tank. I imagine going down on me after a night on the town
must be like Indiana Jones entering some sort of
a cobwebbed room where he'll need to choose a
cup wisely.

This saintlike man looked up at me after I
tapped him. He was hot, so I patted myself on
the back and thought, *Nice job, Schumes*. He
looked up but stayed down there, and for a minute it looked like I was giving birth to him. I
said, "Hi, I'm Amy, I don't believe we've had
the pleasure." He was very confused. As gently
as I could, I explained what had happened. He

left prrrrrretty quick. I stormed into my roommate Denise's room and asked, "Why did you let
me bring some random guy home? You know I
have a boyfriend!" She was in shock and immediately defended herself. Apparently I hadn't even
seemed very drunk and had walked around the
bar with this guy all night, our arms around each
other like we were a couple. Denise assumed I
had consciously made the choice to be with this
guy and ditch my boyfriend. I literally didn't
remember meeting him. I saw him a few years
later in a bar and apologized profusely. He
seemed a bit unnerved but tried to pretend like
he didn't mind. Knowing what he'd encountered
between my legs that night, I'm guessing he was
probably thrilled to have received such an easy
get-out-of-jail-free card from me. He probably
shuddered at the sight of me and started having
sudden memory flashes of deep-sea fishing and
an old sunken ship covered in plankton and kelp.
I'm not ashamed of this, either. Vaginas are supposed to look and smell like vaginas. Keep your
strange scented washes away from me, women's
magazines. I'll allow my vag to keep its natural
aroma of chicken noodle soup, thank you very
much.

There were other notable blackouts during college, like the time I ate an entire Papa John's pizza,
or when I ditched a cab and skinned my hands
running from it. I also once went home with some
dude who owned more than two pit bulls, which

is the reddest flag there is, and my sister still loves to remind me about the time I put her in a car with strangers so I could stay out longer. My blackouts have usually involved eating like it's my last meal, but the time my brain went night-night while I let a stranger wake up my unwashed vagina definitely still gets the top prize. I want to encourage any young lady reading this to avoid drinking to the point where you're unsafe, especially if you have this cool genetic quirk and are prone to blacking out. It's crazy unsafe, and I lucked out with a nice dude who treated my vaginal area like a Golden Corral.

But let's get back to the part about how I'm a seasoned, smart adult now. I drink wine and scotch fairly regularly—sometimes a martini or tequila, just to mix it up—but not excessively, and I definitely don't drink to the point of blackout. Not only did College Amy teach me a lesson, I truly don't enjoy being drunk anymore. I'm not recommending dead sobriety here. I mean, don't be cray. But I don't like to get anything more than a little tipsy now. I'm in a really good place and have gotten my behavior under major control.

Guys, I blacked out a few months ago.

I'm not proud of this. I don't think it's cute or even funny. But sometimes when a sad and complicated set of circumstances lands you in the emotional and physical gutter, all you can do is laugh. After you cry. And drink.

It all started when a woman named Meg went to

see *Trainwreck* with her friend. Meg has multiple sclerosis and didn't know MS would be such a large part of the movie but ended up really liking the fact that it was included in the story. She reached out to me because she said she wanted to hook my dad up with an incredible doctor in New York who had helped her.

Dr. Sadiq is the only doctor in the US who is FDA approved to treat MS patients with stem cells. To me, the idea that my dad could feel better wasn't even in the realm of possibility. I was grateful to Meg and excited for my dad to meet Dr. Sadiq, but I also didn't want to get my hopes up too high. Over the years, I'd noticed a change in my dad's willingness to take his meds and follow doctors' recommendations. He's offered physical therapy several times a week in the facility where he lives, but he was going infrequently or sometimes not at all. I sent an acupuncturist to him for a few months, and without telling me, he told her to stop coming. One day a couple of years ago, we got into an argument about it, which ended with his shouting that he just didn't want to try anymore.

This crushed me. Realizing that he'd thrown in the towel and wanted to passively allow the disease to do what it would broke my heart. People with MS deal with a lot: difficulty with eating, walking, and controlling their bowels (as has been well documented in this book)—not to mention the toll it takes on cognitive abilities and emotional stability.

My dad was never the kind of guy to have a hopeful outlook on life. He was always dark. Even in his heyday, when he was young, rich, and handsome, he could make Tim Burton seem like Richard Simmons. But this was different. He was telling me to back off and let him decay. I don't blame my dad for wanting to give up, but it still destroyed me to hear him say it.

Since then, I've been mourning my dad while he's still alive. One certainty of his MS is that his physical abilities will decline more and more until they're entirely gone. This has led us to experience a lot of "lasts" together. The most heartbreaking one was the last time we went bodysurfing. We'd always loved riding the ocean waves together, so when it became clear that he wasn't going to be able to walk much longer, he asked me to go to the beach with him one last time. It was a pretty cloudy day, and there was a chill in the air. There were only one or two other people on the beach. I put on a brave face as we walked into the ocean. The waves were rough enough that you had to use your leg strength to make it in past the break. He struggled. It was crushing me to see him getting knocked down. I led us in and turned my face out to the ocean horizon so my dad wouldn't notice my heart falling out of my chest and into the sea. Seeing your parent physically incapable like that is something I wish on no one.

We waited for a good wave. The last wave we would ever ride together. When we saw it rolling in, we made eye contact and nodded to each other like musicians agreeing to play the bridge. We bent our knees, leaned toward the shore with our arms over our heads, and dove. It was a long, hard wave, and we rode it all the way in. We could feel the power of the ocean carrying us. When we stopped, I picked up my head to see where my father was. He was right next to me, squinting through the salt water and wiping the hair out of his eyes. He looked over at me and we smiled big at each other, bugging our eyes out to keep each other from bawling. I took his hand and helped him walk back until the wet sand turned dry. We caught our breath and tried not to take in the gravity of the moment.

I never wanted to give up hope that we could someday go out there again. But none of the MS studies I'd ever read made this seem possible, so I decided that instead of trying to heal him, I'd do whatever I could to make his time on this earth as pleasurable and comfortable as possible. If he asked me to bring him five hundred Werther's Original hard candies to suck on incessantly, I would. If he wanted booze (even though he never asked me), I'd get it for him. If he asked me for pot cookies (which he did), I'd bring them. I'd do anything for my dad. Buy him a lap dance, a lapdog, whatever it took.

So when I received Meg's email about Dr. Sadiq, I thought about the promise I'd made to my dad to let him be, and I thought, *FUCK HIM! He's going to see this doctor!* I didn't care if he had to be brought in on a stretcher kicking and screaming. Well, he can't kick, so just screaming.

I didn't even ask him. I just told him he was going to see this special doctor, and made it sound exciting and magical and as if it were something to look forward to. And he bit.

The next day, he traveled the two hours from Long Island to meet Kim and me at Dr. Sadiq's office in Manhattan. It's always a gamble what version of my father I will get. The medication can often make him out of it and kind of mean, but when he got off the elevator at the doctor's office that day he was smiling and didn't say anything hostile to the staff. My dad can be a huge wiseass who lashes out in a funny way at people, but sometimes it's altogether unfunny and just unkind. I've seen him scream at very gentle, nice orderlies who are just trying to help him back into his chair. He is rude to nurses—dismissive and cold if they're lucky, and flirty and aggressive if they aren't. But that day, he didn't make inappropriate eye or ass contact with the nursing staff. At one point when the nurse asked who was older, Kim or me, he answered, "The big one," as he pointed at me. But other than that fun insult, things were looking up.

My dad and I held hands as Dr. Sadiq explained what the stem cell treatments would entail over the

next six months. Less than halfway through the
conversation, my dad interrupted Dr. Sadiq, who
was midsentence.

"I have to pee."

His attendant wheeled him to the bathroom,
where he stayed for a very long time. Longer than
normal by five times. The doctor continued while
my dad was in the restroom, explaining that the
stem cell treatment could at the very least improve
him significantly, even potentially making it possible for him to walk again. This was amazing news,
of course, but Kim and I must have seemed like we
weren't sold, because Dr. Sadiq started offering up
references who could testify to the quality of his
treatments.

"No, doctor, we aren't worried about you," I
said. I came right out and admitted that I was afraid
my dad would either completely resist the treatment or become so difficult that the doctor would
eventually refuse to treat him. Dr. Sadiq—a man so
determined and dedicated to his work that he often
sleeps in his office—jokingly explained, "Oh, no, I
am treating him whether he likes it or not. He can
punch me in the face and call me names, and I will
not let him get out of this." And then the doctor, in
his matter-of-fact way, said something that should
have been obvious to me.

"Your father doesn't want to get his hopes up."

A pang shot through my entire body. Of course.
Why didn't I see this myself? It's a huge theme in
my own life and even in my movie. *Trainwreck* is in

many ways a love letter to my father. It's my way of saying, *Even though you have wronged people and made mistakes, I love you, and your life hasn't gone unwitnessed*. I wanted him to see himself as I see him, as a human who is sick and flawed but who I think is pretty wonderful, most of the time. I guess the need to protect yourself to the point of being an asshole runs in the family. My dad and I have both been burned so many times that we use humor and darkness to keep potential pain at bay. I'd been giving my dad such a hard time for his unwillingness to fight his MS, but he was being resistant for good reason. He'd already been beaten to the ground countless times. Literally.

Kim and I teared up a little and nodded as our dad was rolled back into the room. I squeezed his hand and could tell his mood had soured a little.

I held my breath and could not bear to look at my dad. Dr. Sadiq explained every detail of the next six months of his life, and while he didn't make it sound easy, he did focus on the results.

Throughout the discussion, my dad kept looking at the floor and Dr. Sadiq would gently reprimand him, "Look at me, Gordon." When he finished his explanation, my dad was looking down again. There was a long silence. We all sat there very still.

And then my father looked up and said: "Okay, I will put my hope and faith in you."

Kim and I couldn't fucking believe it. Never had I ever heard my dad say the words "hope"

or "faith." I think my dad could be at the Wailing
Wall or sitting with the Dalai Lama on a mountain
in Tibet and he'd be annoyed that someone next to
him was humming too loudly or complaining that
he was hungry. What I'm saying is he's not a spiri-
tual guy.

I threw my arms around him and then sat back
down before the tears started falling uncontrollably down my face. I leaned over and said, "I'm so
proud of you! I love you!" It wasn't just that he'd
accepted treatment. It was that he still had some
hope left in there.

We set up our next appointment with Dr. Sadiq
and said our good-byes, and went home to spend
the evening with my very kind boyfriend, Ben. I
was feeling emotional, but I held it together. We
got cozy in the living room and I exclaimed, "I had
a tough day. I want to have some wine tonight!" I
opened a bottle and had a glass. We started watching the latest episode of *Girls*, and it was coincidentally about Hannah's father, who was struggling
with living his life as a gay man, having just come
out of the closet to Hannah. The parent/child roles
were reversed, with Hannah coming to his rescue
when her father was sad and disoriented. The
episode ended with their walking through Times
Square together, him sadly saying, "I don't know
what to do," and Hannah saying, "That's okay, I'm
here . . . and I'll always be here."

Any tears I'd held back in my entire life came
out right then and there. The floodgates opened

and I bawled hard. Thank God I'm a very very pretty crier. Ben was sweet and watched a lot of mucus drain from my nose onto the couch, and hugged me after I finally caught my breath. When I was done crying, I drank another glass of wine and took a hit of weed. I wanted the day to end because it was hard enough having all of those realizations about my dad, but it was also new to have a boyfriend with me, witnessing the whole thing. Being the child of an alcoholic father and *whatever my mom is* has made me almost incapable of believing that the people I love won't leave me or hurt me in a way I didn't think they were capable of. I have to fight against all of my impulses and warped instincts to accept any sort of love. This night was no exception.

It was time to call it a day. And fast. So I took five milligrams of Ambien, which is on the higher end of the normal nightly dosage for me, and I started to get ready for bed. My limbs were a little sore from the eleven-mile bike ride Ben and I had gone on that morning. (Ew, we're an annoying white couple.) I was physically and mentally drained—and a little drunk. Throwing Ambien into the mix was not wise, since, as I learned the hard way, it enhances the effects of alcohol and vice fucking versa. If the details of what happened next were left to me, I'd tell you that I had one more glass of wine and then woke up the next morning.

But according to my loving, patient boyfriend (who was staring forlornly at the ceiling when I opened my eyes the next morning), a LOT happened after that last glass of wine.

According to Ben, shortly after I prayed to the holy trinity of Ambien, wine, and weed, I began dipping crackers into butter as if it were guacamole. While he watched me in this feeding frenzy, I kept accusing him of judging me. He said I was chasing him around the living room saying, "You're judging me!" with a lot of sass and he was responding with "You're getting butter all over the apartment!"

Then I sat down on the couch to watch television and continue eating my buttermole. I turned on *Keeping Up with the Kardashians* (his least-favorite show) and wouldn't shut up about Khloé and how much she's changed. At least that's what Ben thinks I said, because he could only understand about 30 percent of my yammering. I ended up heating up two frozen pizzas, one of which I burned, before he finally convinced me to go to sleep. In bed, I aggressively stacked all the pillows on my side instead of the usual division of two and two. Then I laid my head on top like the princess and the pea. He said, "Amy, we each get two pillows," to which I elegantly responded, "Not tonight, motherfucker!" Cue the Stevie Wonder song "Isn't She Lovely."

Anyway, the lesson here is don't combine alcohol, Ambien, and weed on the same day that you take a marathon bike ride, find out your dad's will to live has been restored, and watch a heartbreaking episode of *Girls* that hits way too close to home. If you learn one thing from this book, let it be that.

This blackout at age thirty-four was a far cry from some of the dangerous situations I got myself into during college, but I still wouldn't recommend that anyone engage in this kind of activity—not even grown-ups who are in loving, supportive relationships and safely drinking under their own roofs. Ben was pretty generous about the whole thing. He wasn't judgmental or critical, but he was concerned. He didn't like that I decided to "check out" on him. With good reason. It's not fair, and I haven't done it since.

It was a hard couple of years, seeing my dad check out on life like that, knowing that he really meant it when he said he was done trying to improve his condition. A part of me gets it. Things are grim for him most of the time. I'm strong and healthy, and I still have to fight the urge to give up about twice a day. Three times a day during awards-show season. In his younger, healthier days, my dad traveled, partied, philandered, and drank. I know he must miss those times. I feel fortunate I'm still able-bodied enough to make poor choices.

Sometimes when I visit him and he's looking particularly dead-eyed or sad, I try to amp up his spirits. Roll him outside for a walk, get him involved, force him to mix it up. He's still in there when he wants to be—and it's nice to see. Knowing there's a possibility he will walk again has made everything brighter, and it feels like he's coming back. I push his wheelchair into the fresh air, and make him look up at the sky. I watch the sun hit his face and he comes alive, every cell of his body lighting up to cause trouble, just like he was meant to do.

AN EXCITING TIME
FOR WOMEN IN HOLLYWOOD

Imagine you just wrote and starred in your own movie for the first time. The movie premieres, it does well, and you feel like you're on top of the world. And you are exhausted because making a movie is a lot of work, and also because you had to lose (and keep off) ten pounds you usually like carrying around with you. (Because no woman is believably lovable unless you can see her clavicles from all angles.) Then, before you're even done celebrating the premiere of your movie, which you poured your guts into, it's explained to you that actors aren't really paid to act. What they're paid for is to do press.

What a gross discovery.

I get it. Movies are really expensive to produce so the studios have to make sure people actually go see them. I apologize if you saw way too much of my face in ads and billboards and commercials in the summer of 2015. If this is how you're feeling, you can thank the marketing people. And trust me, no one was sicker of hearing my voice than I was.

I'd never starred in a movie before *Trainwreck*, so I was virtually unknown in other countries. This meant I had to sign up for an intense international press tour to promote the movie. Press tours consist of visits to multiple cities where you sit in rooms with journalists (usually while on camera) who ask you to talk about your movie so they can go away and write hopefully positive stuff so people will go see your movie. On that press tour, I was interviewed by what felt like every journalist in the world—from the most well-known news stations to dudes who were taping the first episode of their podcast. I had to say yes to everything, because the studio was taking a chance on me. I was a new employee, and that is when you have to act excited for the opportunity and be a good little worker bee.

When you first hear that you're going to Australia, Germany, London, Amsterdam, Dublin, and on and on, you think, *FUCK YEAH! Free trip! I've never been to Berlin!* And then you realize that you will spend every second of every day being asked the same questions by every single interviewer, and you will be expected to perform the answers for them as if they are freshly coming out of your mouth for the first time, every single time. Without fail, every last one of them asked, "How autobiographical is your movie?" I started to feel like a soulless show pony. Talking about yourself all day long like that leaves you with a kind of emptiness that's hard to describe. And it's a lot to take on for someone like me who is so unfortunately prone to honesty.

On top of feeling like it was up to me to convince people to buy tickets, there was the added burden of being a woman. Because every time there is a female lead in a movie, everyone bugs out and says, "Will this be a turning point for women?" or "What does this MEAN for women in comedy?"

So the pressure is on. Because the movie doesn't just have to do well so that I can feel proud of it or so the studio can make money—it has to do well for the 50 percent of the population I am now apparently representing. *What will this mean for our gender for years to come!??* That line of questioning is pretty loaded. Especially since this was my first movie, and I don't even pretend to speak for all women. I write about my life and how I see and experience the world, without assuming that my views are universal.

So anyway, I went on a huge press tour, not just for the movie but for all of female-kind. And just like everywhere else, since the dawn of man, every interviewer's favorite question was, "Is this an exciting time for women in entertainment?" or "What does this mean for women in Hollywood?"

"Isn't this an exciting time?!"

And I wanted to scream, "NO!"

First of all, I don't consider myself a "woman in Hollywood." I'm not even totally sure what that term means. But if I were to play free association with myself and I heard that term, I guess I would think of someone who either has her own abbreviated celeb name, like J. Law/Lo, or someone who has looked very hot in a few movies who also, I don't know . . . has her own lifestyle blog or her own product line? Like an Alba or a Paltrow. I have none of those things. "A. Schu" never really caught on like we were all hoping it would.

Also I am literally not a "woman in Hollywood." As you know, I have always lived in New York, and no, it doesn't feel like an exciting time. The exciting time will come when nobody has to answer that stupid question. Everyone, on the count of three: Stop asking that. Forever. Just stop. One. Two. Three! And besides, Hollywood is not at all exciting for women. I'm sure no one is too shocked to hear that it's an industry of people who judge most women almost solely on their appearance, and where every day women feel themselves barreling toward death and decay while smaller, hotter actresses like Selena keep appearing like Russian nesting dolls. It's an industry where you go from playing a lead love interest to a turtleneck-and-knit-vest-sporting grandmother who, despite missing her husband, still has a lot of love to give to pets, in half the time a leading man turns into a grandpa.

I'm of the belief that in most industries, women have to work twice as hard to get half the credit. After putting in so much effort to make a good movie, it felt pretty demeaning when they called it a "female comedy." This meaningless label painted me into a corner and forced me to speak for all females, because I am the actual FEMALE who wrote the FEMALE comedy and then starred as the lead FEMALE in that FEMALE comedy. They don't ask Seth Rogen to be ALL MEN! They don't make "men's comedies." They don't ask Ben Stiller, "Hey, Ben, what was your message for all male-kind when you pretended to have diarrhea and chased that ferret in *Along Came Polly*?"

On the press tour, many interviewers actually acknowledged this issue and came right out and asked, "Is there a lot of pressure on you to speak for all women?" I appreciated that they got right to it. Maybe it's a good question. I understand that I have enough eyes and ears on me that what I say and do matters. This is a responsibility that I'm honored to have—because it's an opportunity to do my best to help empower women in the only way I know how: by writing a story about a woman from the woman's point of view.

Trainwreck was about equal opportunity. Equal opportunity to be a commitment-phobe—even if you're a girl. But some of the interviewers were thrown off by this. Many of them asked me why I chose to write a role reversal for the guy and the girl. Meaning, why did I make the girl the one who had trouble being vulnerable and the guy the one who wanted more of a commitment? Why was the girl the one who had a bachelor pad and a string of one-night stands, and the guy was the one with a highly respected career and a sober lifestyle? Interviewers were always shocked when I explained that I hadn't done this intentionally, but that I wrote something true to my experience. Women get a reputation for being the crazy, overly sensitive ones in relationships, but in my experience, it's the dudes who do that. Not that I and most of my friends aren't sensitive flowers. We just don't invest as much or as quickly in relationships, and we don't get our egos as involved. I'll admit to exaggerating LeBron James's character. We made him overly concerned about his friend's love life, the way girls are often characterized—and this is something I haven't actually witnessed from my male friends. But that is where the gender role reversal begins and ends in *Trainwreck*. I was writing what felt honest, real, and compelling, coming from my perspective and my real life. And even though I'm not gonna cop to representing all women, I'm also pretty sure I'm not the only chick with these experiences.

Nonetheless, the slut-shaming was off the charts. Maybe it was just a cultural thing that made the foreign journalists seem out of line. Some interviewers brought this vibe: *Well, you talk about sexual subject matter in your movie, so I can say anything I want to you.* Which made me want to shower for the rest of my life. One of the interviews I did in Australia went viral when the journalist asked me the question "So your character is a skank, do you have a word for skank in America?" I told him that it was a rude question and we went back and forth a little bit, and of course, if you do anything other than just smile and nod and thank them for their time, if you actually have an unfavorable or emotional response to a rude question, the shit hits the fan. People react as if you obviously can't take the heat and need to get out of the kitchen. But I've never been a smile-and-nod type of girl, nor have I ever been one to get out of the kitchen.

The worst experience was in Berlin—surprise, surprise—when I sat with the same interviewer twice. He was a man in his late fifties or early sixties, wearing jeans and a button-down. He was balding up top and was letting it grow a little long in the back, half pageboy, half Robert Plant. He wore glasses and didn't let social norms pressure him into smiling, ever. I first sat with him and Bill Hader. He asked Bill if he liked playing a doctor, and then he asked me what I was like to have sex with. Bill didn't like this question and stood up for me, but I said it was fine and explained that it was like being with one of those performers who stand on boxes on street corners spray-painted entirely silver. You can't tell if they're statues or not but every couple minutes they move slightly. The only difference, I said, is that no one ever gave me a dollar. (I need to amend this at this time and say that since then, my boyfriend did, very generously, slip a dollar under my door once after sex. I sat on the toilet and watched it make its way into the bathroom as I waited until my body agreed to pee so I wouldn't get a UTI. I stared at that dollar feeling loved.)

That same Berlin interviewer was, for some reason, allowed to come back later and interview me again, this time with Vanessa Bayer, who plays my friend and coworker in *Trainwreck*. He was immediately abrasive and started asking me things that seemed to express not only his dislike for the movie but also for every breath I had ever taken. He said these exact words: "Why do you think it's okay to make people uncomfortable?" As he said this I caught sight of a large hole in the crotch of his pants and realized that not one but both of his testicles were exposed. I looked him in the eye and said, "I don't want to embarrass you, but I would like you to cover your lap." Vanessa looked down and saw and nodded while her face turned bright red. She concurred that his balls were like the answer, my friend, blowin' in the wind. He looked down, crossed his legs, regained his composure, and said, "Where was I?" I said, "You were asking me why I thought it was okay to make people uncomfortable."

After the three hundredth interview talking about how many people I'd slept with and then awkwardly transitioning to my dad's illness, I thought, *Fuck this, I'm never doing a movie again.* Just kidding! I am going to make more movies. But I'll never do that much press again. And I'll never lose weight again. Well, not that much anyway. I look stupid skinny. My large, Cabbage Patch head stays the same size and the rest of me shrinks to a different proportion. And what's the reward? To be a "woman in Hollywood"? No thank you!

Then again, maybe what it means to be a

"woman in Hollywood" is to be one of the many angry, bemused, and ravenous women who just wanted to be actors or artists, and who were made to believe this option would actually be available to them after they jumped through five thousand hoops in high school and college and in the gross offices of agents and managers and the quiet church basements where they performed one-act plays and musicals within an inch of their lives. Maybe a "woman in Hollywood" is just a person who was going about her business and trying to live her dreams—the same as all her male counterparts—but along the way she got held up, hungry and exhausted, by fending off insane double standards and stupid-ass questions from journalists.

If that's a "woman in Hollywood," then fine, maybe I am one. Guilty as charged.

But even though the foreign press couldn't be more wrong about the "exciting time" all us women in Hollywood are having, not all journalists misunderstood me and my movie. I was so grateful I got nominated for a Golden Globe, which is determined by the Hollywood Foreign Press Association. The night of the Golden Globes was a dream. My whole family came with me, and even though I didn't win, I was lucky enough to lose to a friend whose work blows my mind. Some of the journalists from the Hollywood Foreign Press Association who were there that night were amazing. I spoke with many of them and left the interviews feeling nourished, grateful, and understood. Maybe I wasn't just a trainwreck of a girl after all! I started to feel better and comforted myself by trying to see myself through their eyes, remembering some of the kind things they'd said to me. But I was promptly brought right back down to earth when I saw how *Trainwreck* had been renamed in some of the foreign markets:

Italy: *A Disaster Girl*
Bulgaria: *Total Damage*
Czech Republic: *Derailment*
Russia: *A Girl Without Complexes*
Germany: *Dating Queen*
Finland: *Just the Night*
Portugal and Poland: *Derailed*
Hungary: *Disaster*
France: *Crazy Amy*
French Canada: *Hopeless Case*
Argentina: *This Girl Is a Mess*

So since I didn't win the Globe that night and get to stand at the podium to make a speech, I want to take this opportunity to thank all the journalists in all the different countries I visited. First, I'd like to thank all the people who pointed out that I was a woman. Your compliments were phrased very precisely so that I was never just described as "funny," but rather, a "funny *woman*." You made sure I didn't lose sight of my ovaries. Thank you. Without your constant reminders, I may have just forgotten my uterus on a crosstown bus, but you guys made me perpetually aware that I bleed once a month *and* I can tell a joke! I also want to thank the guy who called me a skank. I could see how unhappy you were in your own life, and I deeply felt for you. If you're out there, I want you to know that I am very happy and experiencing a good time in my life. And lastly I want to especially thank the balls of that journalist in Berlin. If it weren't for you guys I would probably be able to sleep at night, and who the hell wants that. *Auf Wiedersehen.*

MAYCI AND JILLIAN

It was July 23, 2015, and *Trainwreck* had been out for about a week. I was so happy to be home, having just landed in Los Angeles after spending the aforementioned week doing very tiring press for the movie, this time in Australia. It was especially sweet to be home since that trip had not been too uplifting. I was supposed to go out to dinner with my friend Allan that night. He's one of my very good friends, though I don't know if his name is spelled Alan or Allan. I also have major questions about how to spell his last name.

I was jet-lagged and having some hard-core back pain from all the travel, so I booked a massage. I walked out of the hotel spa feeling great—generally excited about life, fortunate, and rejuvenated. I looked at my cell phone and had a lot of missed calls from my publicist, Carrie, who'd also sent me many texts telling me to call her right away. I started giggling. If she was trying to contact me that urgently, I was certain that a naked photo or a sex tape of me must have gotten out. I had sex with my boyfriend on a computer camera once when I was twenty and it was totally awful. We were in no way focused on each other. We were looking at ourselves on the monitor. I'd bought black lacy lingerie with a garter belt. I didn't understand that you have to be a Victoria's Secret model to not look insane in a getup like that. A still of Rupert Murdoch in a rocking chair would have looked sexier than I did in that outfit. All in all, it was a horrible sight and I apologize in advance for that sex tape in case it ever does get out. I have major, major sympathy for anyone whose phone or computer has ever been hacked, and I really hope it never happens to me. But nude photos don't scare me. I'm sure they will leak someday, and I don't know how I'll feel then—but on this particular day at this particular moment in my life, I think I'd laugh if it happened. And apologize to all who had to see the footage or shots.

So on July 23, 2015, I was preparing myself for news of my sex tape leaking and was gearing up to calm down my publicist and let her know I didn't care. I dialed Carrie and I was already smiling. My giggling had become a full laugh by the time she answered.

Then she said, "There was a shooting in a theater in Lafayette, Louisiana, at a showing of *Trainwreck*."

My heart broke right then and there. I mean it. The only other times I felt sadness that heavy in my

life were after a surfing accident when I was sure I
was losing my leg, and upon hearing of the deaths
of a couple of close friends. The news crushed me.
I went to my hotel room, turned on CNN, and
became almost catatonic. I didn't yet know that
two beautiful, smart, strong women would die that
night. I didn't know about Mayci Breaux, who was
just twenty-one years old and a sweet, kind, gorgeous churchgoing girl who was set to marry her
high school sweetheart. And I didn't know about
Jillian Johnson. She was just thirty-three years old
and an active member in her community. A great
wife and stepmother, she was a smart and creative
business owner, a musician, and a beautiful artist.
I needed to know every detail, and I wanted to fly
straight to Louisiana to be with the families who
were affected by this tragedy.

My friend Allen came over to my hotel room
and let me put my head on his lap while I cried. He
called the necessary people and took care of me. I
was pretty out of it for a couple weeks. I had more
press to do for *Trainwreck* and a vacation planned
with friends, but I wanted to cancel everything.

I read about the disturbed man who killed Mayci
and Jillian and injured nine other people. I don't
believe in giving mass shooters their moment in
the sun. I don't want to write his name. I never
have and never will say it. But I do want to out-
line some facts about him. He loved the Tea Party.
He publicly hated women and praised Hitler. This

man purposefully selected my movie as a place to shoot and kill women.

Here are a few other facts: In 2006, he was arrested for arson (and was denied a concealed weapons permit in Russell County, Alabama, as a result), though the arson charges were eventually dropped. In 2008, his family members asked a court to involuntarily commit him for mental health treatment because he was a danger to himself and others, but he was only committed on an emergency basis and never reached the stage of having a judge rule on his mental competence. Also in 2008, his former intimate partner filed a protective order against him—but no final order was issued by the court. Despite all that, in February 2014 he was able to legally buy a gun in a Phenix City, Alabama, pawn shop—the gun that would become his murder weapon.

He was not prohibited from having guns, but he was precisely the type of person who should be barred—a person with a dangerous criminal history who abused and threatened family members, and who had contacts with the mental health system. Several states have passed laws often referred to as "gun violence restraining orders," which allow family members of these types of dangerous people to ask a court to temporarily prohibit the person from having guns. If granted, not only do these orders prohibit the person from buying a gun, but they also require the person to turn in the guns they already own. Had this tool been available to this man's family members when he threatened them, maybe everything would have turned out differently for Mayci and Jillian.

Knowing this is unbearable. Knowing this is enough to make me want to do something.

And yet, gun-violence restraining orders are just the tip of the iceberg. Because even if every single state had more laws like this in place to keep guns out of dangerous hands, there's still a gaping loophole that makes it easy for *anyone* to buy guns through unlicensed sellers, perhaps at gun shows or online—because for those sales, there are no background checks and no questions asked. Surveys conducted over three decades consistently show that 30 to 40 percent of US gun transfers take place without a background check. In many states getting a gun is easier than getting birth control. Read on. It gets even better (worse). In several states in this country, it's legal to buy a gun if you're completely blind, and in most states it's legal to buy a gun if you're on one of the terror watch lists. I'm going to tell you that again. If you can't see *anything at all*, you can buy a gun. If you're on not just the "no fly" list but literally the list of people our government suspects are terrorists, you can Legally. Buy. A. Gun.

Don't get it twisted. I'm great friends with plenty of gun owners. I believe law-abiding Americans have every right to own a gun. But I think there is room for improvement. Don't you?

Haven't enough shootings happened? You know who says no? The people who profit the most from gun sales. But 92 percent of Americans—including 82 percent of gun owners and 74 percent of NRA members—support criminal background checks for all gun sales. Yet the gun lobby opposes this most commonsense of policies. And their lapdogs in Congress—whom they've bought and paid for—fall in lockstep behind them. As you may have noticed by now, there are a lot of lists in this book. I've included another one at the end of the book on pages 376–377—it's a list of congress-people who've taken money from and been influenced by the gun lobby. Enjoy!

It was especially striking to me to learn that gun violence is specifically a women's issue: women in America are eleven times more likely to be murdered with guns than women in other developed nations. In the eighteen states that require background checks for all handgun sales, 46 percent fewer women are shot and killed by intimate partners than in the states that do not.

Do you know much about all of this? Before the Lafayette shooting, I didn't. You owe it to yourself and your family to be educated about it, because it's a problem we can chip away at, together. For more details on how to get involved, see page 375.

As I've documented in this book, I've mostly been able to find the humor in the absolute darkest moments. It's hard to do that with this, though. I know that for many of you, this might not be a chapter you signed up for and you may be thinking, *Get back to telling your vagina jokes! Make us laugh, clown!* I hear you. When I've written sketches about gun safety on my TV show, people have responded by saying they wish I'd just be funny. They tell me to stick to comedy because that's what they come to me for. I'll tell you what I tell them: No! I love making people laugh and am grateful that I'm equipped to do that. But when an injustice affects me deeply, I will speak about it—and I suggest you do the same. I wish I could muster the energy to put a clever and sarcastic spin on some of the grave statistics about gun violence in America, but I have to tell you, I just fucking can't. I was able to write a funny scene about gun safety on my TV show this year, and if you want to laugh along, please watch, but for this chapter in my book . . . I'm not laughing. I think about Mayci and Jillian every day. I carry pictures of them on the road with me, and when I see that yet another American or several Americans were killed senselessly and avoidably by guns, all I can think is enough is e-fucking-nough. Period.

I began working with Senator Chuck Schumer, a distant cousin of my father's, to advocate for sensible ways to stop gun violence. I sit on a committee for Everytown—a movement of Americans working together to end gun violence and build safer communities. As I was drafting this chapter, no lie, I got an invitation to the White House to meet President Obama and was there when he announced a set of new executive actions to address this national crisis.

The White House allowed me to bring a few guests, so I brought my sister, my brother, and Ben. There are few people I'd drop everything and fly across the country for on such little notice. President Obama is one of them. Common and Tatiana Maslany from *Orphan Black* are two others. What I'm saying is, it was thrilling to get to be there. We were joined by the rapper Wale and two guys from the Washington Wizards basketball team who are advocates to end gun violence. I was hanging out with them for most of the visit.

When it was time for the president to come into the room to meet us, we formed a receiving line. I straightened the Wizards' ties and belts and then saw that I had some dirt on my leg, so I quickly licked my finger and rubbed it off because I'm as elegant as I am hygienic. We were all transformed into little kids helping each other on picture day. As we neared the president, we were asked to write our name and occupation on a fancy little card and hand it to a stoic naval officer so he could announce us to the president before we shook his hand. When it was my turn, the officer looked at what I'd written on my card and, without missing a beat, announced with military precision, "Amy Schumer. She is a model!"

I stepped forward, and President Barack Obama smiled at me. We shook hands, and he spoke first:

"You're very funny, Amy Schumer." He sounded just like he sounds on TV.

"So are you."

"We really enjoyed *Trainwreck*," he said.

I said, "You saw *Trainwreck*?!!!"

He nodded and said, "Of course."

I couldn't believe it. He was so cool. He was keeping the conversation going with me and I didn't want to take any more of his time so I rushed our picture together. I was losing my mind in the picture, so moved and thrilled. He thanked me for my work trying to end gun violence, and I thanked him back and walked into the room where the press conference would take place.

A bit later, the president faced the cameras, standing in front of the parents of children whose lives were taken by gun violence—many from the shootings at Sandy Hook Elementary School in Newtown, Connecticut. He delivered the most eloquent, honest speech I will ever hear. He talked about the first graders who were killed. He repeated the words—"*first* graders"—and shed a few tears. I could see them. He wiped away the ones on his left side but not the right. After a few beats, he wiped both eyes. He spoke about how it was all too easy to get firearms on the Internet or at gun shows without a background check. Then he outlined the plan to fix that and much more.

When the press conference was over, I stood in the room for a while and was approached by people wearing buttons with the pictures of their slain children on them. Parents, wearing their dead children on their lapels. They just wanted to tell me about their kids. Some had lost their kids in Columbine. A nice couple whose daughter was killed in the Aurora movie theater shooting told me she had been a fan of mine. I listened and hugged them and promised I would keep fighting with them.

During the entire day at the White House, I was thinking of Mayci and Jillian. I'd been holding back tears for hours but when the president mentioned the shooting in Lafayette at the press conference, I couldn't stop myself from crying. Those women will always be in my thoughts. I will not forget them. I'll work hard every day to honor their memory and live in a way I hope would make them proud.

In the months since the White House, I've said many things about guns onstage or aired those gun-related scenes on my TV show. I'm always immediately hit with criticism from people on the Internet. That's putting it very lightly. Many of them feel incensed about the idea of the government wanting to "take away [their] guns," which is not at all what I'm advocating for. What most people in this movement care about is ending gun violence and making our communities safer. People rage at me on Twitter (and this is actually one of the nicest, most sanitized kinds of insults I get): "You're out of your league, Schumer! Stick to what you know!" Of course most of them call me a fat cunt, which I have grown to love.

But they are wrong (not about my being a fat cunt; that's subjective). They are wrong to say that I'm out of my league. Because I *do* know this issue. And you do too. Anyone who lives and breathes and has an opinion about whether or not first graders should get shot at school is qualified to speak on this issue. I'm not a politician nor an NRA-hating shifty Jew, as some people see me in certain parts of the country. Most members of the NRA are great people. But their leaders are the cuckoo birds. I'm just an American who thinks we can have more common sense about keeping our families, children, and friends from being shot to death by an unstable person who never should have been able to get his hands on a gun in the first place.

Mayci Breaux

Jillian Johnson

I want to thank Jason Rzepka and Noelle Howey at Everytown for helping educate me about gun violence statistics and gun laws. I also want to thank the families of Mayci Breaux and Jillian Johnson for providing these photos and allowing me to honor the memories of Mayci and Jillian.

THINGS
THAT MAKE ME HAPPY

---

1. My toddler niece laughing or doing pretty much anything. I love how she pronounces my name and yells, "Mimi!" when she sees me. Also her hair, which for a while looked like Benjamin Franklin's.

2. Scones. And not the store-bought ones that come six to a plastic container. I'm talking Alice's-Tea-Cup-in-NYC scones, either the vegan one (not because I'm vegan but because the texture is dope) or one with some form of chocolate (not white chocolate, real chocolate). Also, fine, the store-bought ones.

3. Seeing the people I love happy.

4. Riding a horse. We had a little farmhouse upstate when I was a kid, and I learned to ride at a local stable where I would go around in circles on the smallest horse. Since then, I'll get on a horse any chance I get. Zero questions asked. One day a few years back, I was lying on the couch watching *Game of Thrones* at my sister's house, and she came into the room and said, "Babe, do you wanna ride a horse?" She lives in a normal neighborhood in Chicago where there should never have been a horse

nearby, but I silently got up and followed her outside and there was a horse across the street. His name was Norman. We are now friends.

5.   Telling a new joke that I'm excited about onstage, even if it doesn't do well. Telling a new joke never gets old.

6.   Hearing my brother, Jason, play his horn. We both love Miles Davis, John Coltrane, and Thelonious Monk, but Jason plays really loose, crazy stuff called "free jazz." It's the kind of jazz you hear in the background when Claire Danes is very stressed out on *Homeland*. But I just love hearing him play it. Doesn't have to be onstage either. Sometimes at his house, I will all of a sudden hear his horn from another room, and the beautiful sound instantly makes me feel at peace.

7.   Watching British or Irish sexual-assault-based crime shows at my sister and brother-in-law's house. The thicker the accent, the thicker the reason I need to change my underwear by the end. (Ewwwww.) I mean it. I have to watch these shows with subtitles.

8.   Sitting with my friends at the Comedy Cellar and making fun of each other. Particularly Keith Robinson, who is never, ever

right about anything but still commits to his arguments as if his life depends on it.

9. Coming.

10. Being on a boat or Jet Ski that is going way too fast and screaming my head off.

11. Snuggling on the couch with my sister's three-legged dog, Abbott. We have this really cool relationship where I don't give him treats, so I know his love for me is entirely non-food motivated.

12. Making people laugh to the point of wiping tears away.

13. Waking up next to the person I am in love with and immediately rolling away from him to hide my busted-ass morning face and baby-diaper breath. But he pulls me toward him, cuddling my butt into him, not caring at all.

14. My sister. Playing volleyball with her, watching *Orphan Black* and eating pasta with her. Drinking with her. Smoking pot with her. Traveling the world with her and making TV shows and movies we are proud of together. Making her laugh on camera. I will sometimes force her to be in a sketch for my TV show and one of my favorite things is making her laugh during the scene, ruining as many takes as possible. I know she

panics and is worried that she's wasting everybody's time by laughing, but I can't help myself.

15. I like when a small animal rides on the back of a larger animal (think Sir Didymus and Ambrosius in *Labyrinth*). Or a video of a lion and a seal becoming friends or something like that.

16. When someone in a motorized wheelchair passes, I like holding my hand up to cover the person's body, so it just looks like a head whizzing by.

17. When the dog bites. When the bee stings. Sorry.

18. Laughing and yelling at my girlfriends from high school when they try to smoke pot in the bathroom of wherever I am performing, no matter how classy. They tried to smoke pot at both *SNL* and Carnegie Hall.

19. Hearing my sister on the phone with a delivery place after they bring the wrong food or don't include enough sauce. She starts out very calm and rational but then spins the fuck out after thirty seconds.

20. Sitting on the couch with a girlfriend, facing each other, and having long conversations about what's going on with the guys or girls in our lives. Yes, with wine. I didn't think I

needed to add that, but if you're gonna make a big deal about it, yes, of course, with wine, unless scotch is needed.

21. Making a new friend. When you're over your twenties it's hard, but once in a while someone comes along that you really want to invest time in and it's so special.

22. Smoked salmon.

23. Watching Dave Attell onstage. No one makes me laugh harder.

24. Sex. I know I already said coming, but sex is pretty great and should be mentioned.

25. Falling in love.

THE SUN WILL COME
OUT TOMORROW

I'd been single for about three years when I met Ben. Well, that's not totally true. There are three dudes who might read this and say, "WHAT THE FUCK, SCHUMER?!" And I'd be like, "Don't call me 'Schumer,' that is part of the reason why we broke up!" I'm kidding, but there are three guys who were my boyfriends over the course of those years. Whoops! I mean four. I just remembered another one. But each was over after a couple months, and I never got to the point of feeling like a real couple with any of them. We played at it. We tried it on like jeans to see what it would feel like. After a month or two, one of us would call the other one "baby," or meet the other's friends, or make hypothetical future plans, but we never got there. I never made it there with anyone during the last few years before Ben.

I found myself feeling very satisfied in my work during that time. I know that sentence may sound like a cry for help. "I'm just happy really throwing myself into my work right now" (*as she chases a bottle of pills with a liter of Jack Daniel's*). But I mean it. This kind of unlikely satisfaction can actually happen. It was almost unsettling to be so okay with being single. I was almost certain that I'd start needing some sort of romantic stimulation or sexual activity to feel totally good about myself, but the need never came. I was feeling great, working my ass off doing stuff I was really proud of. (Such as a scene on my TV show depicting a girl who uncontrollably farts when she's scared, which ultimately leads to her being murdered.) It helps that my work is actually fun.

I'd already been through the panic that sets in when all your friends get married in their twenties and start having kids. This was then followed by the even worse panic when you turn thirty and you're still single. During that phase, I was terrified, and I started making pacts with male friends that if we were still alone in our forties, we'd get married and allow each other to see other people but keep our commitment to grow old together. Compared to the marriages I witnessed growing up, a prearranged, late-in-life marriage with a friend (or two) actually didn't seem that crazy. It was, however, probably a little nuts that I started making so many pacts for marriage. I was setting it up so that my forties could be a sort of reverse *Big Love* situation—a bunch of real live brother-husbands. How does that not exist?!

My parents have both been married. A lot. Three times each, to be exact, which teaches you never to invest too much in loving someone because he may be replaced within a couple months. I've had UTIs that lasted longer than some of my parents' marriages. And these marriages have led to a constant revolving door of siblings. The first time your parent is dating someone long enough and seriously enough for you to meet his or her kids, you invest. You think, *Wow! This person may become my new sister or brother. Maybe we'll share clothes and get tea together on Tuesdays at Alice's Tea Cup!* You show interest in them as human beings. You ask them questions like "When is your birthday? Do you like beets? Ever used a vibrator?" Okay, not the last one. But by the time marriage number three and stepsibling number whatever come around, you just kind of learn their name and maybe, if you're up to it, you get a feel for their general vibe.

By the time my father met his second wife, Melissa, I'd already learned this strategy. Dad's marriage to Melissa happened, in no small part, so he could benefit from her health insurance. What could be sexier and more romantic than that? Meet-cute alert! If I had to make a three-second movie to illustrate this relationship, it would open with a very unlucky woman dropping her wallet. Her Blue Cross Blue Shield card dramatically falls out, and my dad slowly picks it up without making eye contact with her. When things became official between them, Melissa introduced us to her daughter at a dinner at Ruth's Chris Steak House.

My father has been to most of the restaurants in this chain all over the country, a point of pride for him, and he'll tell you—if you'll listen—how many and which cities he has yet to visit. It became a tradition that our dad would take me and Kim there, and we would start with the calamari (I like the ones with the legs because I'm gruesome; I'll also eat cow tongue sandwiches and gefilte fish. I don't give a fuck!), then have potatoes au gratin, creamed spinach, and filets, still loudly crackling from all the scalding-hot butter they are drenched in. So when my dad introduced us to the person who was to be our new(est) stepsister, he naturally chose Ruth's Chris. Kim and I were already wise to the fact that this insta-sibling wouldn't be in the picture for long, so when she started talking about how excited she was because she had always wanted sisters, it kind of broke our hearts. We drank underage and choked down our steaks as fast as we could to get through the meal.

The marriage with Melissa lasted a few months and out went that sibling. I still think of her every time we . . . NEVER. I never think of her.

But back to my parents and their parade of marriages. My mom was already one divorce deep when she met my dad. Her first husband's name was David and they had one son together—my brother, Jason. When Jason was a few years old, they divorced, and my mom married my father soon after that. I was born a year later, and then Kim somehow snuck into this world. We're all four years apart. When Jason was eleven years old, he lost his dad, who died suddenly of a heart attack at the age of thirty-nine. After my parents divorced, my mom dated several dudes.

There was, of course, the first man she dated after the divorce, named Lou, whom I told you about in the chapter "Mom" and who also happened to be the father of my best friend, Mia; and then John, who wound up being at the very least a cokehead, but my siblings and I think more likely a crackhead. My mom thought it was time to move this guy in with her children after knowing him a few months. One weekend when my mom went to a volleyball tournament with my sister, she left me alone with John and he took off to indulge in a weeklong drug bender, leaving me at home. I was a teenager at the time, so I was psyched. But still, it's probably better not to live with a crackhead. To give my mom the benefit of the doubt, I suppose there are worse things than moving a crackhead into your house with your children, like maybe . . . no, a crackhead is the worst thing. After he left me alone, my mother ended their engagement briefly, until they got back together and he did the same thing again a few months later.

Then there was Andrew, who was very, very slow. I mean, I Am Sam would have schooled this guy in a game of Heads Up. There was Doug, my mother's childhood sweetheart who resurfaced for a brief time, and Hank, whom we nearly moved in with.

There were a few more, none of whom I liked, and in fact I'd try to scare the suitors away. As soon as my mom would introduce me I'd call them "Daddy" and do anything I could to weird them out. I'd look them in the eyes and say, "My mom makes men fall in love with her and then gets tired of them. She will dispose of you like Kleenex in a week." They would giggle, thinking it was cute. Until they hit the bottom of the bin.

Our mother's third marriage was to her boyfriend Moshe, a Persian Jew from Israel who owned an auto mechanic shop in Queens. Moshe was stubborn, loud, embarrassing, and full of strong convictions. He and my mom were a real couple and genuinely loved each other. I found out they had gotten married by looking through photos she left on the counter one weekend when I was home from college. One photo showed them with two witnesses standing in front of a justice of the peace. I yelled into the other room, "Did you and Moshe get married?!" She shouted back, "Yeah!" They did it so that he could stay in the country, but then 9/11 happened and no one was too keen on granting citizenship status to an Iranian Jew. After a handful of years they divorced, and shortly thereafter Moshe had to go back to Israel to take care of his parents and was never allowed back in the US. I still miss him to this day. He was kind, and he loved us and our mom so much.

Since Moshe left the picture, my mom dates from time to time, and I hope she finds someone to grow old with, if that's what she wants. Sometimes it seems like she may just want to be alone, and I understand that instinct, too. As someone who is on the road all the time, I know very well how difficult it can be to share your life with a person once you've become so used to being on your own. You have to ask questions like "What do you want for dinner?" or "Can I have more of the blanket?" or "Can I have more of your dinner?" or "Can dinner be pigs in a blanket?" And that can be harder than you think. But it can also be really nice. I'm getting distracted. What is better than pigs in a blanket? Read my next book for the answer; my next book's title is *NOTHING*.

Then one day, out of nowhere, the fear I had of growing old unmarried just faded. My life was feeling full. Despite my parents' various attempts at marriage, I'd hear stories of happy second marriages, or tales of people not meeting until they were in their fifties or sixties, and feel calm about the whole thing. I was settling nicely into my thirties. I was dating a little but was not at all as consumed with it as I had been in my teens and twenties. The days of *He didn't call me today and it's three p.m.—what does that mean?!* were truly behind me. I realized that nothing was missing. I felt pretty and strong in my own skin. From the inside. Not from the reflection I saw while staring into some dude's pupils. I was feeling like I had it all.

I had a pretty big year. You've already heard all this earlier in the book . . . My movie came out, I hosted *Saturday Night Live*, and I filmed a one-hour special for HBO directed by one of my idols, Chris Rock. So many of my dreams were coming true all at once, and a lot of people were paying attention to me, including Barbara Walters. She'd just labeled me one of the "most fascinating people" of the year. Sure, why not? I didn't feel particularly fascinating, but if Babs thought so, it must have been true. I taped an interview with her during which she asked me one of those questions about where I saw myself in five or ten years. I answered that I would want to be writing, producing, directing, and creating. She was surprised. She said, "You didn't say married and with children." I was surprised too, because the thought hadn't even occurred to me. I laughed to myself and said to her, "Yeah, I guess you're right. I would love to have those things but I don't know how realistic that is for me."

And maybe I gravitated toward that answer because my job isn't exactly compatible with married life, and mostly because I was beginning to think that my parents were, at their core, both loners. Maybe I was like them. What's wrong with being alone anyway? Being alone is sometimes a great place to be, but people are always trying to correct this "problem" for you, even if you yourself don't have any kind of problem with it.

Seeing my parents as "a unit" these days is even more of an argument for remaining alone. Sometimes my mom will help me out by bringing supplies to the hospital where my dad lives, and watching them interact is strange. They were married for fourteen years and had two kids together, but now they talk with all the warmth and recognition of two people who maybe attended the same high school for a year but at different times. Their distance from each other probably started on day one of their marriage, something I really don't need all the details of but I'm sure one day I'll hear, because my dad likes to share. One day he told me about this woman, Lana, who went on to become his third wife. They had dated in the seventies back when my dad was hot shit. Tan and athletic, funny, and rich to boot. (I don't know what "to boot" means. But you already bought this book and you can't take it back—it's too late.)

Lana was crazy about my dad. Back in the seventies she'd bring her pots and pans over to his bachelor pad and cook for him. She was head over heels, and she hung around long enough and forced herself into being my dad's girlfriend. I have no judgments about that, by the way. As you know by now, I have moved to Astoria, Queens, to trap a man into a relationship and cooked him skirt steak with creamed spinach and a baked potato, because that is the one meal I know how to make. (And if you come over and notice out loud that I have never used my stove I will cut you with a never-used kitchen knife.) Anyway, one day, Lana's parents came to Manhattan to visit. Lana and Dad had been up in his penthouse apartment hanging out and smoking "grass," as my dad calls it. "And, Aim," he said, "this was really good grass." They were all heading downstairs in the elevator to go out to dinner, and when they got down to the lobby, a beautiful woman walked into the building. My dad said he stepped away from Lana and her parents, and walked right up to her and said, "Excuse me. Have you ever seen the penthouse in this building?" She said no. He asked, "Would you like to?" She said yes. The next thing my dad said to me was, "And that was the only time I've ever been tied up."

So to reiterate the facts here: My father left his girlfriend and her parents in the lobby of his building in order to go upstairs and have sex with a complete stranger, who apparently loved bondage. And he felt the need to tell his daughter all about it, thirty-plus years later. Lana's father was pounding on the door and calling my dad nonstop, so he locked himself in the apartment with the stranger for hours. And yet somehow, thirty years later, Lana still wanted to reunite with him and became my stepmother number two.

ABOUT A WEEK after the Barbara Walters interview, I was hanging out with my friend Vanessa Bayer, and we were talking about the latest with dudes. We both always had a guy or two we were juggling but not excited about. Which, by the way, means just texting and not actually meeting up. I realize it may have sounded like I was trying to say, "Vanessa and I were dealing with a bunch of different dick," but we weren't. We were always texting people. Not that there's anything wrong with juggling dicks. Which is the title of my third book—*Juggling Dicks*. So Vanessa said she'd heard of a dating app for your phone specifically aimed at creative people that attracted a lot of celebrity members. We decided to sign up. You pick some pictures of yourself to post and a song that will play if people click on your profile. I chose the song "Dirty Work" by Steely Dan thinking this was pretty funny to put on a dating site. In my main profile picture, I was wearing sunglasses and a baseball cap with no makeup. It was a selfie and I made a gross face, looking as though I were dying, because I was hiking, so I was. I also put up a picture of Sophia from *The Golden Girls*, Claire Danes making her cry face on *Homeland*, and one more normal photo where I was smiling and wearing a sweatshirt. Vanessa and I posted our profiles at the same time and scream-giggled like little girls.

We clicked on the profiles of a couple guys who looked cute, and it seemed like every dude was either a model or a photographer. They all posted the same two Rolling Stones songs and the same photos of themselves riding a motorcycle, chilling with a bulldog, holding an old-timey camera in Europe, or doing a cannonball off cliffs somewhere tropical. They were attractive—too attractive— and clearly a bunch of full-time pussy magnets. It was very discouraging. Vanessa and I had only been on this app about four hours and already I was feeling ready to throw in the towel, loofah, and disposable razor.

But I decided to hang in there. I made myself click the "like" button on maybe four guys' profiles, and within forty minutes, I got my first match. The guy was Ben. He was dancing with his grandmother in his profile picture at what looked like a wedding. His song was "LSD" by A$AP Rocky, my favorite song on that album. He wasn't an actor or photographer by trade like all the other guys— and he didn't live in LA or New York. He was a Chicago guy. We sent each other very simple hellos and short, funny messages.

A few hours passed and we were still messaging each other. He was funny, kind of odd, and interesting, and that made me paranoid. *This must be a trick. I'm a celebrity, and I will be reading this whole conversation on some trashy website tomorrow.* I had slowly worked myself into a full frenzy. I told him that I wanted to FaceTime to make sure I wasn't being catfished by a basement-dweller with a comedy podcast. He said, "Sure, no problem." We tried, but the Wi-Fi in my ancient apartment building wasn't working, so he called me instead and we spoke on the phone the old-fashioned way for a few minutes. He sounded like Christian Slater and was just as funny on the phone. He had heard my name but had never seen my movie, stand-up, or TV show. I liked talking to him. We hung up, and I thought he seemed cool and that I'd like to meet him at some point, but I didn't think much more about it.

I messaged with a couple other guys on the app and even made some loose plans to meet a few of them, but I never followed up. I took my profile down in under forty-eight hours. The experience was too intense, and if I saw one more guy looking off into the distance on a boat, I was gonna open my wrists and get into a warm bath. A few weeks later, I reached out to Ben because I was going to Chicago to visit my brother. He told me that he was actually driving to New York City. He is a furniture designer and was bringing something he'd constructed to a client. We made plans to meet for a drink at my place the next night. My sister immediately vetoed this dangerous idea and made me suggest a small, quiet restaurant to meet at instead.

I know it was a bold move to invite a guy I'd never met in person up to my place for a drink, but it does not really compare to my dad acting out *Fifty Shades of Grey* in his penthouse. Speaking of which, I'm sure you're dying to know if Lana forgave my dad after he ditched her to be hog-tied by a total stranger. The answer is yes, and she is N to the U to the T to the S. She had an adopted Vietnamese daughter, who was about seven years old. Her name was May, and when we all found out our parents were getting married, May was very much under the impression that Kim and I were to be her sisters for life. She clung to us in a heartbreaking way, and we played along even though you didn't have to be a psychic to guess the fate of this union. I'd have loved to have kept in touch with May, but her mom made sure this didn't happen.

My dad was in his late fifties and already in a wheelchair and very sick by their wedding day. We went to a place on Long Island that was part chapel, part someone's living room, and mostly haunted house. The person who married them seemed like he would be a waiter at the Jekyll and Hyde Club—very creepy looking and overweight, like the guy in *Beetlejuice* in the dinner-table scene where they all sing "Day-O." Lana, our shiny new stepmom, wore a white dress, a veil, and dramatic makeup, including a drawn-on mole.

The reception was at a Chinese restaurant, and there were about forty people there who were 98 percent Lana's guests. Lana's friends were all very strange with a hint of disturbing, and they were mostly people from her community theater. After her thespian friends gave toasts, Lana got up and read a—no exaggeration—twenty-five-minute speech, which was meandering and pointless. Nonetheless, I thought my dad should at least look in Lana's general direction while she read to him, her new *husband*. He never even glanced at her. Not once during the whole damn rant. He just ate moo shu pork and shrimp fried rice, and never acknowledged her presence during the whole speech. She didn't seem to mind too much. It was clear that she was just giving a performance, and she was thrilled to have so many eyes on her, even if none of them were my father's.

It was a rough day, and it turned into a rougher night. It seemed like things couldn't get much worse. Kim was nearly catatonic by the time the evening wound down. We'd both drunk as much boxed white wine as we could get our hands on, and that's when events hit rock bottom. I felt a tiny hand on my shoulder and a sweet voice ask, "Amy, will you sing 'The Sun Will Come Out Tomorrow' with me?" It was my new sister, May. She was such an innocent, beautiful little angel. I could not fucking believe I was about to sing a song that I loathe in a Chinese restaurant on Long Island with my temporary Vietnamese stepsister. I wanted to turn to her and say, "I can't! That song is a lie! You have such a hard road ahead of you! Your mom is cray-cray, and I'm going to take you out of here and raise you myself so you have a shot at happiness in this awful world!" But instead I said, "Yep." She stood up on a chair and held hands with Kim and me, and we all sang, "When I'm stuck with a day that's gray and lonely, I just stick out my chin and grin and say, *OHHHHHHHHH!*"

In the end the sun didn't come out tomorrow on this relationship. Six months after Lana moved my disabled dad all the way to New Orleans, she decided she'd had enough of him and kicked him out. He ended up on the curb. Literally. She up and left him alone in his wheelchair and he wheeled his way to the side of the road. After that, he moved to a hospital on Long Island, and I haven't heard from Lana or May since.

And I wouldn't say the sun came out when I met Ben either. Not because things weren't awesome, but because I try not to talk in metaphors about my relationships anymore. After everything I've witnessed with my parents, I like to keep things super basic—no solar analogies or rose-colored filters of any kind. Just the Valencia one on Instagram, because I look super good in that one. But the night I first met Ben in person, there was no literal sun to speak of; it was raining. I'd just had acupuncture, so there was oil in my hair and there were deep red lines on my cheeks from being facedown on the table, but I put on jeans instead of sweatpants and walked downstairs to meet him outside. I got out into the rain, and Ben was standing there, no umbrella or hood, with a soggy paper bag with a bottle of wine in it. We smiled at each other and in that moment, everything felt right.

I didn't lie to Barbara, but my thoughts on love and marriage are always evolving. I'm sure in the past I've said marriage is stupid. Marriage makes someone sign a contract promising something they really can't deliver. I'm sure I will again say marriage is dumb. But I can also imagine why it could be lovely. There's something beautiful about truly being there for another person. In the movie *Moonlight Mile*, Susan Sarandon and Dustin Hoffman play a married couple who fight a lot but still really love each other. They talk about how they're there to "witness each other's lives." I love that description of commitment. I don't think my parents ever signed up for that. They didn't show me what a good marriage looks like or how to stick it out to the end. When you have a sick parent, you can't help but think of the end. Like literally, the final moments of life come to mind when I begin to love someone. I think, *Will this dude push my wheelchair?* And even scarier, *Would I be willing to push his?* These are not light thoughts, and they're not easy to sort out when you're in the early stages with a person you care about.

I don't know what will happen with Ben of course. Maybe we'll grow old together, or maybe we'll be apart before this book is on shelves next to Godiva chocolates and gift cards. I would like to think that good things can happen for me in relationships with men, but maybe I think too much about the wheelchairs. I might just be a product of my parents. But it still seems worthwhile to suspend my disbelief for as long as I can—to keep myself open to accepting love—and to give mine every day.

WHAT I WANT PEOPLE
TO SAY AT MY FUNERAL

Amy is dead, and we can all sleep a little easier. She was honest and fair, and she demanded the same from all of us. But it was exhausting. Even though she made everything more fun and exciting, it's a relief in some ways that she's no longer with us. We all get lazy with our lives and stuck in what we think we deserve. We all accept too easily that life has to be hard and forget to make sure we have the most fun we can. Amy made sure we laughed and didn't take any shit. If she was your friend, she'd do anything for you. She'd defend you and die for you, even sometimes when you didn't want her to. She went above and beyond, at times even making things harder. She once wrote a Facebook post congratulating her friend on getting a role in the new Woody Allen movie even though her friend was not going to be in that movie. She did it because her friend was in pain from a recent breakup and Amy knew her friend's ex would read the post and be jealous. That is an inappropriate thing to do. That is one of the reasons we will be able to continue on without her.

Amy would give you the shirt off her back, even if you didn't ask for it, and never mention it again. She was generous. She was also pushy and would talk shit to anyone in her way. She was fun to drink and smoke pot with. She was fun to eat mushrooms with. She was not fun to watch television with because the whole time she'd say, "Wait, who is that? What did he just say?" She was not a good listener. She was so easily distracted that you had to say, "Amy, I need you to really listen," to get her attention, and even then there was only a 40 percent chance she'd hear you.

She made us feel better. She demanded that we feel better. It could be exhausting. But we will miss it. We will miss her. But she'll always be with us. But not really, because as I mentioned up top, she's dead. Does anyone know if they're validating parking? Oh, it's New York, and you guys don't do that here. Well aren't you so lucky. You guys are smarter for living here and not LA.

RIDER FOR THE FUNERAL OF AMY SCHUMER

First and foremost, no one should call this a "celebration of life" or a "memorial." It may only be referred to as THE FUNERAL OF AMY SCHUMER. No bells or whistles.

There is a zero-tolerance policy on flowers. No wreaths, bouquets, corsages, single carnations, greenery, or flora of any kind is allowed. Everyone should bring some sort of a pasta dish and pour it into the casket. Not a pasta salad. Don't be an asshole.

The actual body of AMY SCHUMER should be propped up on a chair in the northwest corner of the room, wearing aviator sunglasses and her trusted snow hat that reads, "No Coffee, No Workee," a motto in life that she will continue to stand by in the afterlife.

WARDROBE
All guests should be comfortably dressed. Think sweatpants, velour,

and comfy socks. Absolutely no high-heeled shoes are permitted. No guest shall be permitted entry if they are wearing a waist trainer, unless they are AMBER ROSE. She can wear whatever the F she wants.

CATERING/HOSPITALITY

Please provide at least two (2) sandwiches per guest. Sandwiches must be from Defonte's in Greenpoint, Brooklyn, and should be either the prosciutto or the mozzarella.

The signature cocktail of the night should be a Moscow mule.

Amazing appetizers should be abundant. For example, those puff things where you're not sure if you are eating bread, cheese, cream, or all of the above. Do not be sparing with things that you dip in crème fraîche or anything truffle-based. Absolutely no French macarons are permitted, but the Jew kind are okay. None of these foodstuffs should require the use of utensils. Pigs in a blanket as far as the human eye can see. I repeat, pigs in a blanket as far as the human and pig eye can see.

Please provide:

- Twenty-two (22) cases of Rombauer chardonnay. Oaky as shit!!!!
- Fifteen (15) cases of Opus One cabernet, the kind John Cena introduced to the deceased.

FACILITIES

There shall be no bathroom attendants permitted in the bathrooms. Please make two (2) fun side rooms available, with one (1) room providing trivia and the other providing hair-braiding stations. HARPISTS should play background music, but only in the bathrooms, which should be small—such that the presence of the HARPISTS prevents everyone from washing their hands.

TALENT

The following people should speak at the funeral:

- Keith Robinson
- Rachel Feinstein (because she will trash Keith)
- Jimmy Norton
- Colin Quinn (because he will trash Norton)
- Vincent Caramele

- Cayce Dumont
- My niece
- Lena Dunham
- Mark Normand
- Allan Haldeman
- Kevin Kane to close it out

MUSIC REQUIREMENTS
During the ceremony, BRIDGET EVER-ETT will sing "That's All." Intro, outro, and other interstitial music to be provided by a great bluegrass band—STEVE MARTIN AND THE STEEP CAN-YON RANGERS if they're up for it.

SECURITY
The following people (who never did anything to the deceased, but she just doesn't want them there) are not per-mitted at the funeral, nor may they attend any after-party-type event:
- Donald Trump
- Mario Lopez, unless he brings Elizabeth Berkley
- The boyfriends and girl-friends of AMY SCHUMER's friends are only permit-ted to attend if she liked them. In order to qualify for this status, they must

be very kind and loving to said friends exactly all the time. If they are ever not nice to said friends, they must stay five (5) football fields away from the funeral.

- Anyone who has ever gotten laid because they teach improv, with one exception being Neil Casey

MISCELLANEOUS REQUIREMENTS

Please post signs around the room(s) stating, "No small talk, no inside jokes." Please provide a large glass bowl at the entrance for those who wish to participate in an optional key party.

AFTER-PARTY AND BURIAL

After the funeral, guests will participate in an Edward Forty Hands party. All guests should have forties of Olde English duct-taped to their hands and are not to be untaped until said bottles are completely empty. This party should be DJ'd by Questlove and there needs to be ample room for everyone to dance.

First song should be "Put It in Your Mouth."

Immediately following the Edward Forty Hands party, guests should proceed to the ocean in Long Beach, New York, for a Viking funeral. The body of AMY SCHUMER will be transported to the beach by horse-drawn carriage, because she was "worth it," and will be laid to rest in a tiny boat. The boat should be set on fire with a flaming arrow and gently pushed out to sea.

FORGIVING
MY LOWER BACK TATTOO

When I was on the Comedy Central roast of Charlie Sheen, I told Mike Tyson that he had a slutty lower back tattoo on his face. I said, "Men don't know whether to be scared of it or finish on it." He heckled me for a minute, shouting high-pitched insults I couldn't understand, before I improvised a way to stop his interruptions, asking, "Is his interpreter here?" Now, that is just not a smart thing to say when you're twenty feet away from an ear-biting ex-con who was described as making a "comeback" after serving six years in prison for rape. But I did what any desperate comic would do. I committed to the moment, put myself in immediate danger, and went for it—which is exactly how I wound up with my own slutty tattoo, right where the good lord intended: on my lower back. Yes, I have one. What a hypocrite I am. I roasted Tyson while sporting my very own shitty, humiliating, not-even-on-straight, slightly-raised-because-the-guy-sucked-and-went-too-deep-and-it-got-infected tattoo of my own.

I'd wanted one for years. I saw so many tribal varieties while I played beach volleyball with my sister on Long Island, and I thought they looked badass. I wanted to get a tattoo that communicated "Don't fuck with me, because I don't give a shit about anything and I've been through it all," even though I was only eighteen and all I'd been through was the cereal aisle at Key Food. I was not a badass. I didn't feel strong or confident or particularly tribal. I thought I could literally stamp myself with those qualities, and if I could fake it long enough, they'd become real. And, unlike with an orgasm, I think that tactic works sometimes. The point is, my heart was in the right place seeking those things. Too bad my lower back got in the way.

The summer I was eighteen, Kim and I were on a road trip passing through Myrtle Beach. We decided to get some tattoos after careful consideration that consisted of seeing the shop; saying to each other, "Should we get tattoos?"; nodding; and going in. We browsed around, looking in different books and examining the designs on the wall, before we picked out the "art" we wanted on our bodies for the rest of our lives. I thought the guys who worked in the shop were just being cool allowing us to look around, because at fourteen, Kim was so clearly too young. I figured once they knew we were serious about getting all tatted up, they'd tell Kim she couldn't get one since she was a minor. We walked up to the counter and with confidence that can be described as wavering at best, I told the sun-damaged muscle-bound surfers that we'd like them to deface our young bodies with the two worthless designs we had so painstakingly chosen. "Cool," one of them said. "Let's go."

What the fuck? Was this a game of chicken to see who would break first? I tried to hide my confusion and appear bold and skeptical by asking: "How long will it take to get them put on?" The reddest-faced one pointed at me and said, "Yours will take ten because it's bigger, but hers will take about seven." "Ten hours?!" I shouted. "Minutes," red-faced-emoji man replied. Kim had picked out a little fairy that she wanted on her hip, but mine was a big tribal motherfucker, the size of a small possum. Ten minutes seemed like a very short amount of time, but what did I know about tattooing? "And how much will they cost?" I asked, projecting a lot of authority, amping up my New York accent so they wouldn't overcharge us. He said mine would be twenty dollars and Kim's would be ten. WHAT?!!?

I was beyond confused. Kim and I looked at each other and had the same thought, but as the big sister, I spoke up. I proclaimed, "We're not gonna do anything with you guys. We'll pay the full price!" The whole shop stood still. It was like a record had scratched. I looked around and noticed we were by far the least attractive girls in there, and if they were going to try to get sexual favors it wouldn't be from the two busted-ass Long Island teenagers. Then the man whose tank top exposed his nipples said, "You know this is a *temporary* tattoo shop, right? Tattoos are illegal in South Carolina." At that moment, I became the one with the reddest face. We slowly backed out of there like cats. Kim and I didn't speak on the walk back to our bedbugged hotel. It was too embarrassing.

When we finally got our real tattoos one year later (when we were ready to make great permanent decisions), we actually went to our mother for permission. I told her we'd wanted them for a really long time and had selected exactly the right designs and placement. You'd think a year would have matured our aesthetic, but I was still set on a big tribal configuration and Kim still wanted that dumb fairy. Upon hearing this request our mother responded like any parent and told her teenage daughters, "No fucking way. You smell like pot! Go to your room, you're grounded, you no-good skanks!" Oh, wait, nope, not our mom. Our mom responded with, "Well, what are we doing just sitting here talking about it? Let's get in the car!" She drove us to the East Village, where we went into the back room of the shadiest shithouse and got our "ink," as the douchebags call it.

I went first. When I say it killed, no, it fucking KILLED. It was like being stung by a thousand bees every second, or dozens of tracker jackers for all you young adult–fiction fans. The guy doing it wasn't very skillful, so he went way too deep, which caused the tattoo to keloid and scar. *Hawt, Aim, tell us more!* Okay, he was also very drunk, so the tattoo came out crooked. The guy's name was Kurt and he looked like an overweight asthmatic Son of Anarchy. I was dying from the pain, but I wanted to be brave for Kim so that she wouldn't be scared. So while tears ran down my face I smiled, saying that it wasn't that bad. The whole time my mom was beaming at both of us, so happy to be a part of this wonderful event we'd live to regret immediately. Naturally, my tattoo got infected and hundreds of tiny bumps formed around it, and it healed horribly. This display of rash and inflammation is exactly what every sexy young lady wants floating just above her ass. To this day, it's still raised like a *Mad Max* war boy's head scar.

So now, fifteen years later, I'm thirty-five, and any time I'm in a bathing suit people immediately know in their hearts that I'm trash. Any time I take my clothes off for the first time in front of a man and he sees it, he also knows in his heart that I'm trash and that I make poor, poor decisions. And now that the paparazzi think it's interesting to take photos of me doing absolutely nothing noteworthy on a beach somewhere, the whole world has been treated to photos of my lower back tattoo hovering crookedly over my bikini bottoms. But I promise you from the bottom of my heart I don't care. I wear my mistakes like badges of honor, and I celebrate them. They make me human. Now that all of my work, my relationships, my tweets, my body parts, and my sandwiches are publicly analyzed, I'm proud that I labeled myself a flawed, normal human before anyone else did. I beat all the critics and Internet trolls to the punch. I've been called everything in the book, but I already branded myself a tramp, so the haters are going to have to come up with something fresh.

The summer before eighth grade, in my pre-tattoo days (or, as I call them, my PTDs), I landed the nickname "Pancakes." A large group of my friends and I—and the boys we liked—were walking around the neighborhood on a warm night with beer in our book bags, ready and willing to run from the cops when they found us, as they often did. On this particular night, we'd just enjoyed Dr Pepper shots and Irish car bombs at my friend Caroline's house. For those who grew up Amish, a Dr Pepper shot entails dropping a shot glass full of amaretto into a pint of beer just moments before chugging the whole thing. Somehow it tastes like Dr Pepper. Add Bacardi 151 and a lit match to make it a Flaming Dr Pepper shot. Also say good-bye to all your loved ones. The Irish car bomb is a shot of Bailey's dropped into a pint of Guinness— and is also highly, highly offensive to any Irish person who has lost a friend that way. Once a year I'm provoked to drink one of these terrible combination drinks with little to no convincing needed.

We walked up the block to an elementary school on Caroline's corner, sloppy and excited by the drinks and the freedom. While we were hanging on the playground, the ten guys some-how convinced the six girls to lift up their shirts and show them their boobs. They'd presented the very good argument of "Why not?" We had no counterargument for that, so we lined up and, on the count of three, lifted our shirts.

I wrapped my fourteen-year-old fingers around the bottom of my Gap tee and yanked it over my pimpled, plump face with abandon. I was nervous and excited, and probably buzzed. I peeked at the boys over the top of my sensibly priced T-shirt and realized they were all looking only at me. Not at Denise, who had the biggest boobs, or at Krystal, who had the greatest abs, or at Caroline, whom they were all fighting over at the time. I was in the solid-medium range, boob-wise, so I was shocked by how much attention mine were getting. I can remember the boys' faces: they looked as if some-one had just done a sick move in a basketball dunk-ing contest, like "Ohhhh!!!!" They covered their mouths and high-fived one another. I then looked down the line and realized that all the other girls had just shown their bras. In a perfect metaphor for my life, I had revealed too much. I'd pulled up my entire bra too. I was the only skins player on the team. That was also the moment I learned the unforgettably fun lesson that I had larger-than-average nipples.

The nickname "Pancakes" (and also sometimes "Silver Dollars") stuck around long enough that its life span and evolution could have been slowly, carefully chronicled in a Ken Burns–length documentary. At least that's how it felt. But really it was just the remainder of the summer. I was HUMILI-ATED and didn't think I'd ever live it down. Of course, by now I've been around a lot of different women and watched a lot of porn, and I know that our body parts come in all shapes and sizes. (Men's too! Did you know their body parts *also* come in a wide variety of shapes and sizes, but strangely, the media almost never discusses it?) At the time, I was stunned to learn that my silver dollars were not the norm.

Anyway, that day on the playground turned out to be prophetic for me. I displayed everything to everyone and learned that there would be a price to pay for doing so. This was my very first experience of the stripped-down, cold, unprotected space where vulnerability meets either confidence or shame. It was my choice, and I had to learn (I'm still learning) how to choose to be proud of who I am rather than ashamed. Lucky for me, I'm a woman, so I've had the opportunity to practice this lesson over and over and over and over and over and over and over and over and over and over again. Ultimately, I just decided, fuck it, yeah, that's my body, so what? There was more power in that position than I realized at the time.

As women, most interactions from around age eight on teach us to keep things cool so no one is inspired to, God forbid, call us the U or F words:

"ugly" or "fat." I'm not the first to point out how women are taught that our value comes from how we look, and that it takes a lifetime (or at least until menopause) for most women to undo this awful lie. As someone who is crazy impulsive and incapable of taking any shit from other people, I've been criticized from so many angles and laughed at for all the wrong reasons. But, as many comics have realized, there is a gift in being laughed at, or heckled, or even booed off the stage. When your fears come true, you realize they weren't as bad as you thought. As it turns out, the fear is more painful than the insult. I boxed for a few years, and when I started sparring, I was so afraid of being hit, of experiencing that physical pain. But I learned that trying to avoid the pain didn't protect me from it. Oddly enough, getting punched in the side of the head or taking a shot to the gut *did* protect me. I got hit and it hurt for a second, but then I realized I was okay, that I could take it. And then the pain passed. After having all my fears realized and being insulted to no end, I got stronger. Being scrutinized for the ten years since I was first on a reality show has made me feel invincible. There's nothing left. So what if someone says you're fat or you're ugly? SO WHAT? Most women I know are far less afraid of being physically hurt than they are of being called ugly or fat.

I have a tramp stamp and I'm on the cover of *Vogue*. The puffy blue-green tendrils of ink underneath my skin weave together in a meaningless formation, but I've found the meaning in it. I fully accept myself as the girl with the lower back tattoo. This is not to say that I don't have regrets. Fuck yes, I regret getting this ugly tattoo that I thought signified toughness when it really just symbolized how lost and powerless I was when I was an eighteen-year-old girl. But I forgive that girl. I pity that girl, and I love that girl.

Ironically, the tattoo represents the opposite for me today. It reminds me that it's important to let yourself be vulnerable, to lose control and make a mistake. It reminds me that, as Whitman would say, I contain multitudes and I always will. I'm a level-one introvert who headlined Madison Square Garden—and was the first woman comic to do so. I'm the "overnight success" who's worked her ass off every single waking moment for more than a decade. I used to shoplift the kind of clothing that people now request I wear to give them free publicity. I'm the SLUT or SKANK who's only had one one-night stand. I'm a "plus-size" 6 on a good day, and a medium-size 10 on an even better day. I've suffered the identical indignities of slinging rib eyes for a living and hustling laughs for cash. I'm a strong, grown-ass woman who's been physically, sexually, and emotionally abused by men and women I trusted and cared about. I've broken hearts and had mine broken, too.

Beautiful, ugly, funny, boring, smart or not, my vulnerability is my ultimate strength. There's nothing anyone can say about me that's more permanent, damaging, or hideous than the statement I have forever tattooed upon myself. I'm proud of this ability to laugh at myself—even if everyone can see my tears, just like they can see my dumb, senseless, wack, lame lower back tattoo.

ACKNOWLEDGMENTS

I would like to express my most sincere thanks to the following people:

Mayci Breaux and Jillian Johnson, you are always with me and will forever be at the top of every list I make for the rest of my life.

Everyone at Everytown, especially Jason Rzepka and Noelle Howey. Also, Chuck Schumer and all the other people in America who fight every day for more sensible gun laws.

Howard Stern, who opened up my world to these opportunities.

Estee and Noam at the Comedy Cellar.

All the comics who make me a better and worse person: Jim Norton, Dave Attell, Bobby Kelly, Keith Robinson, Colin Quinn, Jess Kirson, Kurt Metzger, Pete Dominick, and Judy Gold.

Opie and Anthony and Chris Mazzilli.

Mark Normand, love you, brother.

Chris Rock, you are just the best guy.

Judd Apatow, you changed my life. Thank you for seeing something in me.

Eddie Vedder, I want to thank you for being the kindest human being I have ever met; for being the reason my dad, sister, and I used to sing together in the car at the top of our lungs; for taking the time to call my dad—a person you'd never met who is stuck in a hospital and can no longer drive around with his girls—just to make him smile.

Carrie Byalick, how did we get here? Thank you.

Allan Haldeman, Josh Katz, Guy O, and Berkowitz, I can't believe it but I love you guys. Thank you.

Everyone at Comedy Central, especially Kent Alterman, Doug Herzog, and Michelle Gainless—but even more than them, Anne Harris and JoAnn Grigioni.

Everyone at Universal, especially Donna Langley, Ron Meyer, and Erik Baiers.

Everyone at Fox, especially Stacey Snider.

Alison Callahan, for editing this book and seeing a higher order in the chaos of content I created. Making sense of my life is a gift you didn't know you were giving me. Thank you also for laughing in all the right places and encouraging me when I needed it.

Everyone else at Simon & Schuster and Gallery Books, including Jennifer Bergstrom, who is the best and most beautiful cheerleader anyone could ever want for their book; Nina Cordes; Jennifer Robinson; Carolyn Reidy; and Louise Burke.

You Gallery Gals are funny and creative, and were very supportive of my writing the book I wanted to write. Thank you.

To Elisa Shokoff, Jules Washington, and Chris McClain—the team who recorded the audio version of this book—thank you for allowing me to sob openly, and for providing tea and hugs when I needed it.

David Kuhn, who believed in me and this book from the very start.

Kate White, thank you for giving me my first writing job and supporting me through the years.

Mark Seliger.

Marcus Russell Price.

My parents.

My high school volleyball coach, Cheryl Scalice, who taught me so much about working hard and getting better.

Cydney, thank you for supporting me through my life for the last seventeen years. You are a great mother and friend.

Vickie Lee, I love you.

Kimmy Cupcakes, Dre Money, and Kyra for elevating me and listening to me all the time.

Leesa Evans, thank you for always making me look good, but more importantly thank you for always making me feel good.

Lena Dunham, thank you, my love. You get me through.

To my hoes Rachel Feinstein, Bridget Everett,

Nikki Glaser, Jenny T., Angie Martinez, Sappy, Feiny, Ca, D., Kati, Kate, Jessi Klein, Jennifer Lawrence, Jessica Seinfeld, Amber Tamblyn, Natasha Lyonne, Chelsea Peretti, Natasha Leggero, America Ferrera, Vanessa Bayer, Kyle Dunnigan, and Dan Powell. Yes, Kyle and Dan, you are my hoes.

To the people who influenced me the most: Lucille Ball, Gilda Radner, Carol Burnett, Miss Piggy, Gloria Steinem, Whoopi Goldberg, Goldie Hawn, Shari Lewis, Ani DiFranco, Joan Rivers, and Janeane Garofolo.

To the people I admire, some of whom gave me chances early on, and all of whom inspired me to do better: Ellen DeGeneres, David Letterman, Jimmy Kimmel, Stephen Colbert, Jon Stewart, Jay Leno, Seth Meyers, Tina Fey, Julia Louis-Dreyfus, Jerry Seinfeld, Anne Sexton, Sarah Silverman, Margaret Cho, Parker Posey, Wu-Tang Clan, Steve Martin, Chris Farley, and all the Muppets.

Kevin Kane, my life partner, you make me better in every way.

Vin, thank you for talking sense into all the crazies around you.

Cayce Dumont, thank you for making this book possible with all your hard work and for getting me through this. You made this happen and I love drinking with you and talking shit and watching bad TV. You are the smartest person I know and I love you. Also, thank you for giving birth to my favorite person.

Ida, we can't wait to see what you do.

Jasy, you are the coolest, greatest brother in the world and I can't believe I get to hang out with you.

Kimby, thank you for keeping me laughing and happy and alive. You are half of me.

And Jesus. JK.

ENDING GUN VIOLENCE ISN'T EASY, BUT A MOVEMENT HAS SPRUNG UP OVER THE LAST FEW YEARS THAT IS ACHIEVING REAL VICTORIES AND MAKING US SAFER. IF YOU WANT TO GET INVOLVED, THE THREE MOST IMPORTANT THINGS YOU CAN DO RIGHT NOW ARE:

1/ JOIN THE MOVEMENT. Millions of people are getting organized and demanding that our elected leaders do more to address the gun violence crisis that claims ninety-one American lives every day. The largest organization fighting for this change is Everytown for Gun Safety—which I work with. Most of the key gun safety battles play out at the state level, and if you want to get involved in your area, text JOIN to 64433. Everytown will keep you updated on what you can do now and in the future.

2/ BE HEARD. You may not realize it, but oftentimes the difference between a law passing or not is a few hundred phone calls. The average congressperson represents fewer than 750,000 people. The NRA is great at getting their supporters to reach out and help stop or pass gun legislation. But gun safety advocates need to be just as vocal. You can dial 1-888-885-4011 to be connected with your senator. Tell them you want them to vote for a criminal background check on every gun sale now!

3/ VOTE FOR GUN SAFETY. If our current elected leaders won't address this crisis, then we need to elect new leaders. It's generally wise to vote against the congresspeople who have taken the most money from the gun lobby and for those who have voted in favor of universal background checks. Senators who voted for universal background checks in the strongest background check bill to date (in 2013) can be found here: http://politics.nytimes.com /congress/votes/113/senate/1/97.

And finally, here is a list of people in Congress who have taken money from and been influenced by the gun lobby:

Kelly Ayotte

John Barrasso

Dan Benishek

Sanford Bishop

Roy Blunt

John Boozman

Ken Buck

Richard Burr

Ken Calvert

Shelley Moore Capito

Bill Cassidy

Thad Cochran

Mike Coffman

John Cornyn

Tom Cotton

Ted Cruz

Steve Daines

Sean Duffy

Michael Enzi

Joni Ernst

Deb Fischer

Jeff Flake

Cory Gardner

Lindsey Graham

Chuck Grassley

Heidi Heitkamp

Dean Heller

Jody Hice

John Hoeven

James M. Inhofe

Johnny Isakson

Ron Johnson

John Kline

James Lankford

Mike Lee

Mia Love

Thomas Massie

Kevin McCarthy

Mitch McConnell

Martha McSally

Alex X. Mooney

Jerry Moran

Markwayne Mullin

Rand Paul

Stevan Pearce

David Perdue

Rob Portman

James E. Risch

Pat Roberts

Mike Rounds

Edward Royce

Marco Rubio

Paul Ryan

Ben Sasse

Tim Scott

Richard Shelby

Michael Simpson

Daniel Sullivan

John Thune

Thom Tillis

Scott Tipton

David G. Valadao

David Vitter

Tim Walberg

Roger Wicker

PHOTO CREDITS

INTERIOR

Photos by Marcus Russell Price: pgs. 193 and 348; photo taken in an amusement park photo booth: pg. 239; pg. 325: photo of Mayci Breaux by Coco Eros Boutique; photo of Jillian Johnson by Lucius A. Fontenot

PHOTO INSERT

Photo by Ben Hanisch: pg. 7 (bottom); copyright © 2015 Universal Pictures, courtesy of Universal Studios Licensing LLC: pg. 10 (bottom); photos by Marcus Russell Price: pgs. 13 (bottom), 14 (bottom), 15 (both), 16

ABOUT THE AUTHOR

AMY SCHUMER has become one of the most influential figures in the entertainment industry as a stand-up comedian, actress, writer, producer, and director. Her smash hit television series, *Inside Amy Schumer*, has won a Peabody award, a Critics Choice Television Award, and two primetime Emmy awards. She wrote and starred in her first feature-length film, *Trainwreck*, which dominated the 2015 summer comedy international box office and was nominated for two Golden Globes and won both the Critics Choice award for Best Actress in a Comedy, and a Hollywood Film Award for Comedy of the Year. She earned a 2018 Tony nomination for her performance in *Meteor Shower* on Broadway, and starred in the 2018 summer hit, *I Feel Pretty*. As a stand-up comedian, she continues to perform to sold-out audiences around the world. Her 2016 tour was voted Pollstar's Comedy Tour of the Year. Schumer was raised in New York City and Long Island and loves her brother and sister the very most.